PENGUIN BOOKS

TURN RIGHT AT LAND'S E

Over the last seven years John Merrill has successfully
completed many marathon walks in Great Britain. He is
unquestionably the greatest long-distance walker in this
country and has walked all of Britain's long-distance
footpaths. He has also created his own Peakland Way. He
has achieved many notable 'firsts' including the Derbyshire
Boundary walk and the East of England Heritage Route.
He is also interested in natural history, folklore and
customs, historical buildings and industrial archaeology
and photography. He has written over thirty books, many
of which are about his own county of Derbyshire, and has
contributed to several major walkers' handbooks. He
appears frequently on both television and radio.

John Merrill

Turn Right at Land's End

Penguin Books

Penguin Books Ltd, Harmondsworth,
Middlesex, England
Penguin Books, 625 Madison Avenue,
New York, New York 10022, U.S.A.
Penguin Books Australia Ltd, Ringwood,
Victoria, Australia
Penguin Books Canada Ltd, 2801 John Street,
Markham, Ontario, Canada L3R 1B4
Penguin Books (N.Z.) Ltd, 182–190 Wairau Road,
Auckland 10, New Zealand

First published by Oxford Illustrated Press 1979
Published in Penguin Books 1981

Typeset by CCC, printed and bound in Great Britain by
Cox & Wyman Ltd, Reading

To Sheila

Contents

Maps

Acknowledgements

A walk of such large proportions, lasting almost a year of one's life, relies heavily on the spontaneity and generosity of people met on route. To all of you I met or received help from on the British Coastal Walk, may I simply say a very big thank you.

My thanks, too, to the police, coastguards and rotary clubs who greatly assisted me throughout; to Blacks of Greenock who helped me so much when I discovered the fatigue fracture; to Sheila Milne who took me in when I was immobilized and acting like a caged lion; to Sandra French and the Cumberland Hotel who put on two splendid functions at the beginning and end of the walk; to my sponsors the Milk Marketing Board, Blacks of Greenock Ltd, and Berghaus Ltd, and the following companies who gave me equipment: Raven Foods, Silva, Camping Gaz, Trafalgar Watches, C.Z. Scientific Instruments Ltd, Ilford Ltd, Blacks of Greenock and Berghaus; and finally to my secretary Christine Reeve who played such an important role in the preparation, the smooth running of everything while I was away and who dealt so diplomatically with the press and media. Her dedication to the walk relieved me of numerous problems and to her enthusiasm I owe a great deal. Thank you.

1. Planning and Preparation

A journey all the way round the coastline of England, Scotland and Wales is the longest continuous walk that can be done in Britain. Since taking up marathon walking in 1972, I have walked all of Britain's official long-distance paths and some 'unofficial' ones, which include several sections of the coastline. My major walks comprise several journeys through the remote parts of Scotland and Ireland and their islands (Hebridean Journey, 1,003 miles, Northern Isles Journey, 842 miles, and Irish Island Journey, 1,578 miles), the Parkland Journey (2,043 miles) which linked the ten National Parks and a 1,608-mile walk from Land's End to John o'Groats. The latter I did as preparation for the coast walk. Having completed all of these, to walk the entire length of the coastline was the ultimate challenge left to me in Britain. No one had walked it in its entirety before, and certainly no one had attempted it as a continuous walk.

To walk anti-clockwise is the Devil's way. That is one reason why I chose to do the walk in a clockwise direction. It also helped me psychologically for in those terms walking north seems to be 'uphill', and south 'downhill'. When I reached John o'Groats I had to control myself from rushing 'downhill' all the way to London! The significance of beginning and ending at St Paul's Cathedral was entirely personal, but there were practical reasons for choosing London. I started out in early January because it seemed wise to walk the south coast and the West Country during the winter months. Beginning in January also meant that the shortest day would be past and, moreover, I would be starting the New Year with a new project.

I firmly believe that marathon walking as I practise it is principally a mental exercise. Obviously it is necessary to be an athletic type and extremely fit, but if the mental approach is not right then the whole undertaking is in jeopardy. For this reason I will spend as much as a year preparing myself for a major walk. In fact I spent a total of fourteen months on the coastal walk, though the physical work started in earnest nine months before setting out.

A 4,000-mile training programme, which also served the purpose of helping me select equipment and food, began on 1 April 1977 with an eleven-day hike up the length of the Pennine Way. During May and June I organized four separate parties of twelve people to walk a hundred-mile circular route, which I devised myself, around the Peak District National Park – the Peakland Way. On 14 July I set off from Sudbury Hall to walk the boundary of the county of Derbyshire, in aid of the National Trust's Derbyshire and Peak District Appeal Fund. This walk, which took ten and a half days, was 281 miles long and raised about £5,000. Four days later I was at Land's End to begin my fifty-seven-day, 1,608-mile walk to John o'Groats. I purposely took a route which included the whole of the South-West Peninsula path from Land's End to Minehead, the Cotswold Way, Offa's Dyke Path, the Pennine Way, the Cairngorms and the North-West Highlands. I finished this in late September, by which time it was scarcely three months before departure day for the coastline. From then on I did a daily two-and-a-half-mile run before breakfast and a twenty- to twenty-five-mile walk every Sunday. Just before Christmas I did a final training walk (following my usual pattern of a one hundred to two hundred-mile stint two weeks before a major walk) and for a change I headed south to walk the Pilgrim Way, reaching Canterbury Cathedral on Christmas Eve.

The training schedule was but a part of the preparation: I had started planning the coast walk on paper much earlier. Before I could begin to work out a daily schedule, I had first to decide how closely I could keep to the coastline, what I should do at river estuaries, whether to include islands, whether to walk round every single peninsula, and what bridges I should use. Ferries, of course, were out – I had decided, as on all my previous walks, against 'mechanical' assistance of any kind.

Unlike walking long-distance footpaths, for much of the coast I would have no established route to follow. The way would sometimes be along main roads or promenades, over sand or shingle beaches, cliff tops or mudflats and, where the shore or cliffs were impassable, I would have to walk inland through open country, fields or forests. I even needed to use a compass on occasion! But, whatever problems were presented by the terrain, they were dealt with by the following rules which I drew up:

1. In England and Wales I would use the nearest right of way to the coast. In Scotland, where the trespass laws are different, I could walk as near as I liked to the shoreline.
2. At Ministry of Defence property I would seek permission to walk through ranges and training grounds as and when I reached them. I would only make a detour inland if I was refused or if they were actually firing.
3. At estuaries or other water inlets I would walk inland and cross by the first bridge passable by foot. This did not include motorway bridges, though occasionally rail bridges. It sometimes meant enormous detours – one was 142 miles!
4. Islands were not to be included – there are *942* of them off Britain's coast.
5. I would always walk round every peninsula and, to sum up, keep as near to the coast as humanly possible for the whole way.

I should also add that I determined to take no rest days as I don't find they are a help. My aim was to keep up an average rate of walking every single day.

Using a map measurer, I estimated the coastline of Britain to be 6,180 miles. I also asked the Ordnance Survey for their estimate of the total mileage, and they arrived at 6,095 miles (England and Wales 3,240 miles, Scotland 2,855 miles). On the ground I did 6,824 miles (England 3,363 miles, Scotland 2,695, and Wales 766 miles). I always use a pedometer, set to my average pace, and this tells me exactly how far I have walked between points A and B. No one walks in a straight line, and neither can a map measurer record all the indentations, so I relied on this piece of equipment to give an accurate account of the distance walked.

With the guidelines given above, I worked out a continuous walking schedule from 3 January 1978 to 15 September 1978, a total of 256 days. The distance was broken down to an average of between twenty-three and twenty-five map-measured miles per day. I knew from experience that for every thousand miles worked out with a map measurer, another two hundred would be added on location. Therefore, a twenty-five-mile day on paper would represent something like thirty in the field.

With the 256-day itinerary compiled, I worked out nineteen suitable post offices to where, according to schedule, Christine Reeve, my secretary, would despatch parcels containing supplies of food, maps and equipment needed over a two-week period. Parcelling the contents into the right order was a major task, but it proved to be the key to a smooth operation. The post offices were also vital communication points where I could be contacted, and I in turn used them to return my used maps, films, boots and socks to base.

I knew that for at least half the walk I would have to be totally self-reliant, and in fact I was prepared for this for all of it, if need be. Food, therefore, was a most important consideration. Not wishing to carry tins, I selected Raven dehydrated foods, which I had tried during my 1977 training walks. Choosing my favourites from their range, I sorted 120 main courses and 120 desserts into batches ready for parcelling. On the walk I purchased food locally wherever possible, but I always made sure that I had three or four days' supply of dehydrated food with me at any one time.

While all the training, planning and sorting was continuing, I had other work to do: writing articles and books and touring the length and breadth of the country to give lectures. I had also agreed that the walk could be used by the Royal

Commonwealth Society for the Blind (RCSB), for fundraising purposes. This also entailed a lot of work and meant that the walk had to be well publicized. Thousands of press releases were printed and sent out to all interested parties. Being a rotarian myself, I had secured the support of all the rotary clubs, and ideas on how to use the walk for fundraising were sent to the seven hundred or so clubs that were on or near the coast. I secured the interest of several newspapers and magazines at both local and national levels; I approached regional and national radio and television programmes and eventually some of them, too, agreed to follow the walk. Regular phone-ins with 'Today', 'Start the Week with Richard Baker' and my local radio stations Radio Derby and Radio Sheffield were arranged. The working out of the master itinerary was essential to arranging publicity, and it enabled Christine to send out press material ahead of me together with monthly progress reports.

Further information on equipment, food, maps, my own approach to marathon walking, the charity involvement and statistics about the walk can be found in the appendices, pages 263–309.

2. London to Bournemouth

On 2 January 1978, the eve of departure, I arrived at the Cumberland Hotel, Marble Arch. The object was to spend the night prior to setting out around the coast of Britain in luxurious surroundings and I wasn't let down. A suite of rooms was placed at my disposal, along with the services of the floor manager and other members of staff. It was all done entirely for publicity; an extraordinary beginning, but the press had a field day.

The hotel buzzed with photographers and pressmen firing questions about the walk and the charity involved. It was quite overwhelming, but when they left I joined my group of friends and supporters to enjoy a sumptuous dinner. I will never forget that meal. We started with grapefruit and orange segments in wine, followed by a fish course, then large succulent steaks, red wine, sherry trifle, petit fours, cigars, liqueurs and several cups of coffee. The service was immaculate – even the linen serviettes were changed after each course. When I finally retired to my bed, there were only ten hours left to the moment of departure.

3.1.78

I was awake at seven o'clock and ready for an elaborately staged breakfast in bed, so that 'Nationwide' could film the proceedings. Pandemonium broke out as the film crew arrived with lights, cameras and cases of recording equipment. In the midst of the confusion a delicious-looking breakfast arrived, but with so much happening it was left to get cold. A second breakfast was brought up to my room but that also was ignored as the film crew prepared a rapid sequence of shots of me washing and packing my rucksack.

Time was racing away as the one and only golden taxicab in London collected me from the hotel and whisked me to St Paul's Cathedral. I arrived there at a quarter past ten and found that I had to fight my way through a crowd of people and photographers to attend morning service. I was late, but the Priest in Ordinary to her Majesty the Queen was able to give me a private blessing. This moved me deeply for it was important to me to begin the walk with a few moments of quiet and prayer and I planned also to end the walk in this way.

I stepped out of St Paul's at 10.30 a.m. ready to set off and found myself confronted by a barrage of reporters, newsmen, photographers, and film crews. Microphones were thrust in front of me and I answered the rapid questions as quickly and as best I could. I was amazed at the amount of interest the walk had generated and it was a tremendous send off. An hour later I left the now deserted steps of St Paul's and walked quickly to the Mansion House where the Lord Mayor was waiting to wish me well. He helped me on with my pack and I gave him a sealed envelope which contained the predicted date for my return to London.

I set off past the Tower and over Tower Bridge to begin the first day's walk to Gravesend. The day was sunny and warm. Once across the bridge the last of the newsmen and the 'Nationwide' team left and I was on my own. The walk had begun!

It was then well past one o'clock and I had thirty miles to walk, with only fours hours of daylight left. I had to walk along the road all the way to Gravesend and I was joined by my first five-mile sponsors, who in fact completed eight miles with me.

Crossing Greenwich Park I couldn't fail to notice the extent of the skateboard craze. Young children were flying down the paths in all sorts of dangerous-looking positions and I retreated to the safety of the grass. Ten months later, when I returned to London, the craze was over.

I reached Gravesend in the early evening, tired but delighted

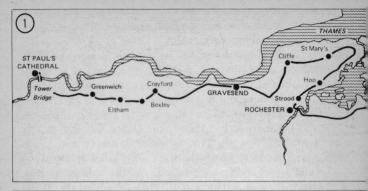

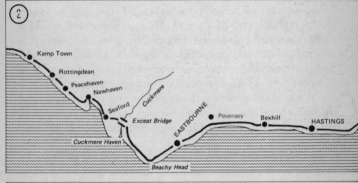

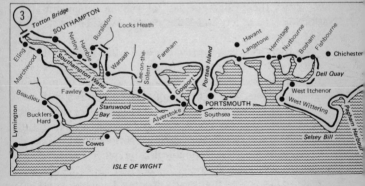

18

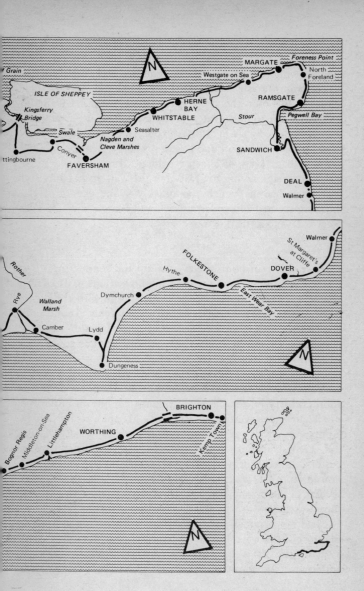

that the first thirty miles were behind me. The rotary club president, Walter Woods, was waiting and took me to a member's house for a meal. Although a bed was offered I felt it was important to sleep out on my first night and much to their amusement I put the tent up on their lawn. BBC Radio Medway came to do an interview and together we arranged a radio-sponsored walk in two days' time. By eleven o'clock I was too tired to do any more and I went to bed. Stretched out in my sleeping bag, I lay awake for a long while, absorbing the atmosphere and trying to grasp that the walk had begun. But too much had happened too quickly – the events of the morning seemed a long way away – and I knew it would take several days to settle down.

4.1.78

After only four hours' sleep I was up and conducting a live interview for one of my own local radio stations, BBC Radio Sheffield. Fifteen minutes later I was speaking to the other, BBC Radio Derby. This was to become a weekly event. I only missed them on a couple of occasions when I couldn't reach a telephone. I enjoyed doing them although I was sometimes tired and then it was a strain. I'm sure this must have come across, but I always tried to do my best.

From Gravesend I could at last get onto the sea wall. It was another thirty-mile day as in clear, sunny conditions I followed the Thames past Cliffe and St Mary's Marshes, to the Isle of Grain. Already I was beginning to see a wide variety of bird life: wrens, blackbirds, ringed plovers, lapwings, curlews, snipe, oyster-catchers, cormorants, grey herons and shelduck. As I neared Hoo, a *Daily Express* photographer appeared and took several dramatic shots of me silhouetted against the setting sun. I carried on to Strood where I stopped for the night.

I had not originally intended to do such a large mileage at the start of the walk. I usually prefer to do about twenty miles a day for the first week. This time however, I was feeling so fit and eager to be on my way that the miles seemed to disappear easily.

5.1.78

As I walked through Rochester to the BBC Radio Medway studios, the impact of appearing on television became apparent. Walking through the streets people called out 'good luck' or even stopped to shake my hand. I enjoyed the attention but at the same time found it rather disturbing. Waiting outside the studio were the station manager, Harold Rogers, and an interviewer. They were both sponsored to walk with me for fifteen miles and we were accompanied by a radio van which put out an hourly bulletin on our position and condition. We walked over the Swale towards the Isle of Sheppey where we parted company at Kingsferry Bridge. Their walk with me had raised over £200.

I turned to Sittingbourne and from there back out to the sea wall. It was getting dark as I approached Jarman's boatyard at Conyer and the last two miles were very difficult as the earth wall was slippery. Although I carry a torch I rarely use it, for I find it a nuisance to hold and the light it gives is often misleading. I prefer to trust to instinct.

6.1.78

I continued along the sea wall to Faversham. I was alone, thoroughly enjoying the solitude and looking forward to reaching the coast proper, at Herne Bay. The quiet was interrupted, however, when a reception committee met me on the outskirts of Faversham and walked with me to the town centre. There I found a crowd, a film crew and the mayor all waiting to welcome me. This was totally unexpected: I had to do several retakes of meeting the mayor for the benefit of the film crew, before I set off beside the creek to get to Nagden Marshes. On the way I did a television interview and that night I had the dubious pleasure of seeing myself on the 'box'.

After crossing the Cleve Marshes the coast lay before me – at last! I walked round Seasalter Bay, Whitstable Bay and Herne Bay, and although the rocky coast was not very dramatic, I was thrilled to be on the coast where I could smell the sea, hear the waves breaking against the shore and the pebbles being sucked back, and see the sum shimmering over the water.

For the next ten months, the sea on my left-hand side was to be my constant companion.

7.1.78

Leaving Herne Bay I walked beside more marshland, including the intriguingly named Plumpudding Island, to reach Westgate on Sea. I saw several greenfinches, sanderlings and black-backed, black-headed and herring gulls. From there, as a direct contrast to the quiet marshland where only the sound of the gulls broke the solitude, I walked through fifteen miles of built-up coast to round Foreness Point and North Foreland, the most south-easterly point of Britain, and between these two places I literally turned right for Land's End. There was no dramatic scenery as there is at the three other extremities of Britain: Land's End in the south-west, Cape Wrath in the north-west and Duncansby Head in the north-east. In fact my rounding of the Point hardly registered for I was still not fully aware of having begun the walk. It usually takes me a good five hundred miles before I start adjusting to my new way of life.

The sun shone from an almost cloudless sky and the temperature was extremely mild for early January. It was strange walking through such popular seaside haunts as Margate, Broadstairs and Ramsgate, and seeing everything shut and boarded-up for the winter. Very few people were about and, seeing the deserted sandy beaches, it was hard to envisage what it would be like in mid summer when crowded.

8.1.78

I left Ramsgate early in the morning and set off for Dover. As a contrast to the good weather of the previous day, it was cold and a sea mist hung over the land for most of the day. My route took me inland past the hoverport at Pegwell Bay to Sandwich where I was to cross the river Stour at the first road bridge, and so get back to the coast. Sandwich is one of the five original Cinque Ports of the south-east coast, the others being Hastings, Romney, Hythe and Dover. Winchelsea, Rye and Seaford were added later. In Norman times the ports were granted special privileges in return for supplying ships for war.

Due east of Deal lie the Goodwin Sands, famed for their legends, treacherous waters and visible wrecks. To many the area is known as 'Calamity Corner', and they were famous for their hazards even in Shakespearean times as this quotation from *The Merchant of Venice* illustrates:

... Antonio hath a ship of rich lading wrecked on the narrow seas— the Goodwins, I think they call the place; a very dangerous flat and fatal, where the carcases of many a tall ship lie buried.

Deal Castle was particularly attractive; it is the largest castle of the Tudor coastal defence system, and was built in 1539 on the orders of Henry VIII. A little over a mile later I reached Walmer Castle, which was also built by Henry VIII, and which has been the official residence of the Lord Wardens of the Cinque Ports since 1708.

Even though it was late in the day I carried on past St Margaret's at Cliffe and on to Dover. Through my binoculars I could see kestrels and ravens flying over the Dover cliffs. Never having been to Dover before I was looking forward to seeing this historic port which is often called the 'Gateway to England'. I had trouble finding the correct path down in the dark but after fighting my way through the undergrowth I reached the port gates. Although it was a hazy evening, a blaze of lights lit up the docks and town, whilst behind me towered the imposing floodlit castle. I stood awhile to watch the bustle of cars, lorries and people at the docks before moving into the town to stay at the youth hostel.

9.1.78

Leaving Dover shortly after eight o'clock, I was looking forward to climbing the first real cliffs of the walk: Shakespeare Cliff and Abbot's Cliff. I found their ascent to be easy, even though it was wet and windy, and I was well pleased with my form. I was also walking along the start of the North Downs Way. As a rule I was always walking by 8.30 a.m. and never stopped before five o'clock, although it was often as late as seven or eight. Despite the short daylight hours in January and February, I didn't let the darkness call a halt to my day's walk.

As I walked round East Wear Bay to Folkestone I realized I had been walking seven days and had put my first two hundred miles behind me. This initial stage is crucial on a major walk, but I felt fit and had no blisters and was generally pleased with the way I was settling in. I stayed in Dymchurch that evening.

The day started peacefully enough with a slight wind blowing and the sun shining through the clouds. From Dymchurch I began the long haul beside the pebbled shore to Dungeness. I knew that beyond Dungeness was a military danger area, but was unaware exactly what went on there or whether it was being used. On reaching the end of the road I discovered that the army were busy firing on the range, and so for the first time on the walk I had to back track and walk up the road to Lydd and down the edge of Walland Marsh to Camber. Walking round the range I saw and heard the army exercising with guns and I passed the mock Irish street used for training for Ulster duty. Having walked all the way round, a sergeant ran up and expressed his amazement at my speed round the range. We sat in his observation post and drank tea as we watched the worsening weather.

At Camber rain began to fall and the wind rose as I plodded on to Rye to cross the river Rother before regaining the coast and staying on Winchelsea Beach. What I could see of Rye through the torrential rain made me want to stay and look round at leisure. Its cobbled streets, the many ancient buildings, together with the museums and its historical associations with the other Cinque Ports, make it a place of particular interest. I was fascinated to discover that both the town and Camber Castle were once on the coast, but that due to silting they are now almost three miles away. By the time I reached Winchelsea Beach I was drenched – the first of many soakings!

I woke to find the rain had ceased and had given way to clear skies but that there were galeforce winds. I was joined for much of the day by a schoolmaster who walked twenty-four miles with me to within five miles of Eastbourne, where I ended the day's walk. We had to fight against a force eight gale all the way. In Hastings and Bexhill, the sight of the swollen seas crashing over the sea wall and esplanade was spectacular. I found a shelter and filmed people being caught by the waves and spray. Damage from the gales could be seen everywhere: beach huts were upturned, caravans were blown about and many fields were flooded.

At Pevensey I was joined for the last five miles of the day by the Eastbourne Rotary Club president. It was late afternoon, cold and starting to rain. He walked in a sports jacket, no waterproof clothing, and carried a large golf umbrella, which a gust of wind turned inside out and wrecked after a mile. The rain came down harder and as we neared Eastbourne a blizzard raged. Admirably, my companion stuck it out to the end, even though he was cold and wet, and we parted at Eastbourne. I went to a nearby hotel to stay, have a bath, eat and phone Christine. Waiting for me at the hotel were four photographers and reporters. I answered their questions, posed with my feet in a bowl for the cameras and went for a bath. I hadn't been in it for a minute before there was a knock at the door. I opened it and in walked another photographer. He wanted a shot of me in the bath complete with soap bubbles! I leapt back in the bath while he set up his camera, but fortunately the steam misted up his lenses, so I never appeared in *Playgirl*! Not to be outdone, he opened the door and photographed me in a towel with my feet resting on the bath instead. It appeared in the following day's *Hastings Evening Argus*. Refreshed, I went downstairs and joined a reporter and photographer from the *Eastbourne Herald* for dinner.

12.1.78

The wind was still at galeforce strength as I made my way on to Beachy Head where the South Downs Way starts. The traverse of the Seven Sisters was to be one of the highlights of the south-east coast, and I was not let down. The day was exceedingly cold and for the first time I wore my duvet and gloves. The clarity was good and the sun shone, enhancing an already stunning piece of coastline; the chalk cliffs were pure white and the heaving seas a rich blue topped with white waves. I bent into the wind but I was often alarmed by its power as it tugged at me on the cliff top.

At the end of the Seven Sisters I walked up beside Cuckmere river to Exceat Bridge. Waiting for me there was another five-mile sponsored walker. Unfortunately he was under the impression we would be road walking, and had come dressed accordingly. The footpath along the west bank of the river to Cuckmere Haven was very muddy and made for difficult walking, but my companion agreed it was worth it when we saw the classic but impressive view back to the Seven Sisters.

We parted at Newhaven and I began the final miles of the day to Brighton via Peacehaven, Rottingdean and Kemp Town. I kept to the cliff top all the way, and was able to see the full extent of the coastal erosion in the area and man's efforts with concrete to stop it going any further. I reached the centre of Brighton at about 6.30 p.m. and walked through a line of scouts to a tape where my time was recorded for a lottery; it raised £1,800.

After a few words with the scouts I was ushered across to the Dome where the Mayoress of Brighton and other officials were waiting to welcome me formally to the town. The press asked me to put my muddy boots up on one of the civic chairs for a photograph, which I did. I was offered a drink, and much to their amusement I refused the alcohol and instead accepted a still orange. I was hungry but I was asked to give a talk to the newly-formed rotoract club and so put off my meal. The talk seemed to go down well and at the end I was presented with £400 in cheques. By this time I was ravenous. I had not eaten at all during the day (apart from chocolate), and I was tired after walking the thirty-three miles and doing my various charity duties. I finally ate at ten o'clock and resolved to make sure that I ate before any further assignments.

13.1.78

I slipped away quietly and headed for Worthing. The wind had dropped but the perfect sunny, clear weather was still with me, and I was uncomfortably warm in the duvet jacket I was wearing. As I neared Worthing a BBC TV film crew emerged and I was filmed walking and talking as we moved along to Worthing sea front. Later in the day I went through Littlehampton to Middleton-on-Sea, where I stopped for the night.

14.1.78

Bognor Regis has always been the epitome of the early twentieth-century coastal resort. I was very disappointed therefore when I found a ghost town in bad repair. To get to Selsey Bill I walked round the edge of Pagham Harbour, a largely marsh-filled lake with a small outlet to the sea. The area is a popular nature reserve and many bird watchers were standing on the banks looking for wintering birds. I saw avocets, brent geese, mute swans, and many shelduck. The latter I was to see almost daily for the next five months. Rounding Selsey Bill I could see the Isle of Wight for the first time. Six miles later, and in the dark, I erected the tent above the sands near West Wittering. While cooking my evening meal I looked out from the door of the tent across to the flickering lights of Portsmouth and Ryde.

The next three days saw me working my way round the many islands and harbours that lie between West Wittering and Southampton. Although I walked some eighty miles, I only moved about fifteen miles westwards. It was an exercise that was to happen often on the walk. This could have been soul destroying, but by dealing with only a day at a time, it did not affect me.

15.1.78

From West Wittering I rounded Chichester Harbour via West Itchenor and the yacht basin, with its thousands of yachts, to Dell Quay and Fishbourne. On route I saw my first mallards, coots, moorhens, great tits, pheasants and a spotted woodpecker. Next was Bosham Hoe and the pretty village of Bosham. From Nutbourne I followed the road to Hermitage and Langstone (missing out Thorney and Hayling Islands) where I stayed the night.

16.1.78

I continued along the road to Havant and on to Portsea Island and Portsmouth. Although one of my rules had been not to walk around any islands, Portsea Island and Portsmouth are usually considered as part of the mainland, so I decided to treat them as such. From Portsmouth Harbour I walked through Fareham to Gosport and Alverstoke, where I stopped, having achieved thirty miles that day. I was relieved this difficult section of city and industry was behind me.

17.1.78

From Alverstoke I walked in mild and sunny weather beside Southampton Water through Lee-on-the-Solent and Warsash to Locks Heath where I was to stay the night and be guest of honour at an international evening. This had been arranged before I set off, for I knew that I would be able to maintain the schedule for the first two weeks. After that I had no ties and could go at my own speed and get ahead if I so wished.

The function was held at the nearby Botleigh Grange Hotel. Having packed no special clothing for this kind of event I naturally arrived in my anorak, breeches and muddy boots, although as a gesture I had combed my beard and hair and brushed my teeth! As I was guest of honour I stood at the door and welcomed the three hundred guests, most of whom arrived in long dresses and lounge suits. I felt decidedly out of place. Having received the guests I joined the chairman on the platform and gave a twenty-minute talk on the walk. This time my pleasure in giving the talk wasn't marred by pangs of hunger as I had taken the precaution of having a light meal beforehand. Following questions we all adjourned for a buffet. About an hour later we reassembled for the prize draw. A raffle had been arranged to raise money for R C S B and the first prize was a cruise for two, for two weeks, worth £1,400. With considerable excitement and tension, the lucky number was drawn. The winner was the treasurer of the organizing club! The booby prize of a ticket for two to the Isle of Man was won by a man from Ayr in Scotland and amid much laughter I offered to deliver the prize. I finally got to bed after midnight and slept fitfully, although I was overtired from the strain of the walk and from talking about it. The evening had raised more than £800.

18.1.78

I was away early to get through Bursledon, Hamble, and Netley to reach Southampton by lunchtime. Looking across Southampton Water I could see the Esso refinery at Fawley, where I knew I would be walking the following day. I reached the centre of Southampton via the Northam bridge where a surprise reception committee was waiting. I confess that I was getting rather weary of the publicity side of the walk, I was only just coping with the events that had been planned and for which I was therefore able to prepare myself. These surprise functions, although well meant, really were coming as a shock. But the District Rotary Conference were waiting in the Post House Hotel, and I could not let them down. I walked into the crowded room to a burst of applause. A microphone was passed to me and I began my talk. Fifteen minutes later, to more generous applause, I climbed down from the platform and shouldered the rucksack. I was close to tears; the strain had proved too much. I rushed out and it was only at Totton Bridge that I finally calmed down. In the late afternoon I walked through the village of Eling as a light sprinkling of snow began to cover the ground; it was the first of the walk. A grey squirrel darted up a tree and, entering a field just as the sun set, a red fox ambled nonchalantly past. I stood still and watched it disappear. Perhaps life wasn't so bad after all.

19–21.1.78

From Marchwood to Bournemouth required three days' hard walking. First I had to pass Fawley refinery which emitted a strong smell of petrol. Back on the coast at Stanswood Bay I could see Cowes on the Isle of Wight quite clearly before turning inland to Beaulieu to cross the river. I returned to the coast via Bucklers Hard to Lymington and Milford on Sea. From Milford I had a good view of the Needles before rain poured down and obliterated the view. I walked round

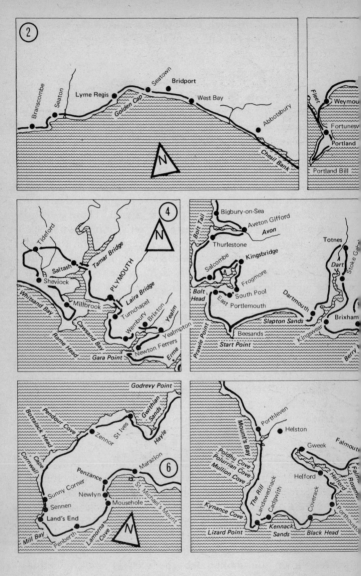

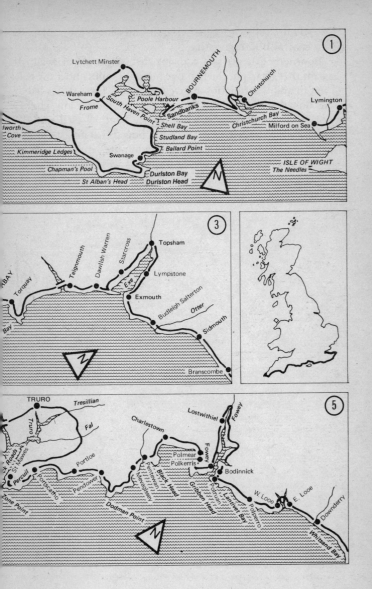

1

Lytchett Minster

Wareham
Frome
South Haven Point
Poole Harbour
Sandbanks
BOURNEMOUTH
Christchurch
Lymington
Christchurch Bay
Milford on Sea

Iworth Cove
Kimmeridge Ledges
Shell Bay
Studland Bay
Ballard Point

Swanage
Chapman's Pool
St Alban's Head
Durlston Bay
Durlston Head

ISLE OF WIGHT
The Needles

3

Topsham

BAY
Teignmouth
Dawlish Warren
Starcross
Exe
Lympstone

Bay
Torquay
Exmouth
Budleigh Salterton
Otter
Sidmouth

Branscombe

5

TRURO
Tresillian
Lostwithiel
Fowey

Truro
Fal
Charlestown

ck Roads
St Mawes
Portloe
Polmear
Polkerris
Fowey
Bodinnick

Percuil
Porscatho
Pendower
Pentewan
Mevagissey
Black Head
Fowey
Polruan
Polperro
W Looe
E Looe

one Point
Dodman Point
Gribbin Head
Lanivet Bay
Downderry

Whitsand Bay

Christchurch Bay to Christchurch and along the esplanade into central Bournemouth.

Bournemouth marked a major first stage of the walk. It meant that I had put the first five hundred miles under my belt. I felt fit and was functioning well, although I was still jaded by the unexpected demands being made of me for my charity work. But ahead was the whole of the South-West Peninsula Coast Path to look forward to, and I hoped that at last I would be able to relax and enjoy some seven hundred miles of solitary footpath walking to Land's End and the west coast of Britain. Content in this thought I slept soundly for the first time for several days.

3. South-West Peninsula Coast Path

22.1.78

The previous night's heavy rain had given way to a still, sunny day. Avoiding the ferry from Sandbanks, I set off on a thirty-six mile detour of Poole Harbour. From Bournemouth to Wareham, I had to walk along the road, and it was a relief when I reached the peace and quiet of Lytchett Minster. Walking through the village I passed a forge, outside which was an enormous mound of used horseshoes. Today it is rare to find even one and I was tempted to put a couple in the rucksack to post home.

Entering Wareham I came to St Martin's church. It is only forty-five feet long and is believed to owe its origin to St Aldhelm, the first bishop of Sherborne, in AD 705. Apart from wanting to see such an historic building my main purpose for the visit was to see the effigy of T. E. Lawrence which was presented by his brother in 1939. It shows Lawrence in full arab dress with his head lying on a camel's saddle and his right hand holding the hilt of a curved dagger.

Once across the river Frome I followed byways to the heaths of Slepe, Wytch, Rempstone and Newton and so to South Haven Point and Shell Bay, the start of the Dorset Coast Path. I reached Shell Bay in the late afternoon and was surprised to see lots of people on the beach enjoying the January sun. I carried on to Studland Bay and to Swanage where I was due to meet the mayor at 4.30 p.m. Rounding the corner of Shell Bay I could see one of my favourite stretches of coastline ahead, Old Harry Rocks. In the bright sunshine these white chalk cliffs and rock stacks made a beautiful picture against the motionless blue sea. Within an hour I rounded Ballard Point and could see Swanage ahead.

Although I had offers of accommodation at Swanage I decided to walk a further six miles to St Alban's Head. I would then be nicely placed for reaching Weymouth the following evening where I had agreed to attend a dinner. After a few words with the mayor I set off for Durlston Bay and Head. Night was falling but I was in high spirits, enjoying the stillness of the evening and walking with only the moon lighting my path. I would have liked to have seen this area in daylight: the Tilly Whim Caves, Anvil Point and the sea cliffs of Dancing Ledge are all popular climbing areas. Two hours of walking in the dark brought me to the coastguard and to remark how peaceful it was before staying in Corfe.

23.1.78

The weather changed dramatically overnight. The wind rose to force ten, the rain lashed down and the once placid seas now looked menacing as huge waves rolled in and crashed against the cliffs. Bent almost double, I struggled to the coastguard station to finish dressing, putting on my overtrousers, gaiters and cagoule inside. While catching my breath I watched the wind gauge frequently top 100 m.p.h. I might have had second thoughts about going for a cliff-top walk in those conditions but as the wind was coming off the sea I felt I would be all right. The guard entered my visit in the log and that I 'was properly equipped'. I bade him goodbye and set off in the storm, bound for Weymouth, thirty miles away.

The gale took a lot of getting used to, and for a while I was blown all over the place. With the hood well down over my face and just my eyes peering out, I fought my way along the saturated path to Chapman's Pool and the Kimmeridge Ledges. In no time I was soaked to the skin. Nothing could keep the rain out with such a strong wind behind it. As long as I kept going my body temperature would be maintained but I knew that to stop and cool down would have been fatal. At times the wind was too strong and it blew me to the ground; I had to fight for every inch I was gaining. But I enjoyed the battle – it was exhilarating – and, looking back now, that particular day was one of the most enjoyable of the walk. It was one person against the elements and it was up to me to make it.

Within a mile I reached a stream which had become a raging torrent. I had been watching it for a long while, for instead of falling down the cliffs it was being thrown upwards at a very sharp angle. There was no way of avoiding it; I knew I was in for a soaking. Steeling myself against the wind and the wet I photographed the up fall.

I battled on towards the Lulworth army range. Before I got there I phoned for permission to walk through and along the coast, but unfortunately there was an exercise on and I couldn't. Instead a sergeant was detailed to meet me and to escort me around the perimeter. The conditions were now even worse than before with the rain streaming down and being hurled furiously into the ground. I stooped to cushion the worst of the onslaught, but frequently had to look further ahead than my feet, and face the full force of the lashing rain. I met the sergeant on schedule and while he drove his Land Rover through the low cloud and rain, I followed him on foot.

At Lulworth Camp I was introduced to the major who immediately ordered a dinner to be placed before me. I ate with gusto while chatting to them about the walk. I still had a good ten miles to do to reach Weymouth and much of it would have to be done in the dark. Lulworth Cove was a seething cauldron. Not a single person could be seen. I quickly photographed the rock folds and the impressive archway of Durdle Door, which was almost awash with spray and waves. Five miles later at Osmington Mills I was in darkness. Thankfully I could see the lights of Weymouth five miles away, and they spurred me on. I reached Weymouth and the hotel just in time, and after leaving my rucksack and waterproofs in a heap, I went straight in to dinner. Before long a pool of water developed beneath me! It had taken almost twelve hours to walk those thirty miles in atrocious conditions. I was elated. I gave a talk about the walk before having a hot bath and falling into bed.

24.1.78

The rain ceased during the night and although there was still a very strong wind, at least the sun was shining. My plan was to reach Abbotsbury. Walking through Weymouth I could see the places where I had played as a child: the roller skating rink, the clock tower on the promenade, the sands, the ruined Sandsfoot Castle and the nearby beach where I had often made sand castles. Looking at the beach I saw the familiar remains of an old boat. It had seemed so tall to me as a child, now it looked pathetically small. It all made me feel rather old and sad.

In time I came to the bridge over the Fleet and the road on to the Isle of Portland. The official Dorset Coast Path omits the island but I was reluctant to bypass a place with such fascinating historical and naval connections, and there is a path all the way round. As I moved on to the island some members of the newly-formed Portland Rotary Club appeared. As I would be walking past their meeting place at lunchtime they suggested that I join them and talk about the walk so far. I agreed and spent two hours with them which was rather more than I had anticipated.

Walking down the eastern coastline, I noticed several winches which, because of the steep cliffs and few sheltered bays, have to be used to get the boats on to the cliff top. I also passed several abandoned stone quarries. At Portland Bill I sheltered behind the tall lighthouse to take some photographs. I climbed Pulpit Rock before walking the west coastline back towards the Fleet. The wind was side-on, making the walking hard. A little way past the Naval Gunnery School I had splendid views north-westwards along the whole length of the famous pebbled Chesil Beach. Darkness was falling as I descended into Fortuneswell. I decided to stay for to have gone on for another ten miles, in the dark, to Abbotsbury, would have been folly. Frustrated, I put my feet up after a lazy day of only twenty miles.

I had never walked the whole length of Chesil Beach before, despite many holidays with my grandparents in Weymouth. The beach is seventeen miles long and the pebbles start small and gradually increase in size to Portland where they are large. It is said that a local fisherman, washed up on the beach, can tell from the size of pebble exactly where he is. Rather than actually walk along the pebbled shore I decided to take the footpath beside the Fleet. After about ten miles' walking I reached Abbotsbury Swannery where I counted at least a hundred mute swans. At the Swannery I left the Fleet behind and walked either beside or on top of the beach. The beach has always had an unnerving effect on me; it is steep and shelves at an acute angle, and I find the noise of the pounding waves and the sucking noise of the pebbles being dragged back very eerie. As a child I would sit on the beach and listen spellbound to the tales my grandfather told me of the shipwrecks and treasure that supposedly lie beneath the stones. Often I would dig frantically for a foot or so, only to find nothing, and give up.

By mid afternoon I had reached West Bay, two miles south of Bridport, where a sponsored walker was waiting. We carried on along the sandy cliff tops to Seatown as dusk began to fall. Although my companion had farmed in the area for thirty-eight years he had never ascended Golden Cap, which is just over 600 feet high, and he was looking forward to it. As he would have to find his own way back in the dark, I carefully instructed his wife to park her car at a farm close to the base of the hill, and to put the headlights on. My partner could then leave the summit and aim for the lights.

The final 400 feet to the top were done in complete darkness. The gorse bushes and slippery surface gave us both an awkward time. At the triangulation pillar we shook hands, delighted that we had made it. I even apologized for a lack of view! We looked for the car and finally discovered it parked at the wrong farm. We descended towards St Gabriel's House and parted company. I hope he made it safely for he had no torch and it was pitch black. I would have liked to have accompanied him, but the London *Evening News* were waiting for me at Lyme Regis, and I had to press on.

After two hours' battling over non-existent paths in darkness, I reached Lyme Regis at nine o'clock. I felt in great shape with thirty-eight miles walked that day. Finding the hotel I walked in to see the manager waiting and obviously concerned that I was late. The reporters were already dining so, leaving my rucksack with the manager, I walked straight in in my muddy boots to join them. Eating a delicious steak, and sipping some red wine, I tried to answer their questions and give a general précis of the walk so far. London seemed a very long way away. It was midnight before I finally slept.

26.1.78

The first few miles were largely through the woodland of the Downlands Cliffs and landslips to Seaton. The area is principally clay, sandstone and chalk, which makes for slippery walking in the wet and helps explain why the area has had so many large landslips. Beyond Seaton I reached Branscombe Mouth and the Hooker Cliffs, the scene of a huge landslip in 1790, when ten acres of land slid into the sea, two hundred feet below.

The footpath along the cliff tops from Branscombe Mouth to Sidmouth was in a terrible state; it was waterlogged and oozing with mud. At first I tried to avoid the path but in the end it was simpler to use it and put up with the mud. I didn't linger at Sidmouth for I was determined to reach Exmouth that night, a good ten miles further along the coast. I could easily have stopped for I was more than a day ahead of schedule, but I had chosen to make for Exmouth and it would have upset me not to. By the time I reached Chiselbury Bay, some three miles from Budleigh Salterton, it was dark. As I neared the river Otter a flashing light could be seen weaving its way along the cliff path. It was Jim Cobley, the president of Exmouth Rotary Club, and an ardent backpacker, who had come to join me for the final five miles of the day.

We sat on a bench overlooking the sea at Budleigh Salterton and shared some chocolate. Two miles from Budleigh we entered one of the largest caravan sites in Britain with literally thousands of caravans covering a vast area. I was thankful that Jim was with me to guide me through. Three-quarters of an hour later we walked into a four-star hotel where I was given a room free of charge for the night. I dropped the rucksack, said goodbye to Jim, and ate a steak before relaxing in a hot bath. I had walked about eighty miles in the last thirty-six hours, and in the last two days had walked harder than ever before with sixty pounds of equipment. Tired, but pleased with my performance, I slept well.

27.1.78

Jim Cobley rejoined me, and together we walked beside the railway with the river Exe on our immediate left. At Lympstone, where the official right of way ends, we continued on along the railway to Topsham where we could once more get onto a path beside the river. After three hours of walking and with ten miles covered, we reached the Countess Wear Bridge just south of Exeter. Jim turned for home and I continued along the west bank of the river to Dawlish Warren. The road sign at the bridge read 'Plymouth 42 miles'; because of the various estuaries I would have to walk round, it was going to take me over two hundred miles.

By the time I reached Starcross, two miles from Dawlish Warren, the weather had taken a decided turn for the worse, and it began raining heavily. In the gloom I photographed the Atmospheric Railway Inn. In the early part of the nineteenth century, Brunel built an 'atmospheric railway' between Exeter and Plymouth. The motive power for the railway was derived from the pressure of the atmosphere, an idea first suggested by the French engineer, Papin, in the eighteenth century. There was a cylinder between the lines and ten pumping stations along its course. One still remains at Starcross. Air was pumped out of the cylinder creating a vacuum, which acted on a piston, which pulled the train. The project was a financial disaster and the line was closed in 1848. One of the problems encountered was rats, which took a liking to the grease used on the airtight seals, and another was that horses had to be used to pull the train in the beginning to get it going.

I splashed on in the rain, feeling the water running down my neck. At Teignmouth I called it a day, well placed to reach Torquay for 11.30 a.m. the following morning when I had agreed to meet Roger Smith, the editor of *The Great Outdoors*.

28.1.78

On the map, Torquay is just eight miles from Teignmouth. But the coastline from Teignmouth to Torquay is very deceptive: it is filled with little bays and is very hilly. It took me four hours of very hard walking to reach there, and so I was late for my meeting. Somewhat embarrassed, I approached the rather dwindled reception committee. Roger Smith was still waiting patiently; he knew I would arrive sooner or later. He was reporting my progress in his magazine, and from now on we would meet monthly. Together we walked round Tor Bay. The weather was excellent and I was beginning to think that perhaps the winter was over and spring was round the corner. At Goodrington Sands Roger left to return to Glasgow and I continued on to Brixham where I stayed the night.

29.1.78

Leaving Brixham I rounded Berry Head and caught the full onslaught of galeforce winds and driving rain. The temperature was barely above freezing. I fastened my cagoule tightly and, with my head well down, battled my way along the cliffs to Scabbacombe Sands and on to Newfoundland Cove at the mouth of the river Dart. Here began my first major trek inland to find a bridge to cross the river, and the detour accounted for much of the mileage I had to complete to reach Plymouth.

Almost two miles from the cove, I walked into Kingswear. A quarter of a mile across the water was Dartmouth and the Royal Naval College, which stands impressively above the town. Not being able to make use of the ferry, I began a thirty-mile walk to get there.

I planned to reach Totnes that night. Now that it was getting towards the end of January, the hours of daylight were increasing noticeably; it was light until 5.30 p.m. Walking up the river valley had its rewards, for I was sheltered from the gales and I saw my first spring flowers of the walk: periwinkles, red campion, violets, and primroses. Flying above the trees near Stoke Gabriel was my first pair of buzzards.

At Stoke Gabriel I was scarcely a mile from Goodrington, which I had walked through the previous day. The final part of the day's walk to Totnes was down a walled lane to Fleet Mill, before the last two miles over the hill to the town. As dusk fell, I walked up the narrow main street and past the pillared buildings to a private court, where one of my relations had invited me to stay.

30.1.78

I was away early, eager to get back to the coast at Dartmouth. The sun shone and the wind had dropped. I looked across the river to Kingswear and noticed an ocean research boat. Almost eight months later I saw the same ship off the Durham coast at Sunderland.

Dartmouth quay was very attractive and beautifully preserved; it looked just like a period filmset with its cobbled streets, gabled buildings and Custom House. Beyond were the rugged cliffs around Combe Point, the village of Blackpool and the Slapton Sands. The road at this point runs along the pebbled shore with the two lakes, Slapton Ley and Lower Ley on my immediate right. At the northern end of Slapton Sands stands a monument recording the American Army's thanks for the use of the beach and area in practice manoeuvres for D-Day.

After three miles of walking in the dark I reached Beesands. I found a telephone box and I decided to camp so that I could use it for my broadcast at eight o'clock the following morning. I checked that the phone was working, and searched for somewhere to camp. I found a site but for some reason the owner would not allow me to use it. I tried elsewhere but without success. Eventually I camped on the only piece of dry grass I could find, and obtained water from the public toilets. In the middle of the night the weather changed: the wind rose to galeforce and the rain lashed down. By morning my site was awash. Just before eight o'clock, I dashed across to the telephone for the interview and found the phone had been vandalized! I could make no broadcast that morning, and I felt totally thwarted.

31.1.78

I packed the tent in the pouring rain with a *Daily Mirror* reporter looking on. He had come for an interview, and wearing waterproofs and wellingtons, he walked with me to Hallsands. The weather was foul and after half an hour he left to return to his hotel. We would meet again next day, hoping for drier weather.

I saw little of the coast that day because of the conditions. My route took me over Start Point and on to Prawle Point and East Portlemouth at the mouth of the Kingsbridge estuary. By the time I got there I was soaked to the skin.

To get to Salcombe required a long walk inland via South Pool, Frogmore and Kingsbridge. Five miles from Salcombe I realized that I was not going to reach the post office in time to pick up my second parcel of maps, films, food and chocolate before it closed. I rang the postmistress and she very kindly offered to take the parcel to her house. I arrived there at 6.30 and, seeing my wet state, the couple invited me in and gave me a tumbler of whisky. I thanked them for helping me out, but ten minutes later I left to walk in total darkness through Salcombe (which was like a ghost town with no lights, cars or people) and up the palm-tree-lined drive to Overbecks Youth Hostel. There were two others staying there but it was too cold to be able to dry out adequately.

1.2.78

The *Daily Mirror* reporter rejoined me and as we left the youth hostel I saw my first snowdrops, and I crouched down to photograph them. Together we walked yet again in gales and driving rain. I felt sorry for him and he left after an hour, very wet, but with enough material. The photographer arrived later and managed to take some spectacular shots of pounding seas, with me in the foreground, all windswept and bedraggled!

On Bolt Head a sea mist came down to add to the poor

weather conditions, and I had to rely on the compass. Six miles later, at Bolt Tail, I descended into Outer Hope and watched the white waves roll relentlessly in. At Thurlestone the *Mirror* photographer was waiting again and took a couple more films. Another mile and I reached the river Avon, where I had to walk inland to Aveton Gifford to cross the river, before returning to the coast at Bigbury-on-Sea. I had lost so much time through all the photography, and I was so wet, that after only twenty-three miles I thought it wiser to stop. The warden of Bigbury Youth Hostel let me stay, and I was at last able to dry out some of my clothes.

2.2.78

Plymouth was just over a day away. It was scarcely twelve miles as the crow flies, yet because of the many rivers that forced me to walk inland, there were still forty-five miles to go. The river Erme was four miles from Bigbury-on-Sea. Rather than walk all the way up to the A379 to Sequer's Bridge, I thought I would try a footbridge marked on the map, one and a half miles further south. Walking along tracks to get there I reached a very unstable-looking wooden bridge. A notice told me that I crossed at my own risk. I started across and the bridge began to sway. Alarmed, I grabbed hold of the wooden rail for support, but it immediately parted company from the uprights and fell into the river. Cautiously, and without further mishaps, I reached the other side.

Back at the coast, I rejoined the Devon South Coast Path before walking up the creek to Newton Ferrers, on to Yealmpton and so into Brixton, where I stayed the night.

3.2.78

Having crossed Cofflete Creek, I walked down river to Season Point and Wembury and was at last able to make an uninterrupted coastal walk via Staddon Heights and Turnchapel to the Laira Bridge, Plymouth. The Lord Mayor of Plymouth had expressed a wish to meet me, and when I arrived at eleven o'clock I discovered the press and television were there to record it all. I had been walking for exactly one month and had clocked 880 miles. I was through the initial stages, had settled down well and was walking an average twenty-eight miles per day.

After my meeting with the mayor, my next port of call was Blacks' shop. As several of their shops are on the coast, it had been arranged that I would call in to meet the managers, talk about how everything was going and in particular how the equipment was standing up to it all. I was also to have whatever I needed from the shop. With the local press looking on, I was presented with a couple of pairs of socks, and a bar of Kendal mint cake.

A little after two o'clock, with a blackening sky, I left central Plymouth via the Hoe. By the time I reached the docks the rain had begun to fall, and within twenty minutes it was torrential and I was soaked. I crossed Tamar Bridge and entered Cornwall, my final county on the south coast of England. Passing through Saltash, the police suggested that because of the bad weather I should stop, but I wanted to get a little further on and so I continued until I reached a small guest house in Tideford. There, for the first time for several days, I was able to dry out most of my equipment. My boots however didn't dry out and it would be a further two months before they did.

4.2.78

Conditions were still poor when I left Tideford and headed down the peninsula via Sheviock and Millbrook to Cawsand Bay. Plymouth Sound lay in front of me but was almost invisible in the low mist. From there I picked up the Cornwall South Coast Path and began the walk to Land's End. From Rame Head the gently curving Whitsand Bay came into view and as the afternoon wore on, the weather brightened and I could at last appreciate the beauty of cliffs, shore and waves. An occasional gull flew past, shags sat on rocks, and my first seal popped up and watched me walk by. At teatime, feeling decidedly tired, I walked into Polperro. It had been a long, hard day.

5.2.78

Setting out from Polperro I knew that I had to reach Charlestown that night. It was thirty-eight miles away and would be the furthest I had ever walked with sixty pounds of equipment in one day. When I was setting off from London, a listener to the Radio 4 programme 'Start the Week with Richard Baker' had written in to offer me a bed and meal at his hotel. When I was three days away I had rung him to say that I was on my way and planned to arrive at about seven o'clock for dinner.

Not far from Polperro, as I came round the cliffs into Lantivet Bay, I saw eleven gannets flying low over the water. They were the first I had seen on the walk. Three miles later I walked into Polruan which sits at the mouth of the river Fowey. I could have thrown a stone across the river at Bodinnick to Fowey, but sticking to my rules it was a twelve mile walk via Lostwithiel to get there. Night was closing in as I reached Fowey and continued on to Gribben Head. At Polkerris it was dark and because I could not find the path to Polmear and Par, I decided to take to the road. In doing this I met a radio reporter from the Radio 4 programme 'Today', who had been looking for me for three hours! I stopped and we recorded a piece about the walk (I had now walked well over 900 miles). I carried on across Carlyon Bay to the hotel, arriving shortly after 7.30 p.m. I dropped the rucksack and sat straight down to dinner. Afterwards I lay in a hot bath, the first for many days, and soaked my aching muscles.

6.2.78

It was fitting that, as the owner of the hotel had heard me on Richard Baker's programme, I should make my first monthly contact with them from his telephone in the kitchen. After completing the broadcast, he kindly gave me some sandwiches and I set off to enjoy some of Cornwall's finest coastal scenery.

At Charlestown harbour I walked across the lock gates and watched a small ship being laden with china clay. The sun was now shining and looking inland I could see the pinnacles of clay near St Austell. Four miles later, just past Black Head, the path ended. The official South-West Peninsula Coast Path which comprises the Dorset Coast Path, South Devon Coast Path, South Cornwall Coast Path, North Cornwall Coast Path and the North Devon and Somerset Path, has been officially opened twice. Yet, parts of it still remain closed or the rights of way are blocked. Just south of Black Head for example, I searched in vain for a right of way and found nothing apart from blocked hedges and tangled brambles. I retreated to the road.

It occurred to me that the South-West Coast Path should be developed as one path rather than being broken down into five separate ones. As a continuous walk (apart from the big cities, such as Plymouth), it would replace the Pennine Way as the longest way-marked path in Britain. As a path it needs to be kept open and not allowed to get overgrown, as this discourages users. It also needs to be waymarked properly, for when it is only spasmodic the user tries to depend on it and eventually either loses his way, or gives up and takes to the nearest road as I was forced to do.

At Pentewan I picked up the coastal path again and rounded the shore of Mevagissey Bay to Mevagissey itself, where I stopped to look at the fish nets draped over the harbour walls and the boats bobbing up and down on the gentle swell. I was now really enjoying the walk and had completely settled down to my new way of life. The rugged coastline was magical and it was good to see the sturdy rock cliffs instead of the frail chalk cliffs and mud flats that I had seen in the south east.

I rounded Dodman Point in the late afternoon and by the time I reached Porthluney Cove the light was beginning to fail. My day's destination, Portloe, was still three miles further on, and I reached it in total darkness. I walked into the centre of the village and began my search for somewhere to stay. I stopped a lady in the street but before she was able to reply the Truro bus arrived and she rushed off to greet someone, calling 'He's here, he's here!' They both came over and the lady introduced me to Ken Johnstone who had been out looking for me to offer me somewhere to stay. What a delightful end to the day's walk. This kind of open generosity was something that never ceased to amaze and delight me, especially as I always expected to pay my own way.

7/8.2.78

Ahead of me from Portloe were several particularly attractive sandy beaches, such as Pendower beach and Portscatho. At the latter I broke my normal rule of not drinking during the day and for the first time since setting out I went into a pub for lunch. I had a half of lager and lime and two 'oggies' (Cornish pasties), which were locally made and extremely tasty. I set off down the remainder of the peninsula to Zone Point feeling much refreshed. I very nearly had to return the same way to get round the Percuil River before heading south once more to St Mawes. Ahead of me was a particularly savage detour, for from St Mawes I could see the lights of Falmouth just two miles away across the Carrick Roads, but to get there by following the coastline and negotiating the rivers Fal, Tresillian and Truro required a walk of thirty-two miles. At Truro I went into the cathedral to look around and also to pray.

I stayed in Falmouth that night, delighted with my performance of 1,028 miles walked in thirty-seven days. My only immediate problem was my colour camera. I carry two 35 mm SLR cameras, one for colour and the other for black and white. The colour camera was giving false light-meter readings but after trying three camera shops I was able to buy a new battery and the camera functioned as normal. Without the camera I felt lost. It is very satisfying to do a major walk but it is essential for me to come back with a photographic record, for I would never do the same major walk twice.

9.2.78

Six miles beyond Falmouth I reached the delightfully named Rosemullion Head, from where I could see the river Helford, the last major river on the south coast of Britain. It is most picturesque, with several wooded creeks, including Frenchman's Creek, and is a popular spot for yachting in the summer. Several of the footpaths in the area, especially near Helford, pass through woodland, and they provided some of my most enjoyable walking in Cornwall. At the head of the river, at Gweek, Helston was only four miles away. Had I not been three days ahead of schedule I would have seen a demonstration of the Helston Floral Dance. A version of the dance played by the Brighouse and Rastick Brass Band was in the top twenty at the time. I stayed in the unspoilt and attractive village of Helford and from my window I noticed a hard frost covering everything.

10.2.78

I left Helford with a jaunty step to begin walking round the Lizard peninsula, the most southerly point of the British mainland. I have often holidayed at Cadgwith and so I was moving into familiar and well-loved territory; for me this peninsula is one of the most scenic stretches of coastline in Cornwall. Although a sunny day it was extremely cold, and I wore my duvet and gloves. My log records two important comments that day: 'Ice – rare in this sector of the country' and 'Rucksack – used to load and walk'.

It was strange to be walking where I had been so often before, and while at times it spoiled my enjoyment to know what lay around the corner, at others my memory played tricks on me and I would discover something I had expected to see a couple of miles further on. It was also strange to be walking there in the quiet season, seeing no tourists and no walkers. In fact I had not seen another walker since leaving London, and I wasn't to see more than a handful on the entire walk!

When I reached Porthoustock I had to negotiate the quarries which tumble down into the sea. Four miles later I entered Coverack, a peaceful, small village with a lifeboat, close to Dolor Point. I carried on round Black Head and across the Kennack Sands, eager to get to Cadgwith. I hadn't been there for five years, and I wanted to know if it had changed. I was relieved to discover that it hadn't – the cluster of thatched houses and cottages was just the same. The only noticeable differences were that some new houses had appeared at the back of the village and that a magnificent thatched house which I always looked for had been burned down. Cadgwith is one of those places where time stays still and where the inhabitants are aware of the beauty of their community and work hard to keep it as it is.

After climbing down into the village and back out again, I regained the cliff tops for the final few miles to Lizard Point. Back on the flat I passed by the Devil's Frying-Pan. It was once a cave but at its furthest point inland it had collapsed exposing a pebbled shore and forming a huge natural archway. Walking around and talking to people it is fascinating to discover the different names for natural features. In the Shetlands this formation would be known as a 'gloup'. Likewise, rivers in different areas may be called streams, becks or burns, and lakes may be called lochs, leys, water and tarns.

A brief descent took me to Landewednack and scarcely two miles further on, I reached the lighthouse and car park of Lizard Point. The sun was setting and as I looked southwards I watched several ships passing by, far out to sea. It was so peaceful that I was reluctant to move, but I had to move inland to stay at Lizard.

11.2.78

The cold weather continued and my duvet and gloves remained on. The ground was frozen hard and was covered with large sheets of ice; the cliffs, especially at Mullion Cove, were draped with icicles. Beyong Kynance Cove and its rock stacks was The Rill, from where the advancing Spanish Armada was first sighted in 1588. Walking up the western side of the Lizard I rounded Mount's Bay, the final major bay on the southern coast of Britain. The coves of Ogo-dour, Mullion, Polurrian and Poldhu are all spectacular with steep cliffs. Very few sea birds were about and I saw only the occasional gull and cormorant. By the one stream which was still flowing I flushed a snipe, and at Mullion Cove a seal was observing the scene.

At Poldhu Cove I reached the plaque which commemorates Marconi's radio station which was in use from 1903 to 1922. It was from here in 1901 that Marconi sent his first message to America. Beyond the cove the rugged coastline gave way to a four-mile stretch of sand, past Loe Bar to Porthleven. Close to

49

the Bar stood a solitary monument recording the hundred lives lost in 1807, when the frigate HMS *Anson* was driven onto the shore and pounded to pieces. Further sandy beaches lay in front of me as I made my way to Marazion, via Praa Sands and Perran Sands. I walked the final stages of the day's thirty-one miles in darkness, along the footpath beside the pebbled shore.

One of the bonuses of the walk was being able to visit friends whom I would otherwise be unlikely to see. Ralph Gould was one such person and he was waiting for me at Marazion where he lived. We had met in 1977 on one of my Peakland Way walks; he had taken up backpacking following his retirement and I had been impressed by his performance. He took me to his house where we sat beside a blazing fire sipping wine. Over a delicious meal we yarned away about the Peakland Way and about my current walk.

12.2.78

After being photographed on the beach with St Michael's Mount behind, we said farewell and I set off for Land's End. I was very excited for this was one of the most significant points of the walk. With Penzance and Newlyn behind me, I was walking along the cliff tops towards Mousehole when I looked down and saw the fishing boat, the *Conqueror*, smashed into the rocks. It had been shipwrecked in December 1977, and within ten hours of being on the rocks £25,000 worth of fittings were stolen. The Cornish Wreckers hadn't lost their knack! The boat was now something of a spectacle and while I was there a continuous stream of people came along to peer down and photograph it.

After walking through the pretty village of Mousehole, I was once again in unfamiliar territory. Two miles further on I found Lamorna Cove which with its sandy beach and rocky foreshore was perfect. The daffodils that grow in profusion, and for which it is justly renowned, were in bud. Another three days and it would have been stunning.

Now there were just ten miles to go to Land's End. I speeded up and the miles disappeared quickly. Occasional flurries of light snow swept across as I passed Penberth, Porthgwarra and

Mill Bay, and in the distance I could see that Land's End and Longships lighthouse were already covered in snow. I could also see snow on the Scilly Isles; it was their first for thirty years. I had planned the walk so that I should round the south-west peninsula in February, as it is normally milder than the rest of Britain at that time, and rarely has snow or ice. But this year was an exception: it was freezing and snow-laden.

I scanned Land's End for people through my binoculars. I had met the Mayor of Penzance as I walked through earlier in the day, and had taken the precaution of telling everyone that I would arrive there an hour later than I actually would, so that I could have a little time to myself. Seeing no people there, I quickly moved on.

Reaching Land's End was a very emotional moment. Behind me was the entire south coast, a distance of 1,138 miles. I was pleased to be able to savour the moment alone and to try to understand the enormity of what I was doing, but it didn't really register. I prayed to give thanks for having had the strength to get there and I asked for help for the days and months ahead. Then I literally turned right for Cape Wrath. I came round to Sennen and walked along the snow-lined shore to Sunny Corner. Waiting patiently for me was the chairman of Penwith District Council. I stayed at Sennen that night, looking out on the winter scene.

13.2.78

Leaving Sennen, it was extremely strange to feel that I was now walking northwards, up the west coast of Britain. There was a definite spring in my step. It was strange, too, to be walking in three-inch deep snow, and to be traversing great sheets of ice. The wind was strong as I set off wearing my duvet and gloves, and although after a couple of miles I was extremely warm inside, I knew better than to take them off. As I neared Cape Cornwall two sea birds shot by playing with the currents of air. When they hovered just above the cliff edge, I suddenly realized they were fulmars, the first I had seen on the walk. I have been fascinated by this sea bird ever since I visited their main nesting ground on the island of St Kilda in the

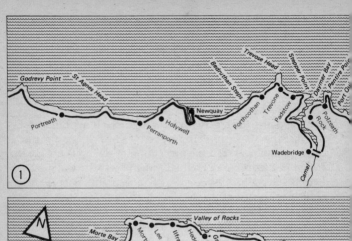

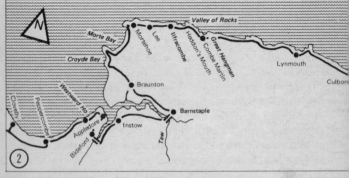

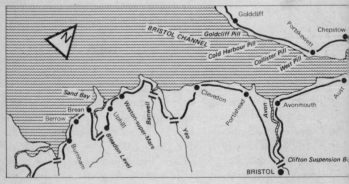

N

Upright Cliff
Hartland Point
Speke's Mill Mouth
Welcombe Mouth
Marsland Mouth
Hartland
Clovelly
Isaac Bay
High Cliff
Widemouth Bay
Bude
Tintagel
Boscastle
Millook
Crackington Haven
Dizzard
Gaverne
Tresparrett

N

Burnham
Start Point
Brue
Pawlett
Parrett
Bridgwater
lock
worthy
eacon
Minehead
Minehead
Watchet
East Quantoxhead
Otterhampton

③

Wye
Tidenham
Woolaston
Alvington
Newnham
Westbury-on-Severn
Minsterworth
ER SEVERN
Sharpness
Gloucester and Sharpness Canal
GLOUCESTER
Upper Hill
Slimbridge
evern

④

N

53

Outer Hebrides. Until the 1890s St Kilda was their only habitat in Britain, but since then they have spread all over the country and they are now one of the fastest growing sea bird populations. There are reputed to be more than 600,000 off our shores but my observations led me to believe there are a lot less.

The scenery at Cape Cornwall, the only cape in England and Wales, was spectacular, with pounding waves and the ground covered with snow. A little under a mile later I reached Botallack Head with its derelict mine shafts and engine houses. The shafts run out under the sea for up to a mile and are so close to the sea bed that the miners could often hear the movement of the sea above them. I quickened my pace as the wind increased and occasional snow showers swept in from the sea. Fourteen miles away in Bottalack Head I reached Pendour Cove and walked inland to Zennor. Although it was not yet five o'clock I broke my rule and stopped early, mainly because it had been arranged for me to stay at the vicarage, but also because the worsening conditions made it foolish to consider carrying on.

Over dinner the vicar told me about Zennor church which is renowned for its mermaid legend and the fifteenth-century carving of a mermaid which can be found on one of the bench ends. According to the legend, Matthew Trewella, a squire's son, was a chorister with a particularly attractive voice. One day a mermaid heard him singing and she found it so enchanting that she came out of the sea to find out who the voice belonged to. Discovering Matthew, she lured him back with her and he was never seen again, although it is said that you can sometimes still hear him singing in the sea.

Noticing some scales, I took the opportunity of weighing myself. I had lost four pounds, and weighed 10 stone 4 lb. Being six foot tall I am light for my height, but I usually weigh about $10\frac{1}{2}$ stones and this was my weight when I set off from St Paul's. Being slightly underweight told me that my body, even after walking more than a thousand miles, had not fully adjusted to the walk. It was to be early March before I was back up to $10\frac{1}{2}$ stones.

14.2.78

Three hours' walking in cold and dry conditions brought me to St Ives. Waiting for me there were the presidents of the St Ives and Hayle Rotary Clubs and the Mayor of St Ives. We adjourned to the council chamber for coffee, and half an hour later I set off again to walk round the mouth of the river Hayle and on to the Gwithian Sands. By this time the weather had cheered up considerably with blue sky and a hint of sun. I called into a baker's shop and treated myself to four cream cakes, which I ate on the beach.

Beyond the beach I regained the cliffs near Godrevy Point and walked along the edge to Portreath, six miles away. Fulmars and a few gulls were flying around and at one point a green woodpecker hopped in front of me. As dusk was falling I walked across the sands to Portreath. There, to my surprise, were members of the Redruth Rotary Club. So instead of having a night in the tent I was royally entertained at a private dinner party. The house was large and encircled a swimming pool. It was quite a contrast to my nights in the tent but even though I was beginning to take such events in my stride they still placed a very great strain on me mentally.

15/16.2.78

The next two days were very cold with torrential rain, and on both days I was soaked to the skin. The first day, from Portreath to Newquay, I had to walk in atrocious conditions and by the time I reached Perranporth there wasn't a dry patch on me. With rain dripping from my nose I crossed the beach and went on to Holywell, where much to my relief the army allowed me to walk through their camp. Six miles later, with twenty-eight miles walked that day, I reached Newquay and dried out. The second day to Padstow was equally filthy: rain streamed down, the wind cut into me and the visibility was poor. At Bedruthan Steps the whole landscape was obliterated by a raging blizzard. It was no place to stop; I hurried on, head down. I rarely looked at the map for it was a major operation just to get it out and when I did it was soaked through before I could even look at it. I simply ticked the places off in my mind, Porthcothan, Trevose Head, Trevone, Stepper Point and Padstow. There I sought refuge and dried my clothes.

17.2.78

Thankfully it was calmer and surprisingly it didn't rain. Little did I know it, but this was the lull before the storm. From Padstow to Daymer Bay, and inland to Wadebridge, was a long detour to cross the river Camel. Rather than walk along the A389, which was the nearest right of way, I decided to follow the course of the old railway line which runs beside the river. It proved to be a peaceful interlude and I saw many birds including buzzards, mute swans, curlews, shelduck, pheasants, dunlins, oyster-catchers, wrens, robins, starlings, herring gulls and a grey heron. The gorse was in full bloom and patches of snowdrops and violets gave the feeling of spring.

After meeting the Mayor of Wadebridge, I headed back out to the coast via Rock, to Daymer Bay and its small interesting church, St Enodoc's, which on several occasions had been almost entirely submerged by the shifting sand dunes. From Polzeath I rounded Pentire Point to Port Quin Bay and Port Isaac. The latter is most impressive from the cliffs, for as you round them you suddenly look down on to this picturesque cluster of buildings, the sea and the boats. I continued on to Port Gaverne where I called it a day.

18/19.2.78

This Saturday was a day I shall never forget. The weather had taken a decided turn for the worse, and it was exceedingly cold with galeforce winds. The prospect of walking in these conditions was daunting, but as I liked the idea of sitting around even less, I set off from Port Gaverne to cross the steep cliffs to Tintagel, six miles away. The wind grew stronger and stronger and in no time I was fighting for my life. I had experienced equally strong winds near Lulworth in Dorset, but there the winds had come off the sea, keeping me on the cliffs and enabling me to make progress. Near Tintagel the wind changed direction and came off the land. I could not stand upright and the only way to safeguard myself from being blown over the edge was to hold onto the barbed wire fence. Bent almost double, and being blown off my footing almost constantly, I struggled on. It began to snow, and then almost immediately to hail; both snow and hail were blown horizontally into my face, stinging it badly. In no time I was drenched and very cold. I called at a friend's house at Tintagel and had a bowl of soup. He pressed me to stay, but I declined and fought my way northwards to Boscastle. Even the birds seemed stunned by the raging storm. Since leaving Port Gaverne I had seen many that just stood still as I passed by; several had lost their tail feathers. At Boscastle I stopped and in my log wrote: 'Foolish to go on – some of the worst conditions experienced anywhere. Stopped at 3 p.m.'

There was no alternative. In front of me was High Cliff; at 700 feet high these are the highest cliffs in Cornwall. In such conditions it would have been folly to attempt them. Everyone was very worried for my safety and the local rotary club kindly took me to the house of one of their members, a few miles inland, to dry out and sit out the storm. I stayed all the next day feeling utterly miserable, pacing up and down and generally hating the inactivity that was being forced on me. I felt quite sorry for my hosts but I think they understood. Outside the snow was falling heavily and the wind continued to blow. News on the radio and television painted incredible scenes of widespread chaos as cars and people were reported lost, telephone lines and electricity cables blown down, villages cut off and animals trapped under twenty-five-foot snowdrifts. These were the worst blizzards to hit the south-west for thirty years.

20.2.78

The snow had stopped, so I resumed the walk. Getting back to Boscastle was difficult because the the roads were blocked, but we managed to get to within four miles and I left my host at Tresparrett Posts. From there I set off walking south to Boscastle along the submerged road, often walking from hedge to hedge with the road six feet below. Once in Boscastle I rejoined my route round the coast. The wind was still strong and as the weather became milder it began to rain. My log describes the day: 'Galeforce winds and rain. Low cloud. Poor visibility. Soaked to the skin. Walked over stiles submerged in snow. Kicked steps in snow up the cliffs. Cornices. Dead birds. Blocked roads.'

I saw very little as I ascended High Cliff, descended to Crackington Haven and went on to Dizzard. At Millook I could at last see the impressive rock formations before carrying on to Widemouth Bay and Bude. I reached Bude at eight o'clock, completely soaked, after taking twelve hours to walk about twenty-four miles. I walked into St Margaret's Hotel, the first hotel that I saw, and found a room. Seeing my state the owners prepared me a meal, ran a bath and opened the bar for me. They also laid out all my clothes and equipment to dry. I could not have wished for anything better.

21.2.78

While eating breakfast I listened to the radio report. Conditions were still very, very bad, and everywhere was still in chaos. At Hartland Point, where I planned to get to that day, it was reported that the coastguards were marooned there and that a helicopter was being sent out to rescue them. With ten bars of chocolate in the rucksack, I set off to fight my way through the drifts and the waist-deep snow to Hartland. On the way it began to thaw, which created the additional problem of swollen rivers. The first one I encountered was at Marsland Mouth, at the border of Cornwall and Devon, where the small stream had swelled to become a fast-flowing river. I waded across only to find, half a mile later, that the stream at Welcombe Mouth had flooded. Taking a deep breath I plunged into the icy water and waded across to the other side.

By midday the weather had brightened and the rain had stopped. I began to enjoy the cliff walk along the Somerset and North Devon Coast Path. At Speke's Mill Mouth I stopped to watch the waterfall roaring down the vertical rock face. Because of the thaw it was in full spate and the light brown water was battering everything in its path. Nearing Upright Cliff, just south of Hartland Point, I watched a beautiful sunset explode across the horizon and saw the fiery ball lower into the sea. I camped near the stream on the driest patch of ground I could find.

22.2.78

I awoke to the sound of beating rain; so much for the omen of a good sunset. I packed everything inside the tent and took down the inner tent. Then, as fast as I could, I took down the flysheet and strapped it to the rucksack.

Near Clovelly, eight miles from my campsite, I came upon an extraordinary scene. Because the roads were still blocked and the farms were virtually cut off, the farmers were having to bring their milk to the tanker. There, by the side of the main road, I stood and watched as they used all manner of containers to transfer the milk from their lorries to the tanker.

Clovelly is one of the most beautiful villages in Britain. Its cobbled main street is lined with white-painted houses, which in the summer are decked with flower baskets. The only trouble is, as everybody knows, that in the summer it is thronged with people who come to admire it. It was nice therefore to see it in winter, when it was almost deserted but still full of character. Looking out to sea I could see Lundy Island. As there is no cliff path I kept to the road and descended to Peppercombe where I picked up the coast path again to reach Westward Ho!

Galeforce winds had raged all day and by late afternoon it was pouring with rain. As the snow began to thaw it brought widespread flooding. Entering Westward Ho! the road was knee-deep with water a hundred yards wide. I waited until two lorries passed and then crossed. Soaked once more from head to toe, I found accommodation at Appledore and dried out while watching the news. I rarely saw television and when I did I enjoyed the novelty. Reports of the south-west were still as bad as ever. Many villages were cut off and sheep were constantly being found dead under the drifts, although some had miraculously survived.

23.2.78

Much of the snow had gone on this section of the coast, so

although it was overcast and raining, the walking was basically straightforward and enjoyable. My route for the early part of the day was largely along roads as I crossed the river Torridge at Bideford and walked beside it to Instow. From there it was part path and part road to get to Barnstaple and the crossing of the river Taw. Another road took me to Braunton where I could at last get onto a path and walk through the dunes to Croyde Bay where I stayed. It had been a messy bit of coastal walking, but it was necessarily so because of the two large river estuaries that had to be crossed.

24.2.78

I had arranged to meet Chris Brasher from the *Observer* at Heddon's Mouth where I planned to camp. It was a thirty-two-mile walk to get there, but at least it was dry and sunny! There was still plenty of snow around and I was still walking through drifts and occasionally sinking up to my waist in snow. First I traversed Morte Bay to Mortehoe and on to Lee, Ilfracombe and Combe Martin. From there I began the ascent of the 1,000-foot Great Hangman. These cliffs are among some of the finest in Britain and, given good weather, as I had enjoyed on my Land's End to John o'Groats walk, they make a scene of unforgettable beauty. The snow made my pace slow, and I did not arrive at Heddon's Mouth until seven o'clock. Chris had not arrived so I found an excellent camp site beside the stream, where I cooked a large meal and, after eating it, fell immediately asleep.

25.2.78

Three miles from Heddon's Mouth, near the Valley of Rocks, I met Chris. He had got to within a mile of Heddon's Mouth by car the previous day but had been blocked by snow. I was slightly nervous of meeting such an outstanding athlete but in no time I felt at ease with him and enjoyed his company as we walked to Porlock. Looking across the Bristol Channel we could see South Wales. With almost 1,500 miles behind me, I was now attuned to the journey and enjoying every stride that I took. At Lynmouth, which, eight days after the blizzard, was still virtually cut off, I went into a shop to buy chocolate. The shelves were bare; supplies had not been getting through and food stocks were low. They still had some boiled sweets, and I made do with those instead.

Beyond Lynmouth the walking was hard as the snow had been blown into the lanes and again we sank up to our knees. At Culbone we paused to have a look round the pottery and the church which has masonry dating back to Saxon times. Accommodation had been arranged at the police station at Porlock, where we were able to dry out and enjoy the luxury of a bath. The station office was soon festooned with my tent and equipment. Within an hour of arriving we sat down to a splendid meal; I was more than grateful for their interest and help.

26.2.78

Chris and I continued on our way to Minehead and the end of the South-West Peninsula Coast Path. I felt sad that this section of the walk was coming to an end. I had really enjoyed the scenery and, amazingly, the conditions. We ascended Selworthy Beacon and continued on over North Hill before descending to Minehead. There I said goodbye to Chris. He had his story and his photographs, but I was sorry that he was going for I had enjoyed his company.

I carried on to meet some other walkers who were sponsored for five miles near Watchet. As the tide was out I collected some ammonite fossils which I gave to one of the walkers to send to me later. Their walk raised £240. At East Quantoxhead I stopped for the day. Behind me lay a major section of coastline; I was sad it was over. But ahead lay the Bristol Channel and the Welsh coast; I couldn't wait to get there.

4. Severn Estuary and Wales

Spring was definitely in the air as I left East Quantoxhead: I saw my first peacock butterfly of the walk, a skylark rose into the air singing and lambs were playing in the fields. The blizzard and its aftermath were now behind me, the weather was milder and as I made my way up the Bristol Channel via Bridgwater to Burnham-on-Sea, it remained dry except for one short, sharp downpour.

By early afternoon I had reached Start Point and began the sixteen-mile walk up the river Parrett to Bridgwater and out on the main A38 to Burnham. At Bridgwater I indulged my liking for cream cakes and bought four which I took to a small park to eat. I looked around the church where, from a lookout on the spire, the Duke of Monmouth had watched his troops being soundly defeated by James II at the Battle of Sedgemoor in 1685, approximately four miles due east of the town. The battlefield is reputedly haunted and many mysterious sounds have been heard. The aftermath of this singularly bloody encounter was that Judge Jeffreys came to Taunton and held the 'Bloody Assize' after which two hundred people were hanged and eight hundred transported.

At Pawlett a car pulled up and out stepped Roger Smith. It seemed incredible that a month had passed since I had seen him at Torquay, and that I had walked 800 miles since then. Together we walked to Burnham and after crossing the river Brue we regained the coast along an extremely muddy path. By this time it was almost dark although the setting sun splashed a brilliant red across the clouds. At Burnham we parted, and I went on to stay with the local baker. My boots were beginning to show signs of wear now that I had walked over 2,000 miles in them, the laces had gone and I was presented with a new pair. I am always reluctant to change laces, as I get rather attached to them and I generally prefer to knot them instead.

28.2.78

Leaving Burnham I made my way with a fellow rotarian to Berrow and Brean. On the understanding that there was no one else to accompany me that day I agreed that he could come with me for five miles. I didn't mind one of these events a day but any more were a strain. It was a pleasant surprise when he was able to contribute to the walk by showing me where the sluice gates were for getting across Bleadon Level, thereby saving me a longer walk inland along the road. At the gates I thanked him for his help and continued on to Uphill and Weston-super-Mare. Rounding Sand Bay, I was surprised to be joined by twenty pupils of Worle School who had arranged to walk to the base of Middle Hope with me. They retraced their steps in the pouring rain while I walked round the point and past Woodspring Priory, to the sluice gates over the river Banwell. Another set of gates took me across the river Yeo to Clevedon, and to another surprise encounter.

Waiting for me there were about a hundred pupils from Clevedon School who walked with me for two and a half miles. Another two clubs joined in on the way. I reached Portishead in the dark, with thirty-one miles walked that day. I was drained mentally and physically from the constant attention. This could not go on, for these unexpected encounters were killing the walk and were imposing an unfair strain on me. I was forced to make my feelings known. The main bone of contention was that everyone had begun to think it was a charity walk and that I was some form of public property. But I was doing the walk as the ultimate challenge to a marathon walker. I had agreed that the walk could be used to raise money, provided I knew what was proposed, and could therefore keep it to proportions I could handle. I realize that everyone was well-meaning, but when a lot of people are arranging things individually and you are the only common factor, there was bound to be some friction – especially when I wasn't told of the arrangements made for me! Unfortunately I didn't gain the control I wanted until I reached Scotland.

1.3.78

I left Portishead early for I had agreed to be at the Clifton suspension bridge at eleven o'clock. On the way the regional BBC television film crew met me and recorded an interview. As I neared the bridge the traffic was stopped and the custodian escorted me across to the waiting reporters and photographers. On the way over he told me I was one of two celebrities to cross the bridge that day: the other was Prince Charles who was due in the afternoon. I was immensely flattered to be paired with His Royal Highness in that way! With the press and formalities over, I descended to the A4 and to the river Avon. I was accompanied by five sponsored walkers who had asked permission to join me. But after the experience of the day before, I found it difficult to give of my best and I was fairly quiet as we walked on to Avonmouth.

The walking now offered a staggering contrast to the remote coastline of Cornwall. I was walking along a main road with heavy articulated lorries thundering by. Either side of me were factories, petrol tanks and chemical complexes belching out smoke and smells. Yet strangely enough the sight did not appal me. The industry was interesting, and I took numerous pictures of the contrasting scenes, for this was still coastline. I camped that night at Aust on the English side of the Severn (M4) road bridge.

Beside the bridge was a sign which read 'Chepstow 4½ miles'. As I had decided against using any motorway bridges, I had to walk inland as far as Gloucester – a detour of some 120 miles!

2.3.78

The day started well from Aust, in bright and dry weather. As I walked along the sea walls to Oldbury-on-Severn, I saw numerous cone-shaped wicker baskets. They are known as putchers and are still used for catching salmon in the Severn. Near Upper Hill, beyond Oldbury-on-Severn I had to dodge a hunting party. I learnt later that it was the Berkeley Hunt, out specially so that Prince Charles could ride.

At Sharpness I joined the Gloucester and Sharpness canal and walked along the tow path, in pouring rain, to Slimbridge Youth Hostel. The conditions didn't warrant a look at the Wildfowl Trust, but overhead I could see the geese flying in and hear their gaggle of voices.

3.3.78

The weather was superb. My log says 'sunny and bright. Spring has arrived'. Pussy-willow was in blossom, catkins hung from the trees, coltsfoot was out and a brimstone butterfly flitted by. It all gave me a sense of well-being. I rejoined the tow path and headed for Gloucester for I had agreed to meet a publisher to discuss the possibility of a book on the walk, at the post office at one o'clock. The canal was very busy with tankers coming up to unload at a small refinery, a tug pulling four heavily-laden barges, and private motor boats passing by.

I reached Gloucester post office in time and called in for my mail. The editorial director was waiting for me and we went to a steak bar to discuss the book and the terms. We agreed upon it in principle and I signed a contract four months later. (This book is the result.)

After two hours' discussion I left, and took the opportunity of looking inside Gloucester cathedral. But I was quite put off by the crowds and didn't stay long. I was decidedly giddy from the wine and in the next three-quarters of an hour I walked four and a half miles out of Gloucester to Minsterworth. There I began to feel better and walked at my usual steady pace of three miles per hour. As I entered Westbury-on-Severn I stopped to look at the canal gardens, made at the beginning of the seventeenth century. They are unique in Britain and are some of the few Dutch-influenced gardens in existence today. The garden was acquired by the National Trust in 1967 and since then they have carried out an extensive restoration

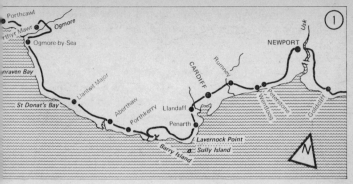

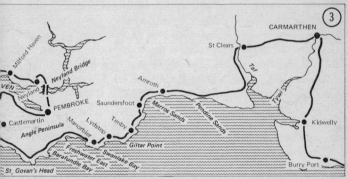

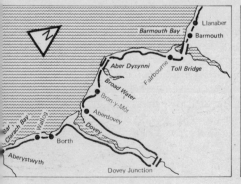

programme. With the sun shining and the reflections of the pavilion on the canal water it looked captivating.

I walked down beside the Severn to Chepstow and Wales in the warm sun. This was to be my last day in England for a month. At Newnham church there was a splendid view down on to the river. Crocuses were beginning to emerge and banks of snowdrops were in bloom. Because of the railway line and there being no right of way along the sea walls, I had no option but to walk along the road to Chepstow via Alvington, Woolaston and Tidenham. Unbeknown to me, my progress was being watched. Just before Chepstow and the iron bridge, I joined Offa's Dyke Path. Suddenly a police car drew up and the sergeant presented me with a leek. 'You must carry your passport into Wales,' he said. Feeling slightly stupid I walked into Wales with the leek. I had it for tea later that night!

I have walked Offa's Dyke Path twice but I have yet to visit Chepstow Castle. Rising from the banks of the river Wye, I consider its location, at a bend of the river with high ground behind it, the finest of any castle in Britain; it is perfectly sited for defence and beauty. It has had a chequered history. The oldest part of the castle is the Great Tower which includes part of the first castle built by William Fitz Osbern, Earl of Hereford in 1067–71. Much of the present building was built in the thirteenth century. In 1690 it was partly dismantled and in 1953 came under the guardianship of the Department of the Environment. It was held for the King during the Civil War and during the latter part of the seventeenth century it was used as a prison for political prisoners.

I walked on through Chepstow and past an unusual inn named 'The Five Alls', which are listed as 'I fight for all, I pray for all, I rule all, I plead for all, I pay for all'.

At Portskewett, four miles from Chepstow, I stopped for the night, delighted to be in Wales.

I awoke to find a glorious sunny day. From Portskewett I

made my way on to the river bank and walked past the stream mouths (known as pills), of West Pill, Collister Pill, Cold Harbour Pill and Goldcliff Pill. Near there I met the press officer for Cardiff, who told me that several city officials would like to meet me on the city boundary. I told him that I would be at the boundary, just past Peterstone Wentlooge, at about 4.30 p.m.

From Goldcliff I made my way inland to cross the river Usk at Newport. Rather than go right into the town to cross the river I wanted to use the transporter bridge. Instead of a moveable swing section to allow shipping through, a transporter bridge has a very high platform with a tower on each bank supporting the cross piece. On the platform runs a moveable trolley from which cables are suspended to a carrying platform. On this the car and passengers are transported horizontally across the river. The Newport bridge was opened on 12 September 1906. Originally there were several of these massive metal constructions around the coast. A famous one ran across the Mersey near Runcorn, but that has been replaced with a permanent high road bridge. The only other remaining transporter bridge in the country is at Middlesbrough, and I used that seven months later.

My rules didn't allow me to use the carrying platform and so I began ascending the zig-zag stairs up to the cross piece, a hundred feet above the river. With a sixty-pound pack on my back, narrow stairs and a hand rail which shook alarmingly, the ascent was an unnerving experience. Yet I would not have missed it for the world! The view was superb and in such clear conditions I could see for miles. I stayed a long time on the platform photographing the landscape and the carrying platform as it transported people across. At first I was nervous when the structure vibrated, but I soon felt quite at home.

Down on the ground again I headed due south back to the sea wall. I was met again by the press officer, who realized I was running late and that it would be nearer 5.30 p.m. by the time I reached the boundary. Two hours later I walked towards a large group of people and a long line of cars parked on either side of the road. Waiting to welcome me was the chairman of

South Glamorgan County Council, the Lord Lieutenant of Glamorganshire, Sir Kenneth Traherne, and other dignitaries. I was rather overwhelmed. In the growing darkness and with flashbulbs popping I signed the city book and was presented with a Cardiff tie, a set of flags, a Parker pen and a book on South Glamorgan. As I couldn't carry them I asked if they could be posted home for my eventual return. Sir Kenneth invited me to stay with him and his wife who was the president of the R CS B Council in Wales. I would have to be taken by car to their residence, but first I insisted on walking to Rumney on the outskirts of Cardiff. Wherever I was taken from I had to be returned to the following day. I was a little overawed by the company I was moving into but it was a foretaste of what was to happen throughout Wales. Being an Englishman I noticed with envy the patriotism of the Welsh and Scottish. They are not afraid to express their love for their country and to sing its praises loudly. The English are more reserved and rarely vent their feelings.

From Rumney the press officer took me to Sir Kenneth's house where I was given the same room that Prince Charles uses when he visits the city of Cardiff. I was informed we would have a simple meal as it was Sunday and the cook's day off. We sat down to a meal of consommé soup, toast and pâté, and a bottle of red wine. I retired to bed just after ten o'clock where I wrote my log and rounded off the meal with two bars of chocolate!

6.3.78

The morning was exceedingly hectic. First I was chauffeur-driven to Llandaff where I did a live broadcast for BBC 'Good Morning Wales'. I literally had to run to another studio where I did another live spot with Richard Baker on 'Start the Week'. I then climbed into the city car and was chauffeured back to Rumney. The morning shoppers looked surprised to see me climb out of the official car in my shorts and lift my rucksack out of the boot. With a cheery wave I set off for central Cardiff and then Penarth.

As I walked out of Cardiff a police car drew up and the

occupants wished me well. Little did I know that my progress was being monitored and that people ahead of me were being kept informed. I was setting a good pace and by midday I was in Penarth, comfortably placed to reach Atlantic College near Llantwit Major where I planned to stay the night. Just as I neared the pier a police car drew up and the constable informed me that I was wanted at the station. A little annoyed that I had to retrace my steps, I went back to the station. There I was told that the mayor wanted to meet me and would be coming shortly with a cheque. An hour later I left, after agreeing to meet him again when I had crossed Barry Island.

The walk out of Penarth along the cliffs to Lavernock Point was delightful, especially as it was warm and sunny. Having never visited this part of Wales before, I was continually surprised at its beauty; it was the reverse of the industrial image I had originally had. Sully Island and Bay were good examples. Beyond was Barry Island and docks and I made my way across the lock gates. On my right I could see numerous steam trains waiting to be dismantled. A sad fate, but one at least, called Peak Railway, was being preserved as part of a plan to bring steam back to the Peak District.

I met the mayor as arranged and we were photographed together for the press. The delay during the day and the late start because of the two radio programmes meant there was little chance of my being able to get to Atlantic College on foot. To solve the problem I walked to Porthkerry Park and agreed to be driven to the college. I would be brought back to the park the following morning. When one of the teachers from the college had contacted my secretary, Christine Reeve, to offer me accommodation and a meal, I had accepted immediately. I spent five years of my school life in a co-educational boarding school in Yorkshire, where everyone was involved in running the school, and working in the gardens, as well as doing academic subjects. The United World College of the Atlantic is run on similar lines and for that reason I was particularly keen to go there. As soon as I arrived, I could sense the friendly atmosphere and I immediately felt at ease. The headmaster, David Sutcliffe, told me a bit about the school.

71

Apart from the academic work, there is a social service syllabus where students help local organizations twice a week, do a compulsory first aid course, and run a rescue service. The college has official responsibility for fifteen miles of coastline, and therefore has inshore lifeboats, and does beach, mountaineering and cliff rescue. There is also estate service and college service whereby the students help to do some simple building or maintenance tasks. The three hundred students do a two-year course culminating in the International Baccalaureate Diploma. It was a delightful and interesting evening.

7.3.78

My chauffeur arrived promptly at 8.30 and I was whisked back to Porthkerry Park. Now I could walk to the college as I had originally intended. Again the weather was delightfully mild and I enjoyed the spectacular coastline of cementstone. My route took me along the Glamorgan Heritage Coast Path past Aberthaw power station to Tresilian Bay and St Donat's Bay. Near Llantwit Major the mayor intervened, and took me to the car park where he sat on the rear of his car and wrote out a cheque! Aware that I was getting late, and sweating profusely, I ran up the steps for lunch in the college. During the meal it was announced who I was and much to my surprise a great cheer resounded through the room.

As I neared Dunraven Bay two officials were waiting: the Mayor of Ogwr and the chairman of Mid Glamorgan Council. While the television cameras recorded the scene, I was welcomed and presented with cheques. Continuing along the coast I saw the path being made and signs being put up. I pressed on to Ogmore-by-Sea but the growing darkness forced me to halt, with only twenty-four miles walked that day. I felt frustrated.

8.3.78

This day proved to be even more frustrating, although I did at least walk thirty miles. My destination was Swansea. First I had to cross Ogmore river near Merthyr Mawr before returning to the coast via the dunes and so on to Porthcawl. Beyond

Porthcawl the golden sands stretched for miles; I could not believe this was South Wales or that I was approaching Port Talbot and its steel works. I walked along Rest Bay, then Kenfig Sands and Margam Sands. Although there was no official right of way I went through the works and wasn't challenged. I spent an hour at the Aberavon Centre where the mayor was waiting and then carried on to the river Neath. From there I could easily do the final few miles past the Ford motor works and get into Swansea before dark.

That was what I had planned, but shortly after crossing the river Neath bridge I was informed that the Mayor of Swansea, the Chairman of West Glamorgan and Lord Lieutenant of West Glamorgan were waiting for me at the city hall. I had no option but to get into a car and meet them. It was dark by the time I was taken back to where I had been picked up and I was then left to walk the final four miles into Swansea. Everything was out of hand. I had a long way to go, and I knew that I wouldn't be able to cope if the pressure didn't ease.

9.3.78

Leaving Swansea after doing four radio interviews, I was cheered by the knowledge that I was moving into an area of exceptional beauty where no officials would be lurking! Over the years many people had remarked on the beauty of the Gower Peninsula, and I was looking forward to the walk very much.

Following the advice of a local, I walked across the beach instead of taking the road to Oystermouth and The Mumbles. At first the sand was firm and progress was good but further on it deteriorated into wet mud. By then it was easier to go on than turn back, so I trudged on taking extreme care. By the time I reached Oystermouth I was completely splattered with mud and looked very dishevelled. Leaving a muddy trail, I went into a sweet shop and stocked up with chocolate. Then, feeling on top of the world, I began my exploration of the Gower coast.

I had only walked a mile when I neared the coastguard station on Mumbles Head. Suddenly a loud hailer pierced the air and a coastguard asked me to call in as they had a message for me! RAF Brawdy near St Davids wanted to come in by helicopter and winch a man down with a cheque for RCSB. Agreeing to the plan, I roughly worked out that in five days I would be at Newgale Sands and said I would meet them there. From then all the stations kept an eye on me, and passed information to the next station. I was flattered by their interest!

From Mumbles Head I entered some truly exceptional coastal scenery. Walking around the cliffs and across the empty sandy beaches to Port-Eynon was very enjoyable and a delight to a weary traveller. I stood spellbound as I rounded the corners and saw Caswell Bay, Threecliff Bay and Oxwich Bay. Finally, in the late afternoon, I walked round the shore of Port-Eynon Bay and stayed at the youth hostel.

10.3.78

The section of coastline in front of me, along the cliffs to Worms Head, should have been superlative. The weather, however, was poor and my log records: 'Drizzle and sea mist – no views – nothing'. I searched in vain for Cluver Hole and its cavern but in the end I simply had to keep close to the cliff tops and concentrate on making progress. Half way to Rhossili I walked above the Paviland Caves once inhabited by Palaeolithic man. At Rhossili I walked into a café (which surprised me by being open in early March and in such poor weather), and looked at the postcards which depicted the magnificent cliffs I should have seen, and Rhossili Bay which I was about to walk round. On the way to the beach I noted a small pool full of frogspawn, the first on the walk. Spring was still making its way north with me.

The next eight miles' walking were across beautiful sandy beaches where only the muffled sound of the breaking waves, deadened by the mist, and an occasional cry of a gull, broke the silence. The few birds that I saw included oyster-catchers, ringed plovers and curlews. At Whitford Sands I headed due east along the northern side of the peninsula. There, the large expanses of marsh were a direct contrast to the dramatic

74

beaches and cliffs of the south side. Perched on a ridge beyond the marshland was Weobley Castle, a ruined fortified manor house dating back to the thirteenth century. Nearby a couple of buzzards flew over mewing to each other.

The geology of the peninsula is interesting, for whereas the whole of Glamorgan is composed of coal measures of the carboniferous period, the Gower has older rocks from the same period and is made up of sandstone, limestone and millstone grit.

At the end of the day I was soaked and as I had been unable to dry everything out adequately the previous night I began looking for a guest house or hotel. By chance I came upon a motel at Crofty and although it was officially closed the owner very kindly allowed me to stay there, free of charge.

11.3.78

I set off on a very full stomach having consumed a magnificent fried breakfast and, feeling in good spirits, started out for Carmarthen, thirty-three miles away. It was a long haul through Llanelli, Burry Port, and Kidwelly, and I finally reached Carmarthen just after seven o'clock. The nights were now getting longer and it was light until 6.30. I had had to walk this far inland to cross the river Tywi, but the most significant point of reaching Carmarthen was that the following day I would reach the Pembrokeshire Coast Path. This has some of the finest coastal scenery in Britain.

12.3.78

By late afternoon the pouring rain gave way to blue sky and sun, just as I reached the Pendine Sands, close to the start of the coast path. As it was low tide I was able to walk round the beach to Amroth where the path begins, rather than having to ascend the cliffs above Marros Sands. Two hours later, having made excellent progress, I was at Saundersfoot and sitting in the harbour master's office sipping tea. I found a guest house to stay in, delighted to have walked the first three miles of the coast path.

13.3.78

The walk to Tenby proved to be very frustrating for several reasons. The first problem I had to sort out was the rucksack. Before setting out, I had planned to use one that was made for me in 1977, but had changed my mind when the makers brought out a 1978 model with nylon fittings instead of alloy, a different type of webbing and zips on the pockets. I had been experiencing stomach pains for some time, but thinking that they were probably due to my not having settled down to the load, I had done nothing about it. However, when after 1,500 miles of walking they still hadn't gone away I rang Christine and asked her to post my old rucksack to Tenby post office.

At Tenby I changed rucksacks and immediately felt the difference. The shoulder strap dimensions had been altered on the newer model and were fitted much lower down the rucksack body; it was this that had given me the stomach pains. An hour later I met the mayor and photographers, but this meeting, together with the unpacking and packing of the rucksacks, meant that I had lost two and a half hours, so I hurriedly set off across the sands to Giltar Point and the cliff path to Lydstep. As I walked I could readily feel that the rucksack was more comfortable and for the next 5,000 miles it did not let me down.

As I rounded Lydstep Haven, I knew I was in trouble. The head-on galeforce winds and the torrential rain meant that progress along the path was slow and hard. I had lost considerable time in Tenby and I knew from past experience that from Manorbier onwards there was nowhere to stay for twenty miles. I would, therefore, be stranded in the dark. I decided to cut my losses and to stay at Manorbier. At the post office I was recommended to try one of the houses in the village, and at 3.30 p.m., with only fourteen miles walked, I stopped. It proved to be a wise decision for the weather got progressively worse.

14.3.78

The following morning I began to walk round the Angle peninsula and planned to camp at Angle. The walk was about twenty-six miles but it took almost twelve hours to accomplish. I was walking straight into a westerly galeforce wind, which meant that each step was a fight. A little over a mile from Manorbier I descended to Swanlake Bay and watched the large breakers thundering in and sending jets of water high into the air. As I stood still, totally absorbed in the scene, a stoat came running up the path and stopped a foot away from me. At first he didn't realize I was there but then he caught my scent and, jumping into the air with fright, he dived back into the undergrowth.

Leaving the bay behind I began walking along the cliffs before climbing down to Freshwater East. There wasn't a soul in sight, but I wasn't surprised for I have walked the whole of the Pembrokeshire Coast four times and hardly ever seen anyone else walking it. Why it isn't walked more baffles me, for the path is good (although in a few places it is now overgrown through lack of use), and its 168-mile length passes through some remarkable and stunning places that even in atrocious conditions are memorable. Beyond Freshwater East I came to two of the most attractive features of this area, Barafundle Bay and its golden beach, and the Bosherston lily ponds. I have been here twice in June when the lilies are in flower and the display is delightful.

My next landmark was St Govan's Head and chapel. There the wind swept unmercifully across the land and met me head on. There were very few sea birds about, one or two were mating, but the rest remained hidden, sheltering from the gale. Who St Govan was is not known, but the chapel, dating back to the thirteenth century, is reached by going down fifty-two steps. Nearby is the Huntsman's Leap where a huntsman is supposed to have jumped across a gap with the sea 130 feet below, and to have died later of nightmares! But the finest part of these limestone cliffs was a further two miles on, where the Elegug rock stacks and the huge natural arch – the Green Bridge of Wales – are. The seas were so high that the arch was almost covered by spray several times and the foamy sea swirling around the bases of the stacks was most dramatic. Beyond to Linney Head the limestone cliffs are spectacular, but because it is part of an artillery range I had to move inland to Castlemartin and walk along the road to Freshwater West. It was worth it, however, for the sight of the pounding seas as I came round the remainder of the Angle Peninsula was fantastic. The final mile was easier, for the wind was behind me; I was heading due east around Milford Haven. I stopped at a camp site at Angle and startled the owner by being the first person to camp there that year. (The site was not officially open until Easter, two weeks ahead.)

15.3.78

Much of the section of the Pembrokeshire coast, around Milford Haven, is beside various oil refineries. Many people prefer to skip walking this stretch and take the bus, but in fact the oil refineries, the tankers and row upon row of pipes have a certain charm of their own; I find the path around the Haven fascinating. I hadn't completed more than six miles when a police car came across the fields to me. 'Thank goodness you are alive and well. Everyone has been very worried about you. It has been on the news that you are lost!' I couldn't understand what all the fuss was about. I knew I hadn't phoned Christine for three days but that wasn't uncommon. However, 'Nationwide' had been trying to find me and as a last resort had rung the police. Somewhere along the line the coastguards and National Park wardens had also got involved for no sooner had the police gone than a warden appeared saying, 'Thank God you are here!' I assured him I was fit and well and that there were no problems, and he went away to notify people. The outcome of it all was that I was to be filmed by 'Nationwide' the following day. Somewhat startled by the recent events, I carried on to Pembroke.

The castle is a very impressive building above the banks of the river Pembroke, and dates back to the twelfth century. The keep is the oldest part with fourteen-foot-thick walls, some eighty feet high. During the civil war it was occupied by both Parliamentarians and Royalists. Cromwellian troops battered it for a month and the Royalists surrendered only when their water supply ran out.

From Pembroke I crossed the Haven via the Neyland Bridge and began the walk back out to the coast via the town of Milford Haven. Near there I came to another oil refinery. The Haven is now the largest oil port in Europe. Esso came in 1960, BP two years later, Texaco in 1966, Gulf in 1968 and Amoco in 1971. Looking down the Haven from near Neyland I could see the jetties in two straight lines on either side of the Haven. Today VLCC (Very Large Crude Carriers) bring in 250,000 gallons of oil at a time. The boats are mammoth constructions: the crew need a bicycle to get from one end of the ship to the other and 160 tons of paint are needed to paint them.

At Hubberston, just beyond Milford Haven, I stopped for the night.

16.3.78

Leaving Hubberston I prepared myself to meet the 'Nationwide' team. No one had been able to tell me when to expect them but I knew that they would have been told my whereabouts, and that we would meet some time during the course of the day.

At Sandy Haven, the tide was too high for me to use the stepping stones across Sandyhaven Pill, so I had to walk three miles inland to cross it there. The next five miles of the coast path to Dale were uncomfortable, for the path is overgrown with gorse and briars and my legs got badly scratched. It was quite a fight to get through.

As I neared Dale at midday, a red Ford Escort came to a screeching halt beside me. It was the producer from 'Nationwide'. We went through their schedule and agreed to meet up at Marloes Sands at about two o'clock. I suggested this location as I knew the beach would make a magnificent setting. I hadn't left myself a lot of time and so after buying some chocolate, I pressed on to St Ann's Head. There the coastguards were waiting to inform me that 'Nationwide' were out looking for me! They asked me to talk to RAF Brawdy about the scheduled meeting at Newgale, which, because of the filming, we changed to St Brides Haven.

Before leaving Westdale Bay for Marloes Sands I had a look

at the Cobbler's Hole, a classic example of rock folding in old red sandstone. Much of Pembrokeshire is volcanic rock, giving very sturdy and stable cliffs with numerous excellent examples of rock folding.

As I neared Marloes Sands the sun came out and the day brightened into a beautiful afternoon. I stood admiring the scene and reflecting on the beauty surrounding me: the sand and the vertical cliffs were in front of me, Gateholm Island was at the end of the beach, and out to sea the reflections of the two islands of Skomer and Skokholm, the haunt of numerous sea birds, could be seen flickering on the shimmering water. Too soon the film crew arrived, and for the next six hours I was absorbed by the film-making. I was filmed walking along the path, admiring the views, talking about the walk, erecting the tent, cooking a meal and finally, in the dark, blowing the candle out.

17.3.78

We continued filming the next morning as I came round Martin's Haven and on to St Brides Haven. Unfortunately the RAF helicopter didn't arrive as at the last minute it was required elsewhere. At 1.30 I was left on my own, having lost a day's walking, and I set off to walk to Solva, twenty miles away. At least by getting to Solva I would rescue a reasonable day's mileage from the disruption of routine. I had found the filming a strain but I had enjoyed the process and contributing ideas.

The first few miles from St Brides Haven to Little Haven is along a high level path on sheer cliffs, often 200 to 300 feet above the sea. The tide was in at Little Haven so I couldn't walk across the beach to Broad Haven, and had to use the cliff path instead. From there the scenery was still dramatic as I walked to Nolton Haven and so on to Newgale Sands. The tide was going out and so I dropped down onto the beach. Beyond Newgale I climbed back up the cliffs and along the path again. Solva was just over four miles away and night was falling, but my effort was compensated by the sun coming out from behind a cloud and sending rays of golden light into the sky. In the dark I reached Solva and a reception committee.

Solva is very interesting geologically for it is a drowned valley. It is the safest harbour in St Brides Bay and is tucked out of sight from the sea, which was very useful in pirate days. The entrance is dangerous but once navigated there is a safe anchorage amid picturesque surroundings. In the early nineteenth century the village was a thriving port with some thirty ships trading in cloth, corn, timber, coal, limestone and culm.

18.3.78

This Saturday was to prove an historic day for me. In the last seventy-four days I had walked just over 2,000 miles and had broken my own *Guinness Book of Records* entry by seven days.

The weather from Solva was some of the best encountered so far on the walk: it was cold and dry, with bright sun and exceptional clarity. With a string of delightful bays behind me – Caerbwdi Bay, Caerfai Bay, St Non's Bay and Porth-clais and its limekilns – I reached Ramsey Sound. Across the Sound glimmered Ramsey Island and I watched as the island's owner busily ferried supplies across on the first good day for three months.

A mile up the Sound I reached the St Justinian's Life Boat Station. There are numerous legends about St Justinian who is reputed to have been a Breton and to have lived on Ramsey Island in about AD 500. One of them relates how, because he was having too many visitors, he prayed that the bridge to the mainland would collapse. The bridge was chopped down and that is why all that remains today is the string of menacing rocks known as The Bitches.

One mile from the lifeboat station I reached the sands of Whitesand Bay. From the bay onwards the coastline takes on a far more rugged appearance and offers some really splendid walking, expecially around Penberry Hill. To get there, I rounded St David's Head where I saw the cromlech. The capstone now rests on just one support, but it is still an excellent example of these megalithic constructions. The next few miles, to Trevine where I stayed at the youth hostel, were memorable for the sight of the gentle blue sea below me, the tall sheer cliffs and the pair of choughs (the first I had seen on the walk).

19.3.78

The beautiful weather of the previous day had led me to think the warm weather was here to stay. I could not have been more wrong. The morning brought a force ten gale with torrential rain. It was distinctly unpleasant and a struggle to walk through. It was a shame for the coastline just north of Trevine and Abercastle is very dramatic, especially near Pwllderi. I had to walk with my head well down and into the wind, oblivious of the scenery. Three miles from Pwllderi, at Strumble Head, I stumbled into the coastguard station. They had been looking out for me and were perturbed that I hadn't been seen. During our conversation I happened to mention that I planned to reach Fishguard at 2.30 p.m. They laughed and said it was impossible – it was already 1.30 p.m. We were now on British Summer Time and I was an hour behind.

Twenty minutes later I was out in the galeforce wind again with the rain lashing my face. At Carregwastad Point I stopped to look at the plaque which marks the spot where the French landed in 1797. A moment or two later a slow-worm crossed my path. At first I thought it was an adder, as I had seen several in the area on previous occasions.

Fishguard Bay is now a ferry port with boats to Ireland departing daily. I had seen two battling their way through the heavy seas from Strumble Head. At Fishguard I stopped and dried out my equipment.

20.3.78

I had reached my final day on the Pembrokeshire Coast Path, and felt sad for it is always heartening to know that you have a long stretch of path before you. The wind had almost blown itself out but it was still very overcast and raining hard as I made my way to Poppit Sands near Cardigan. In Fishguard harbour I could see the sunken cattle boat which had lain there for a year, because of legal wrangling. A determined effort was being made to salvage her and pumps were working continuously to get the water out of her chambers.

Beyond the harbour lay Dinas Island, which is not an island but a small peninsula with a steep rocky coast. The sea birds were beginning to gather on Needle Rock and from there, as the weather improved, I could see across to Newport Bay and the final cliffs of the Pembrokeshire coast. As I rounded the Newport Sands and went on to these last cliffs, I realized I had walked the path four times which meant that I had again broken my own *Guinness Book of Records* entry. I was jubilant!

The cliffs from Newport onwards are steep and dramatic. Near Ceibwr Bay is the Witches Cauldron, which is another collapsed cave, similar to the one near Cadgwith in Cornwall. Beyond Ceibwr Bay, with its rock folds made 450 million years ago by the Great Caledonian earth movements, are the 200-foot high cliffs to Pen-yr-aft. These, too, illustrate rock folding. Scarcely two miles on is another classic example at Cemaes Head. As I approached Poppit Sands, I could see a reception committee waiting. It was the Cardigan Rotary Club and as it was the evening of their meeting they asked if I would join them. I agreed and walked a further four miles to Cardigan, bringing my day's mileage to thirty-three. The president and I were late for the meal and consequently were given a different meal of chicken, which unfortunately was later to prove significant.

21.3.78

My destination for the day was New Quay, twenty-eight miles away. First I had to walk down the eastern side of the river Teifi to Gwbert-on-Sea before following the coast to Aberporth. I had to move inland slightly to walk round the missile range at Penar Uchaf, but the following fourteen miles from Aberporth were exhilarating walking, in dry sunny weather, with very good cliffs and beaches. From Tresaith I crossed a magnificent two-mile stretch of sand before ascending the cliffs to get to Llangranog. The headland beyond Llangranog at Ynys-Lochtyn is very attractive with a circular hill known as Pendinaslochdyn. The final few miles of the day, to New Quay, via Cwmtudu, were along rights of way which seemed to be rarely used. At six o'clock I walked into New Quay and stayed at the youth hostel. I had begun to feel slightly off-colour, so I went to bed early.

22.3.78

I woke up feeling ill. My diary records: 'Decidedly unwell. Slept beside the road for a while before staggering to Aberaeron. Stayed at a B and B. Felt sick, listless, hot flushes and diarrhoea – caused by chicken at Cardigan?' I walked only ten miles that day. On reaching Aberaeron I found a chemist and bought a bottle of kaolin. I drank half of it and went to bed and slept solidly until breakfast the next morning – sixteen hours' sleep. Feeling decidedly better, I continued on my way to Aberystwyth.

23.3.78

The map shows a right of way along much of this stretch of coastline, but on location there is very little evidence of it. Nevertheless, it was a fine walk in force six gales via Llansantffraid, Llanrýhstud and Morfa Bychan to Aberystwyth. By deciding to sleep my food poisoning off, I had unwittingly upset plans ahead of me. However, as I came round the Bar into Aberystwyth, the police spotted me and went ahead to inform people that I was arriving. I spent several hours with the mayor and chairman of the Council, and decided that as I had lost so much time I might as well stay in the town. I had only walked twenty miles but in view of my being unwell it was perhaps wiser to stop early.

24.3.78

The view of Aberystwyth from the summit of Constitution Hill was impressive. The town lay at my feet and in the wild conditions I could readily appreciate the power of the seas and see how vulnerable the houses were. On the way to Aberdovey, the day's destination, I realized that it was Good Friday. There was little sign that spring had arrived in the weather, as gales still racked the shore and rain rarely ceased to fall, but in the fields there was plenty of evidence: I saw lots of new lambs, catkins and pussy willow were in full bloom, and coltsfoot, lesser celandines, snowdrops and daffodils were all bursting out in the hedgerows.

A delightful cliff path via Clarach Bay and Wallog took me to Borth, a unique village built upon a shingle bank. When the tide is out, there is a sweep of four miles of golden sands which are among the finest in Wales. At the northern end of the beach I began walking inland to cross the river Dovey. Aberdovey was scarcely a mile away but it needed a walk of fifteen miles to get there. Rather than do a further eight miles and cross the river at Machynlleth, I sneaked across the railway bridge near Dovey Junction station. This is the one railway station in Britain which can only be reached on foot.

25.3.78

I could tell Bank Holiday had arrived by the milling crowds and busy roads. It was rather a rude awakening after the months of solitude. I left Aberdovey and walked across the sands to Bron-y-Môr. There I picked up the road beside the disused railway line and passed the army's outward bound school. A little over a mile later I reached Broad Water. The railway bridge was almost dismantled but I took a risk and stepped across the steel girders to the other side, and to the army camp which seemed to be used only for part of the year.

The next few miles, to Barmouth Bay and Fairbourne, were along roads which ran close to the shoreline. At the northern end of Fairbourne I followed a path eastwards to the Barmouth toll foot bridge. This took me to the very edge of the Snowdonia National Park. As it was Easter Saturday, Barmouth was bursting with people, and the fun fair and shops were doing a roaring trade despite the cold, windy weather. I didn't linger and carried on, via Llanaber to Llanbedr. I had planned to use the youth hostel but it was full and it took three unsuccessful attempts before I found accommodation.

26.3.78

Three miles' walking took me to Harlech where I entered a

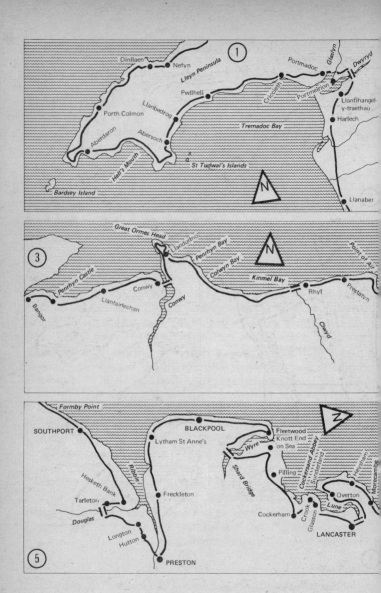

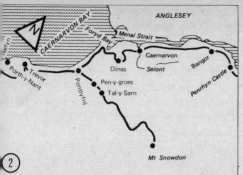

shop to buy some chocolate for the day. The owner recognized me and kindly presented me with eight bars 'on the house'. Behind the shops rose the imposing walls of Harlech Castle. When it was built in 1283, the sea lapped at its base. Today, the sea is a little over half a mile away. As I walked along the golden sands to the mouth of the rivers Glaslyn and Dwyryd I could really appreciate the splendour and magnificence of the ruined castle. Like Chepstow Castle, the position is perfect, not only scenically, but strategically.

A small earth dyke from Llanfihangel-y-traethau took me to another toll bridge across the river Dwyryd. As I walked I looked across through the heavy rain to Portmeirion, the extraordinary Italian fishing village surrounded by exotic plants and woodland. The siting and building of this unique collection of houses was by the architect Clough Williams-Ellis.

Beyond Portmeirion I came to yet another toll bridge across the river Glaslyn and into Portmadoc. As I crossed, one of the steam trains of the Ffestiniog Railway went by. The railway, which was originally opened in 1836 for transporting slate, is now the oldest narrow gauge railway in the world.

In the worsening weather I made my way to Morfa Bychan and the Black Rock Sands. I had played there as a boy as my parents often took us to Criccieth for summer holidays. But the wind and rain didn't encourage me to linger and I carried on across the sands to Criccieth and its ruined thirteenth-century castle.

I noticed that having passed the 2,200-mile mark, which was the longest I had ever done continuously, I had reached a certain state of being which I was not to lose throughout the rest of the walk. I found myself chatting to the sheep, the birds and the cattle, but not because I was lonely or bored; I felt it was more a sign that I was really at one with the countryside and that it was my way of expressing my joy and contentment. But my mind at this particular time dwelt on strange, almost hallucinatory topics, such as riding around in a Land Rover, or wearing very expensive clothes and monogrammed shirts!

Perhaps it was having a final struggle before completely accepting my new way of life.

I continued to Pwllheli and passed the huge Butlin's Holiday Camp. In front of me was the 'finger of Wales', the Lleyn Peninsula.

27.3.78

Leaving Pwllheli, I planned to reach Aberdaron at the far end of the Lleyn Peninsula. With blue sky and mild conditions it proved to be a good day. The coast in this area is nicely broken up into five sandy beaches and rugged cliffs. I walked along the shore of Y Gamlas Bay to Llanbedrog before climbing around the rocky peninsula to an old quarry at St Tudwal's Road to Abersoch. The latter was pretty, with a cluster of colourful boats in the harbour and crowds of milling Easter holidaymakers. Another mile of beach brought me to the headland overlooking the West and East islands of St Tudwal. A few miles later I descended the cliff on to the five-mile beach of Hell's Mouth. Seeing the beach in perfect conditions made the walking much more enjoyable. Ahead were my final cliffs before gaining Aberdaron, where I slept in a caravan.

Aberdaron is an unspoilt village and has a church which is often referred to as the 'Cathedral of Lleyn'. Perched above the beach and dedicated to St Hywyn, it has a Norman doorway though much of the building dates back to the twelfth and fifteenth centuries. A fourteenth-century house on the main street is known as 'Y Gegin Fawr' – the big kitchen. This was formerly a communal kitchen where pilgrims could rest and claim a meal before crossing the sound to Bardsey Island. Remains of St Mary's Abbey stand on the northern end of the island.

28.3.78

My route lay around Bardsey Sound and up the north-west side of the Lleyn Peninsula. On paper it was a good walk but on the ground the first part was very hard to find, and driving rain and galeforce winds did not help. As I rounded the sound I caught fleeting glimpses of Bardsey Island.

The beach at Porthor is known as the whistling sands. I have been unable to discover why it is known as such, but I have been on a similarly named beach on the island of Eigg which is so called because the noise when walking across it on a dry sunny day is said to be like the sound of the dead being released.

At Porthor I found a shop and café that was open, an unexpected bonus as I was cold and wet, and I went inside for a hot drink and something to eat. Continuing on my way, I walked across the beach where disaster very nearly struck. It was high tide, but the sea left a fifteen-foot gap between its highest point and the cliffs. I set off to walk this gap but half way across a large wave rolled in and broke against me, right up to my waist. I was on the point of being sucked down by the force of the retreating wave, when part of the cliff collapsed on me. I shook the mud off and scaled the slippery cliff as fast as I could. It still puzzles me as to how that wave came in unnoticed! For the next quarter of an hour I stood and watched the waves and not one came within fifteen feet of the cliff.

From then on I kept to the top of the cliffs to Porth Colmon and on to Porths Dinllaen and Nefyn where I stayed to dry out my clothes and boots. The right of way along this stretch is rarely used. As I neared Nefyn the sun came out and lit up the cliffs of Yr Eifl which I would cross the following day.

29.3.78

I reached them early in the morning and began a difficult crossing of an area which is riddled with many old slate quarries. At the base of one is Porth-y-Nant, a deserted village, which was once the miners' settlement; it made a sad sight. I had to keep very high up to get close to Yr Eifl quarry, but I had a magnificent view down onto Trevor, Caernarvon Bay and beyond to the coast of Morfa Dinlle.

A further six miles took me to Pontlyfni. There, for the first time on the walk, I deliberately left the coast. My purpose was to climb Snowdon and then return to Pontlyfni to resume my coastal walk. I had decided that as I walked up the west coast of Britain I would climb the three highest mountains: Snowdon, Scafell Pike and Ben Nevis. Apart from adding a bit of fun to the walk, it would also mean I had taken the longest possible route between the three mountains.

I headed inland via Penygroes and Talysarn to the Snowdon Ranger Youth Hostel. I hadn't gone more than half a mile when I realized I was upset at leaving the coast. Tears rolled down my cheeks! It was a great shock to discover just how much I had become attached to the waves, beaches and cliffs. Keeping a tight grip on my emotions, I told myself I would be back the following day.

30.3.78

I left my rucksack with the warden of the hostel and told him I was going up Snowdon and planned to be back within two and a half hours! He laughed at this but I was serious. With almost 2,300 miles behind me I was beginning to feel very fit and without a rucksack I knew I would be able to move quickly. From the hostel I walked up the Snowdon Ranger path, past Llyn Ffynnon-y-Gwas, to the summit. It took one hour and thirty-five minutes! It was freezing, everything was coated with ice and there was no view. I met a few others there before hurrying back down the path to get my blood circulating again. I was down in one hour and five minutes! I didn't feel that I had rushed, but without a load I felt like a mountain goat and revelled in my fitness. The warden was most surprised to see me so soon.

With the load once more strapped to my back I retraced my steps to Pontlyfni. I had, after all, very much enjoyed being in the mountains but it was good to be back by the sea. A little after six o'clock I walked into the camp site at Dinas Dinlle. As I did so I was recognized by the owner who rushed over to invite me to stay, free of charge, and to have whatever food I wanted from the shop. Armed with some tinned food I moved to the site to find a spot for the tent. Before I had even placed the rucksack on the ground a couple came up and offered me the use of their caravan and invited me to join them for tea. They live near Derby and had been following my weekly reports on Radio Derby. I slept peacefully that night, after a really memorable day.

31.3.78

Half a mile after leaving Dinas Dinlle, I found my first violet since Cornwall, almost two months before. Across the sands I could see the mouth of the Menai Straits and the western side of Anglesey. I reached Caernarvon after rounding Foryd Bay. Dominating the town, as I crossed the river Seiont, was the high wall of the castle. Waiting to show me round were the castle keeper and the Mayoress of Caernarvon, who was the first lady to hold the office for 700 years. The southern, eastern and western sides of the castle date from the end of the thirteenth century and the northern side was built soon afterwards and completed in 1323. The western end is dominated by the Eagle Tower. It was in the Upper Ward of the castle that Prince Charles was invested as the Prince of Wales. The last Welsh prince was Llewellyn who revolted against Edward I and was slain by the Earl of Mortimer in 1284. From this time onwards the principality of Wales has been incorporated with England. Since then all male heirs-apparent to the throne have been invested as Prince of Wales.

The remainder of the day's walk was beside the Menai Straits to the outskirts of Bangor where I camped. Anglesey was just across the strait and being so close I walked across the Menai Bridge onto the island. The chief reason for the journey was to see the railway station with the longest name in Britain, Llanfairpwllgwyngyllgogerychwyrndrobwllllantysiliogogo-goch.

1.4.78

From the outskirts of Bangor I walked to the cathedral where I met the Dean. The present building largely dates from the twelfth and thirteenth centuries and stands on one of the oldest ecclesiastical sites in Britain. The founder was St Deiniol, to whom the church is dedicated, and who in about AD 546 became the first recorded Bishop in North Wales. In the nave, in a glass-fronted box, were a pair of dog-tongs. In the seventeenth and eighteenth centuries when such tongs were made, there was an official dog whipper in many Midland churches. His duty was to chase any dogs out of the church prior to a service. Made from oak, they have lethal points at the end to allow the sexton to catch the dog without endangering himself. The dog-tongs in Bangor cathedral are the only ones that I know of.

Leaving Bangor, I was joined by a member of the Royal Welsh Fusiliers, in full combat kit, who was sponsored to walk with me to Conwy Castle. We walked through the grounds of Penrhyn Castle, which commands excellent views to Beaumaris on Anglesey. It was built in the early nineteenth century by Thomas Hopper, who was commissioned by G.H. Dawkins Pennant, the very wealthy owner of the Penrhyn slate quarries. Today this magnificent piece of architecture is owned by the National Trust.

To get to the outskirts of Conwy we went along unused rights of way to Llanfairfechan and from there along the main A55 trunk road. We returned to the shoreline to walk round the mouth of the river Conwy. Entering Conwy, we passed the smallest house in Britain and noticed a sign at the harbour master's office which said 'Out, back at 3 a.m.'! Waiting for us at Conwy Castle was the keeper. Together, in the rain, the three of us had a look round the fortifications. As at Caernarvon, Edward I had played a leading role in the building of the castle. But what impressed me most about Conwy were the town walls. There are some at Caernarvon but, being on a flat site, they are not so noticeable. At Conwy the walls are partly on rising ground which makes them more imposing. Still in pouring rain, I bade farewell to the major and crossed the bridge and walked on to Llandudno.

2.4.78

There was little of Wales left and two days more would bring me back into England. I rounded Great Ormes Head, which is a large mass of limestone. At Marine Drive I was joined by Richard Else of Radio Derby, whom I had been ringing every week; it was nice to put a face to the voice. He was sponsored to walk with me round the headland, and raised about £180. On the way we passed banks of violets in full bloom and on the cliffs saw razorbills and kittiwakes.

As it was Sunday and the weather mild and sunny, I was dreading the crowds that I was sure would be out in the well-known seaside resorts of Llandudno, Penrhyn Bay and Colwyn Bay. Surprisingly, I encountered few people, even though much of the walking was along the esplanades.

From Colwyn Bay I was able to walk along the path beside the shore with the railway on my right. I was also walking through one of the largest concentrations of caravans in Britain. At Kinmel Bay I had to walk through a caravan park to the road bridge across the river Clwyd and into Rhyl. Before reaching Rhyl I called into a shop for some chocolate. I was recognized again, and given a large bagful free. Before the walk I had assumed, like many others, that the Welsh were reserved. The walk convinced me otherwise. For wherever I went I was made most welcome and everyone went out of their way to be helpful.

I walked into Rhyl past the screeching fun fair and Horror Crypt and camped on a lawn, kindly offered to me by a local person.

3.4.78

Five miles from Rhyl I walked into Prestatyn to the post office to collect my map and food parcel. The thought came to me that I had been walking for exactly three months and that, with 2,400 miles now behind me, I had walked more than a third of the way round Britain. Originally I had planned that my second pair of boots should be sent to Prestatyn, but I didn't ask for them as the first pair were still in good order and, as my log records, they 'felt like slippers'! I sat in the office of the local newspaper and undid the parcel. I repacked the contents in my rucksack, and sent the walked-off maps back to Christine.

I returned to the shore and walked along the sands to the disused lighthouse at the Point of Ayr. I had reached the river Dee with Merseyside across the water. The area became more industrial as I made my way via Mostyn to Flint and Oakenholt. The day was quite an eventful one, as first a great friend suddenly appeared, then HTV arrived out of the blue to film me and, at Oakenholt, some friends I had met while on my Land's End to John o'Groats walk found me and insisted I stay with them and eat a steak! A better last day in Wales would have been hard to find. I could relax, content that the whole of Wales was behind me, though I also felt sad for I had really enjoyed its widely differing coastline.

5. Round Lakeland to Scotland

4.4.78

When I left Oakenholt, on a really lovely spring day, two
things were certain: one that Roger Smith would meet up with
me at Queensferry Bridge, and the other that I would be
camping on a friend's lawn in West Kirby that night. After
only one and a half hours' walking through Connah's Quay
and Shotton, I turned left for the Queensferry Bridge and
walked into a barrage of reporters and photographers. Instead
of doing a much longer walk around Puddington and Burton
to avoid British Steel, I was given permission to walk through
the works under escort. At the works gate Roger, the assembled
press and I all signed the necessary form and with a security
van in front we set off through the works. Behind us was
another security van; both had blue flashing lights. All this just
to walk as near to the coast as possible! The *Daily Express* man
and the others had a field day taking photographs of me against
a background of factory buildings. Seeing Roger again made
me realize just how rapidly the weeks were passing by.

After three miles of switch-back walking, I was left to my
own devices to continue into England and the Wirral
Peninsula. I was able to follow a good footpath beside the
marsh and past Little Neston and Parkgate. At Heswall I
picked up the Wirral Way. This is a disused railway line which
has been converted into a pedestrian and horseriders' route. In
the Peak District, where I live, there are three disused railway
lines which have been similarly converted: the Tissington

Trail, High Peak Trail and Sett Valley Trail. The old railway stations have been converted into car parks and picnic sites. One aspect which I felt the Wirral Way had treated well was the combined use of foot passengers and horseriders. In the Peak District the horseriders tend to churn up the surface for the walkers, but on the Wirral Way it is fenced off and the two are kept separate. Near the golf course at Caldy I descended to the sandy shore and walked into West Kirby where some friends run the Outrigger Camping Shop. I was given a couple of pairs of socks, which were most welcome, and I camped on their neighbour's lawn.

5.4.78

As it was low tide I walked round the sands from West Kirby past Hoylake and on to the disused lighthouse at Mockbeggar Wharf. In doing so I looked across at the sandstone islands of Hilbre, Little Hilbre and Little Eye. Hilbre is a very important observation point for migratory birds and more than two hundred different species have been seen, principally waders. On the nearby sandbanks seals often bask in the sun, although I saw none because it was still too early in the year. Three miles from the lighthouse I reached the road running beside the shore to New Brighton. Reaching the Promenade, I could look across the river Mersey to Liverpool and its docks. While I stood there, an Irish ferry went past bound for Dublin. I photographed it, little knowing that at the end of the walk I would take this same ferry to get right away from it all.

The pier at New Brighton was being dismantled. These Victorian constructions seem to have lived their natural lifespan, for in the course of the walk I saw them all and nearly all were in varying stages of decay. Only a few were preserved. I continued on to Egremont and Birkenhead, where I stopped to watch the famous Mersey ferry. Across the water stood the Royal Liver Building. A few minutes on the ferry at a cost of 15p would have taken me to Liverpool, but keeping to my rules it was a walk of some sixty miles.

Because it is an industrial area and a lot of the land is privately owned, I could not walk beside the river and had to content myself with the main A41 road. It made a change to see shops, people and cars. Walking by the hedgerows I could hear lots of birds and noticed that the hawthorn was coming into leaf.

The final few miles of the day from Ellesmere Port took me through the Shell refinery, the largest refinery in Britain. For three miles I walked beside row after row of oil tanks and the smell of petrochemicals hung in the air. I had walked about half way through when a car pulled up and the driver congratulated me on my achievement so far. Twenty minutes later he returned to offer me his lawn to camp on and a meal at his home in Elton. When he offered me the use of his phone for my weekly radio link-up all my problems were solved! In his lounge I put my third pair of laces in the boots. On average the laces were lasting one thousand miles.

6.4.78

From Elton, with a frost covering the ground, I crossed the Ince Marshes to Frodsham, and walked into its colourful and bustling market. The next few miles took me along the road to Runcorn Bridge at Widnes. I took a minor road to Ditton where I came across Beryl's Café. I just fancied a cheese sandwich and a mug of tea, so I went in and sat down quietly in a corner to eat. Before I knew what was happening I was recognized and the press were summoned for a 'scoop'. A hot meal was placed in front of me, on the house, and Beryl gave me strict orders not to leave until the press had been! My simple snack took over an hour in the end, but I didn't mind as it had all been fun.

Approaching Hale, I was reminded of John Middleton, the Child of Hale, who was born in 1578 and grew to a height of 9 feet 3 inches. Numerous legends are associated with him but the most well-known one concerns the chains that were used to secure him to a bed when he had a fever. One chain was later used to hold down the Devil, another to stop the Chester mills floating down the Dee and a third was secured to the Boston Stump of St Botolph's church to stop it from being blown into the sea.

At the western end of Speke I caught a fleeting glimpse of the magnificent Tudor building, Speke Hall. I carried on to the A561 road for the final few miles to Liverpool. As I approached the Royal Liver Building, a taxi drew up and an interviewer from Radio City got out. He wanted a piece urgently for his programme in thirty minutes' time. We made one recording only to find his microphone was faulty, so I made a makeshift repair with my knife and while I held everything in place we did another one which was used.

7.4.78

Before leaving Liverpool I returned to Blacks' shop to do further radio interviews and to be photographed by the press. I was presented with a whistle, badges, boot laces and two pairs of socks. I left the rucksack there while I went off to see the Roman Catholic cathedral. As I walked to the building I passed the almost complete new Anglican cathedral. The Catholic building has always fascinated me, for the shape, the very colourful stained glass windows, the altar and surrounding area all combine to make it a really interesting and exceptional design.

Returning to Blacks' I shouldered the rucksack once more and walked along the docks road through Bootle to Crosby. The docks were a sad sight; they are little used, with large warehouses standing empty and forlorn, and people wandering about aimlessly obviously out of work. While walking past the wharfs an elderly man rushed up to me and handed me a note. It said:

John,
Your British Coastal walk captures manys imagination. In doing so you show people how to give – more than they intended to do.

Proud of you.
Eric Viernon

From Crosby I left the traffic, people and houses behind and walked along the shore, but I had to return inland at Hightown to cross the river Alt. Fortunately there were no army exercises going on at the Altcar ranges and I was allowed to walk through and onto Formby Sands. The next nine miles were along some fine sands to Southport. Looking seawards, I could see the line of buoys marking the channel into Liverpool. For three hours I saw no one as I walked across the sands. I was completely alone and, although I didn't feel lonely, I could sense the solitude.

Being on such a large expense of sand I found it very hard to gauge distances. About five miles from Southport I could see its three-quarter-mile-long pier. It looked quite near but in reality it took two hours to get there. Nearing Southport I was surprised to see cars driving on the sands; planes also land on them. At the pier I walked towards the town, and discovered that the sea front is half a mile from the sea, due to the shifting sands.

8.4.78

From Southport my route took me inland to Hesketh Bank and Tarleton where I was able to cross the river Douglas. I had to continue still further inland to Longton and Hutton to get to Preston where I could cross the river Ribble. Then I could at last head to the coast again towards Freckleton and Lytham St Anne's. As I walked through villages and towns it was delightful to hear people cutting their lawns, and to smell the fresh cut grass.

I was accompanied for the day by an American reporter, Charles Azenby, who wanted to do a profile on me. At first we got on very well but as the miles passed my enthusiasm for answering his non-stop questions became less. I tried to explain about the mental strain of the walk, and how one becomes very drained mentally and physically, but is able to cope when alone. When I reached Freckleton I had walked twenty-nine miles and as there was a camp site I decided to stop. The owner's wife came to the door and summoned her husband from the shed, where he was killing a chicken for their Sunday lunch, to come and attend to me. As the ground was waterlogged he offered me a caravan to sleep in. My American friend went off to find accommodation and I agreed to meet him the next day at nine o'clock.

9.4.78

Charles arrived and we set off. I was not looking forward to the day's walk through Lytham St Anne's and Blackpool as it was Sunday and I was sure that there would be crowds about. Walking along the sands of South Shore we disturbed a huge flock of sanderlings. They scurried along the shore at a rapid pace before taking off en masse and flying low over the sea to another patch of sand a quarter of a mile ahead.

As we neared the central pier of Blackpool, I heard my name called and turned to see three friends from Chesterfield appear. Charles left us and we walked together for a short distance. Five minutes after they left I was hailed again. This time it was a couple from my own village – I couldn't believe it! We chatted for a long while before I carried on to Fleetwood. I reached the ferry point by tea time and for a change went into the café and had fish and chips. Across the mouth of the river Wyre was Knott End-on-Sea. A walk of fourteen miles would see me there next day. For the moment I walked out of Fleetwood on the A585 to a caravan site. Before I could find the owner to seek permission to camp, someone from across the road recognized me and offered me the use of their lawn. In the morning I awoke to find two inches of snow covering the tent.

10.4.78

I crossed the river Wyre via Shard Toll Bridge, from where I walked up the eastern side of the river along minor roads and footpaths to Knott End-on-Sea. The sun had come out but it was still very cold and across Morecambe Bay I could see the snow-clad hills of the Lake District. Just beyond Knott End, near Fluke Hall, I found my first bluebells. A wide variety of birds were active in the area and I saw snipe, shelduck, skylarks, sanderlings, oyster-catchers, black-headed gulls, wheatears, robins and wrens. I walked on beside Pilling and Cockerham marshes before heading to Cockersand Abbey. There were danger signs all the way. One warned me that 'It is dangerous to walk across the marsh and sands. Several fatal accidents have occurred', while another simply said: 'Beware of the Tide'.

Cockersand Abbey was founded in the late twelfth century, and in the sixteenth century was one of the richest monasteries in Lancashire. Little remains of the buildings which originally covered an acre of land; only the Chapter House is anywhere near complete. I pressed on to Crook Cottage where the owners were waiting with cameras poised to catch me as I passed. At Crook Farm, half a mile later, the farmer was similarly waiting – as I moved round the area each rang ahead to let the next person know I was on my way!

I was very impressed with the setting of Glasson Dock: it is beside the river Lune, a large canal basin, and a collection of eighteenth- and early nineteenth-century buildings. A canal links the docks, which was originally the port of Lancaster, to the Lancaster canal, and it is now one of the most important yachting centres in northern England.

I stopped at Glasson for the night.

11.4.78

As I left Glasson under clear blue skies, the canal basin with its colourful boats reflected in the still water created a scene of simple but classic beauty.

As I passed through Lancaster I was greeted by the mayor and we were photographed together near the castle. It was pleasing to see that a considerable amount of restoration work had been carried out in the neighbourhood. Once across the river Lune, I headed southwards to Ovangle Farm, Overton and Sunderland. Beyond the village my troubles began, for the road runs across the marsh and at high tide it is flooded and cuts Sunderland off. I tried to get there before high tide but I was just too late. The road was clear but part way along the sea rolled in at an alarming rate and within seconds was two feet deep. I left quickly. People had often warned me of how fast the tide comes in on marshland but I had never really appreciated the danger. I got to the sea wall and walked along it into Sunderland.

In the late seventeenth century Robert Lawson of Sunderland

Point owned a fleet of merchant ships. His trade was basically rum and tobacco from the West Indies, but he is also reputed to have brought the first load of cotton ever into the country. The cotton lay in Lawson's warehouse for twelve months, whereupon some of it germinated and a cotton tree grew; the tree survives to this day. On one of the voyages, a West Indian slave returned with the ship and stayed in Sunderland. His name was Sambo and, just out of the village, I came across his simple grave, lined with rope and pebbles.

The following poem appears on his grave plaque:

> Full sixty years the angry Winters wave
> has thundering dashed this bleak and barren shore,
> Since Sambo's head laid in this lonely grave,
> lies still and ne'er will hear their turmoil more.
> Full many a sandbird chirps upon the sod
> and many a Summer's sunbeam warms the clod.
> And many a teeming cloud upon him drips
> but still he sleeps – till the wakening sounds
> of archangels trump new life impart.
> Then the great judge his approbation founds
> not on Man's colour, but his warmth of heart.

Leaving Sunderland I crossed the marsh to Potts Corner and on through Ocean Edge Caravan Park to Heysham and Morecambe, where I stopped. Walking along Morecambe front I was amused to see a shop called Snappyland, where below the proprietor's name, A. J. Ryan and Son, had been added 'plus one daughter'!

I had walked more than 2,600 miles and looking at my boots I could see the first major signs of wear. The heels were well worn, and there were holes in the commando-type soles. Normally I would change my boots at this distance, but I thought it might be interesting to see just how far they would last, so I didn't change them.

12.4.78

There is a right of way just north of Morecambe, across Morecambe Bay to Kents Bank, south of Grange-over-Sands.

There was no way I was going to cross this large expanse of sand, which at low tide covers 150 square miles, and risk being caught by the incoming tide. I learnt, as I walked round the edge of the bay, that the guides had not been across for more than sixteen months; there are only a few days a year when a crossing is safe. During the nineteenth century horse-drawn coaches used to cross the bay risking being caught in quicksand or the river channel. I headed for Carnforth to cross the river Keer and went on to Silverdale and Arnside.

Silverdale was particularly attractive and in the cold but sunny weather it reminded me of the Peak District. The trees and limestone rock were identical in setting to my village, but had the added attraction of the sea. An abundance of spring flowers covered the ground: white and purple violets, wood avens, bluebells, lesser celandines and daffodils. Along the shore there were lots of shelduck and mallards and I saw an occasional grey heron poised to kill. At one point I flushed a snipe which immediately burst away in its characteristic zig-zag pattern, while later a green woodpecker kept overtaking me. Out on one particular piece of marshland a moorhen sat on its cluster of eggs. It was interesting to see spring still emerging as I travelled north.

But the biggest surprise of the day came an hour later when snow began to fall. By the time I reached the camp site at Sampool bridge I was putting the tent up in blizzard conditions!

13.4.78

I awoke to find the tent sagging under the weight of snow. Unzipping the door I looked out at a grey sky with four inches of snow lying on the ground. Packing the tent up in such cold conditions was very hard work and, although I tried to do it in the lavatories in an endeavour to get as much snow off as possible, the result was a fiasco. I set off hurriedly to get my circulation going. I went north to Sampool Bridge before heading due south beside the river Kent to Grange-over-Sands. Snow fell gently; everything was silent and nothing moved. It was one of those days when I simply walked hard and had no rests. After Grange I made my way past the Cartmel Sands to the disused railway bridge over the river Leven at Greenodd. By three o'clock I had walked twenty-eight miles and I called it a day when I found a bed and breakfast in Ulverston. The owners were most obliging and I hung the saturated tent in the cellar to dry.

14.4.78

The morning brought sunshine and, as I left Ulverston for Bardsea, the flat-topped snow-covered summit of Ingleborough was just discernible in the east. By lunchtime I was well down the western side of Morecambe Bay, past Aldingham and fast approaching Rampside and Roa Island. Ahead was the Island of Walney and lying in between, in the Piel Channel, was Piel Island. This island has a few sheep and a pub, which must be one of the most remote in Britain. Consequently it is very popular with yachtsmen who often do a weekend trip from Glasson. Surprisingly, Blackpool is only twelve miles away.

I continued peacefully beside the sands from Roa Island towards Barrow-in-Furness. As I neared the town centre I could see the tops of the ships which were being built. It seemed unreal to see such large constructions dwarfing the houses beside the docks. I was momentarily disturbed from my thoughts when a car pulled up and the occupant wished me well and disappeared. Two minutes later I turned the corner to walk towards the town hall and was staggered to see eight hundred cheering and waving children!

Unbeknown to me, my progress had been monitored and the person who had greeted me a few minutes before was in fact the school governor who had arranged it all. I felt very self-conscious walking along the line of children and was relieved to reach the town hall.

A few members of the rotary club were waiting to welcome me and suggested that I join them for a late lunch. As I was well ahead of schedule I agreed. I wasn't too pleased to discover that the hotel was over half an hour's walk inland but after a good lunch I left at 3.30 p.m.

As I left, one of the members, Denis Rose, asked if he could

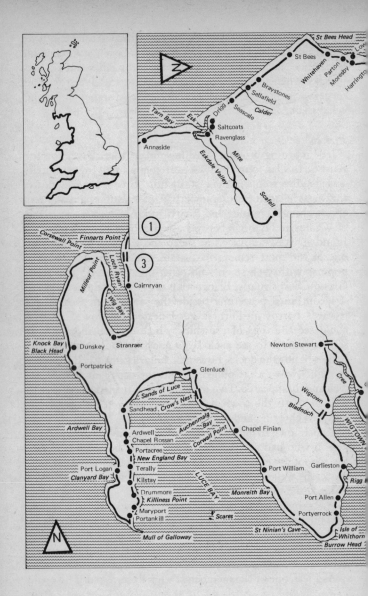

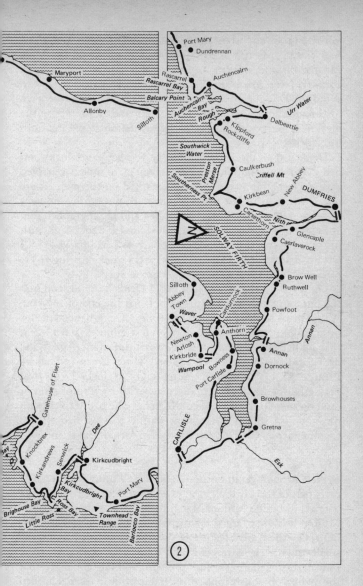

Port Mary
Dundrennan
Rascarrel
Rascarrel Bay
Auchencairn
Balcary Point
Maryport
Allonby
Silloth
Auchencairn Bay
Rough
Urr Water
Dalbeattie
Kippford
Rockcliffe
Southwick Water
Caulkerbush
Griffell Mt
New Abbey
DUMFRIES
Southerness Pt
Preston Merse
Kirkbean
Carsethorn
Nith
Glencaple
Caerlaverock
SOLWAY FIRTH
Silloth
Abbey Town
Waver
Cardrnock
Brow Well
Ruthwell
Powfoot
Newton Arlosh
Kirkbride
Wampool
Anthorn
Port Carlisle
Bowness
Annan
Dornock
Aman
Browhouses
CARLISLE
Gretna
Esk

Gatehouse of Fleet
Dee
Knockbrex
Kirkandrews
Senwick
Kirkcudbright
Kirkcudbright Bay
Port Mary
Ross Bay
Brighouse Bay
Little Ross
Townhead Range
Barlocco Bay

②

join me. I took an instant liking to him and together we walked to Ormsgill. As it was low tide we walked across the huge expanse of sand and began walking due north up very open country. Near Askam in Furness we kept close to the land to avoid the Duddon river channel. From then onwards we were in the middle of the sands and I could readily appreciate the bleakness and vulnerability of our situation if we got into difficulties.

Denis was an ideal companion; he was happy-go-lucky and had a great sense of humour. After about eight miles we arrived at a river channel which was not marked on the map. There was nothing for it but to wade across. To put off the moment of getting wet I waved him across first and photographed him as he stood in the middle holding his shoes and socks and with his trousers rolled up. Once he was across I had to wade in. I left my boots and socks on, as I always do when crossing rivers for I am frightened of stepping on broken glass.

On reaching the other bank I told Denis I would send him the photograph when I returned home at the end of the year. With a great sense of occasion and timing Denis handed me his business card. I burst out laughing. A few minutes later I learnt that he had high blood pressure, was an insurance agent and drove a Rolls Royce! We reached High Cross Inn above Broughton in Furness just after eight o'clock. Denis was perfectly dry and looked immaculate with no sign of sand or mud on his suit. It was difficult to believe he had walked with me, and so I signed a statement stating that we had walked together across the Duddon Sands. We parted firm friends.

15.4.78

I left Broughton in Furness in beautiful sunny weather. The early part of the day took me down the western side of Duddon Sands and beside Millom Marsh to Millom. The area around Millom was once famed for its iron mines and blast furnaces, but today these are a feature of the past. However I found the small town very attractive; its long neat rows of classic industrial housing were full of charm and one could see that the owners obviously took considerable pride in them. I headed southwards to Haverigg and its beautiful sandy beaches and huge sand dunes. Descending to the beach I turned right and began the long uninterrupted walk up the Cumbrian coast to Carlisle and Scotland. For a few days there would be no river estuaries and large bays to walk round; the coast ahead was comparatively straight.

It was Saturday and I was surprised that there were so few people about even though it was a delightfully mild and sunny day. From Haverigg Point it was a long haul up the beach to the shingle and pebble shore of Gutterby Spa. In doing so I walked into the Lake District National Park. Inland I could see the snow-capped mountains. From Gutterby Spa I moved up to the cliff tops to Selker coastguard station and on to Tarn Bay. From there I had to move inland and walk past the Ministry of Defence experimental station at Eskmeals. The red flags were flying and the guns were firing out to sea. My progress had been watched and when I reached the main gate a mug of tea was waiting. The security guards suggested that instead of walking inland to cross the river Esk, I should walk across the railway bridge. I took their advice and reached Ravenglass in the early evening with twenty-nine miles walked that day.

That night I stayed in a bed and breakfast. I had reached the point on the coastline where I would make my second walk inland to climb Scafell Pike, the second of the three mountains that I intended to climb on the walk. The guest house would provide somewhere to leave all my equipment so that I could travel light with just my waterproof clothing.

16.4.78

I left early in the morning and crossed through the mountains of Hooker Crag and Ross's Camp to the Eskdale valley. This time, I didn't experience any of the twinges of regret about leaving the coast that I had experienced when ascending Snowdon. In Eskdale I walked up the road past Dalegarth station, the northern end of the Ravenglass and Eskdale Railway, and on to Brotherilkeld. From there I moved into the mountains to Throstle Garth, Cam Spout and on to

109

Mickledore. I relished being in the mountains and stopped often just to enjoy the stillness and absorb the silence. I hadn't realized how noisy the coast was with the sounds of the sea, birds and wind. After so many muddy estuaries it was refreshing to see the crystal clear water of the mountain streams.

From just above the waterfall of Cam Spout I reached snow. I carried on totally absorbed in the ascent and not bothered by the cold even though I was only wearing shorts. From Mickledore the snow became quite deep and I frequently sank to my knees in it. The summit of Scafell Pike was shrouded in cloud. As I approached I saw a few climbers dressed in breeches and gaiters and armed with rope and ice-axes. Seeing me just walking up in shorts and an open-necked shirt, they fell about laughing. But the most stunning surprise came two minutes later when someone approached me, and said 'Hello John, it's good to see you here!' At first I couldn't place him, then I realized that we had met on the summit of Snowdon a month before! Our parting words were, 'See you on Ben Nevis!'

The cloud was very thick and to get back to Mickledore and its mountain rescue box I had to use the compass. From there I took another bearing to Cam Spout and as I approached the waterfall I walked out of the cloud and could see the path towards Throstle Garth. I retraced my steps back to Brotheril-keld, Dalegarth, Ross's Camp and into Ravenglass. I had walked thirty-four miles, climbed several thousands of feet, and all in the space of ten hours. For the first time since leaving London I felt tired. Overall I had walked almost 2,800 miles, and Scotland was just round the corner. I slept deeply and contentedly that night.

17.4.78

The morning brought a thick sea mist but the temperature was high, and before long the sun burned the mist away exposing one of the loveliest days so far. My route from Ravenglass lay across Mite estuary, where, as it was low tide, I was able to walk across the sands to Saltcoats and Drigg. On my immediate left was the Ravenglass Nature Reserve where during the summer months terns and black-headed gulls nest.

In 1970 there were 11,000 black-headed gulls' nests counted on the reserve, confirming that this was the largest breeding colony in Europe. Natterjack toads are also found in the area.

From Drigg I kept to the shore to Seascale and crossed the Calder river near Sellafield. The low tide had exposed large expanses of sand which offered delightful walking. There is no right of way along this particular stretch of coast until St Bees, ten miles ahead. In time the sand gave way to shingle. Near Braystones I was hailed by a large woman in slippers and flowing dressing gown. She had been looking out for me to wish me well and to take my photograph. She was an avid bottle message finder and had so far found fifty-seven from various parts of the world, stranded on the high tide line where she looks for them each day.

A little over an hour's walking took me to the magnificent sands of St Bees. The last time I was there was Easter 1976, when I was walking Wainwright's 190-mile coast-to-coast walk to Robin Hood's Bay on the North Yorkshire coast. On that occasion the weather had been foul, and seeing it in good weather I was amazed at its beauty. The origin of the name of St Bees is obscure, but one legend says that it is named after an Irish princess called St Bega who was shipwrecked off the nearby coast in the seventh century. She stayed with the Lord of Egremont and pleaded with him for some land to build a nunnery. It was Midsummer's Day the next day, and he told her that she could have as much of his land as was covered with snow on that day. To everyone's amazement, an area of three miles around the castle was covered. He kept his word, granted the land and helped to build the nunnery.

I carried on to St Bees Head and it made a very pleasant change to be on some tall cliffs and to see several gulls flying in the air. Not many other sea birds had arrived, but I did see kittiwakes and herring gulls. Beyond the headland I turned into Saltom Bay and walked through an industrial complex to reach Whitehaven, three days ahead of schedule. Waiting for me at the post office were the local rotary club and my eighth parcel.

18.4.78

It was quite a thrill to set off from Whitehaven carrying the necessary maps to take me into Scotland and along the Solway coast. Much of the day's walk was through an industrial area via Parton, Lowca, Harrington and Mossbay to Workington. The railway runs beside the shore, and on the shore side there is a right of way which I was able to use through to Workington. I continued along the railway line to Maryport where I left the industry behind to enjoy a little-known section of the coast.

From Maryport I carried on to the one-time smugglers' village of Allonby where I slept in a caravan. The final four hours of the day had been in torrential rain so I was glad of the shelter. I arranged to reach the Scottish border two days ahead of schedule on 20 April at three o'clock.

19.4.78

As I left Allonby the sun came out, and as the day progressed it became very warm and I took my pullover off and walked in shirt sleeves. This was the life! Two hours from Allonby I reached the pretty town of Silloth. Built about one hundred years ago as a seaside resort, its wide streets and neat appearance were very striking. The sands, too, were good. The railway has been dismantled which is a tragedy for the town, for only minor roads lead to it. Industrial supplies come in by boat to the docks. From the shore I was able to look across the Solway Firth to Scotland and see Criffell mountain.

Just north of Silloth at Skinburness I moved inland to walk round the estuaries of the rivers Waver and Wampool. This entailed going via Abbeytown, Newton Arlosh and Kirkbride to reach Anthorn and Cardurnock. It was a long walk, and the hours were rushing by. I had worked out that I must reach Bowness-on-Solway by nightfall, otherwise I stood little chance of reaching Scotland at the scheduled hour. It was dark by the time I reached Bowness. As I entered the village a fisherman walked down the road carrying a haaf net which is used to catch salmon. Regrettably it was too dark to take a photograph. In Bowness-on-Solway I searched in vain for a plaque or sign stating that this was one end of Hadrian's Wall. I hurried on in the dark to Port Carlisle and the Cottage camp site where, because I couldn't find anyone to ask, I camped without permission. I was feeling tired after walking thirty-seven miles, and at 9.30 p.m. I cooked my evening meal. Across the estuary, six miles as the crow flies, was Gretna and Scotland. I had seen the lights of Annan as I came through Bowness; and it had brought home to me the fact that I had come a long way from London.

20.4.78

I was away early in the morning to walk the twenty-five miles to Gretna via Carlisle. I didn't stop in Carlisle for it had been raining all morning and the weather was generally miserable. From Carlisle I kept to the minor roads and paths to the Metal Bridge over the river Esk. From there I had no alternative but to walk beside the busy A74 to Gretna. Waiting for me at the river Esk was a crew from Border Television, who filmed my final steps in England.

At three o'clock exactly, with almost 2,900 miles behind me and the sun shining, I stepped into Scotland. A large crowd had gathered to join the press, photographers and film crews who were there. I was a bit overwhelmed by the welcome, especially when the Junior World Champion bagpipe player piped me into Scotland. But I was ecstatic, for I looked upon Scotland as a chance really to get away from everything and enjoy walking a remote and rarely visited coastline.

Also at the boundary were Andrew Nicol and Mrs Sheila Milne, from R C S B. I was all geared to do battle for I had been continually swamped by people and clubs ever since the beginning of the walk and they had been partly responsible for this. We adjourned to the hotel for a meal and discussion. They were very sympathetic; they understood my criticism of the fundraising so far and promised that they would do their utmost to see I was no longer imposed upon in the way I had been in England and Wales. From then on I knew that it would be controlled and that the walk would come first. I felt much relieved and was grateful to find that I had support for my aims.

I put the tent up beside the First House in Scotland, delighted that I was about to embark upon the most exciting coastline in the whole of Britain. I slept very contentedly that night.

6. South-West Scotland

21.4.78

Before I left Gretna, the occupants of the First House gave me a lavish breakfast. I visited the wedding room and saw the anvil where more than 10,000 people have been ceremoniously married. A little after nine o'clock I set off to walk along the north bank of the Solway Firth past Browhouses and Dornockbrow to Annan. I reached Annan in the early afternoon where I was welcomed by the local rotary club. While enjoying a round of sandwiches, I was presented with my Scottish passport, signed by the Chief Haggis Protection Officer. On the description page under the sub-section 'peculiarities' it states 'likes to walk'! In the 'vaccinations' column, it says I am immunized against: Scottish Tsetse Fly, Malt Whisky Malaria, Haggis Hypochondria, Tartan Tickle, Sporran Rash, and Heather Hooping Cough! The passport does not expire and entitles me to report sightings of the Loch Ness monster, and to hunt haggis, but I am cautioned not to disturb or annoy Scotland's only ferocious native beastie – *Ferocititus midgus Caledonius* – the midge! It was all good fun.

Having crossed the river Annan, I walked along its banks and returned to the channel to make for Powfoot, before walking inland slightly to avoid the marsh just south of Ruthwell. Although it was 6.30 p.m. I noticed that the small, long, whitewashed cottage where the first Savings Bank in Scotland was opened in 1810, was still open. I knocked on the door and was ushered in. Another item of interest in Ruthwell

115

is the seventh-century cross regarded by some as the finest example of very early Christian art, but which unfortunately I didn't have time to see. A mile from Ruthwell I came to Brow Well where Robert Burns took the healing waters in an attempt to cure himself. He died at the age of thirty-eight on 21 July 1796, and is buried in St Michael's church, Dumfries.

I camped on the lawn of Stanhope Farm. Across the river at Caerlaverock Nature Reserve I could hear the gaggle of pinkfoot geese. I was really at peace with the world and very pleased to have spent my first full day in Scotland.

22.4.78

The weather was beautiful as I passed the nature reserve to the magnificent Caerlaverock Castle, built in the thirteenth century of red sandstone on a wooded mound. Four miles away, due west, was New Abbey where I planned to camp. But first I had to walk beside the river Nith via Glencaple to reach Dumfries where I could cross it. The weather was now really warm: perhaps at last winter had finished and spring had arrived in the north. People had shed their overcoats and jackets, and many were busy in their gardens.

In Dumfries I made my way to St Michael's church to see Robert Burns's tomb. The church was built at the end of the eighteenth century and had replaced a much older building which had been in a dangerous condition. The work was carried out by local craftsmen and cost a little over £402. When it was only partly built, in 1746, Prince Charles had camped beside it before moving on to his defeat at Culloden. The church has eleven very good examples of Victorian stained glass windows. Near the church I crossed the river Nith and headed due south to New Abbey where I camped beside the ruins of Sweetheart Abbey.

Entering the village I noticed above a doorway, presumably once a blacksmith's shop, a plaque dated 1775. In the middle was a crown with a hand and hammer below. Around the hand were the words 'By hammer and hand, all carts do stand'. The abbey, like Caerlaverock Castle across the river, is built from red sandstone. It was founded on 10 April 1273, and the charter

116

was granted by Dervorgilla, the wife of John Balliol of Barnard Castle in northern England. It was through their devotion to each other that the abbey became known as Sweetheart Abbey. On the death of John Balliol, his wife Dervorgilla had his heart removed and placed in an ivory casket. This became her 'sweet, silent companion', and remained with her until her death in 1289. She was buried in the abbey with her casket.

> She founded in Galloway
> An abbey of the Cistercian order:
> Dulce Cor she made them call (it),
> That is Sweet Heart, that Abbey,
> And now the men of Galloway
> Call that place the New Abbey.

23.4.78

Before continuing my walk southwards from New Abbey, I walked to the northern end of the village to look at the pine trees of Shambellie Wood, and in so doing I caught sight of a red squirrel. A short distance out of New Abbey I could see the slopes of Criffell mountain. On the shore of the Firth I had seen several pole constructions in the exposed mud, secured by ropes. They were salmon nets with a line of poles and nets leading to a square. When the tide covers them, the salmon come up against the line and have to turn until they eventually find an opening in the square, which leads to a one-way trap. Some of these constructions were two or three hundred yards long with three or more square traps. I also came across several haaf nets which are only found in the Solway Firth area. They are rather like a huge children's shrimp net with a short handle, and again are used for catching salmon. I saw dozens of people fishing on the coast throughout the walk, but at no time did I see anyone catch anything!

Just beyond the slopes of Criffell I came to the village of Kirkbean. Almost two miles away, but within the parish, is the cottage where Paul Jones, the legendary figure of the US navy after whom the dance was named, was born in 1747. A little over a mile away I reached Carsethorn which, as the following verse tells, was once a busy port:

> Old sailing schooners, seen no more,
> Coasting along the Solway shore –
> Criffell, Petrel, Havelock, Venus –
> They fade: the sea-mist comes between us.
>
> (Henry Truckell)

Three miles later I approached the magnificent sands round Southerness Point. Near the lighthouse and just inland is now a popular camping and caravan area. The sands were really very impressive and as I continued beside Preston Merse, the sun shone and I walked in my shirt sleeves. From there I had to make a detour inland to Caulkerbush to cross Southwick Water. The next few miles were over some impressive cliffs to Rockcliffe and Kippford. I had now almost left the Solway Firth behind and was coming back to the open sea; the large expanses of tidal estuary were now giving way to cliffs and breaking waves. On the cliffs I saw herring gulls, a fulmar, razorbills and cormorants.

Approaching Barcloy Hill, I saw a monument recording 'Schooner Elbe, Captain Samuel Wilson of Palnakie after providentially landing her crew here backed off the rocks. Sank off Rascarrel 6th December 1966.' I was to reach Rascarrel the following day. Both Rockcliffe and Kippford were surprisingly busy with people taking their Sunday walk along the promenade; they are also active sailing centres. Off-shore was Rough Island, now owned by the National Trust, where scaups, shelduck, mergansers and waders are seen. I passed through unnoticed and went inland again to Dalbeattie, where I camped.

24.4.78

I crossed the Urr Water and went down the western side of the river towards Auchencairn Bay. It was another really warm day and my log records: 'Nose peeling!' Further signs of spring were in evidence: marsh marigolds, primroses, blackthorn and a cherry tree were all in flower. I got to Palnackie and five miles later I was in Auchencairn. Near there I had agreed to walk with the head boy and girl from the Castle Douglas High School, who had been sponsored to walk for five miles around Balcary Point to Rascarrel Bay. I enjoyed their company very much and learnt later that their walk with me had raised a staggering £703; by far the greatest single effort over the whole walk.

The cliffs around Balcary Point were full of nesting sea birds: fulmars, herring gulls, cormorants, kittiwakes and guillemots. As if to add to the children's education a three-foot long adder crossed the path: it was the first they had seen. I tried to get a picture but as always it was too quick. I said goodbye to the children at Rascarrel, and was just debating how to cross the burn to continue round the coast to Port Mary, when the local farmer passed by in his tractor and trailer. Seeing my predicament he backed the trailer into the water and I walked along the top!

Near Port Mary I had to leave the coast and cut inland to Dundrennan. The reason for the detour was because I could not get permission to walk through the Townhead Range. It did have the advantage that I could look round Dundrennan Abbey, founded by Cistercian monks in 1142. As at Sweetheart Abbey, the monks came from Rievaulx Abbey in Yorkshire. Dundrennan Abbey is particularly interesting because the last abbot, Edward Maxwell, allowed Mary Queen of Scots to spend her last night in Scotland there. She left the next morning for England where she spent the next fifteen years 'imprisoned' in several Derbyshire halls and castles.

From Dundrennan I walked along the road round the range to reach Kirkcudbright Bay. A further three miles took me to Kirkcudbright where I camped overlooking the town.

25.4.78

As I made my way through the town to cross the river Dee, I was impressed by the character of the typically Scottish buildings. Hanging on the sides of the tollbooth were some neck clamps. In olden days people who had misbehaved were clasped in them and had to suffer abuse and rotten fruit and eggs being thrown at them. Near the waterfront, which is now becoming a popular sailing centre, I passed the sixteenth-century ruins of McLellan's castle. Leaving Kirkcudbright I went down the side of the river Dee back to Kirkcudbright Bay. In doing so I went past the entrance to Upper Senwick farm. A notice stated boldly 'No hawkers or politicians beyond this point'! For the first time I was beginning to feel tired – I didn't realize it just then, but I had walked 3,000 miles.

Just beyond Senwick I walked round the shore of Ross Bay and on to Meikle Ross overlooking the island of Little Ross. As I made my way to Brighouse Bay, two miles further on, I had to negotiate a field full of cows and bulls. Usually if there are cows in a field with the bull, the bull is believed to be docile and more interested in the females than a walker. Nervously hoping it was true, I began walking through the field. Suddenly the bull noticed me and charged. Despite my heavy rucksack I sprinted to the edge and climbed over the stone wall just before he reached me! But worse was to follow. I had leapt into another field which was also full of cows – and two inquisitive bulls! I backed away as quickly as possible and, with a pounding heart, got into the next field, which was thankfully empty.

Brighouse Bay has one house overlooking the peaceful, unspoilt beach and its occupants recognized me. As we chatted I mentioned the plastic litter I had seen on the beach. This kind of litter is one of the saddest sights I saw on the coastline and I very rarely found a litter-free beach. My companion informed me that he and his wife had personally filled sixty large plastic bags full of rubbish. On the Lancashire coast, on one beach alone, I counted approximately one hundred plastic liquid soap bottles in just a mile. It is a great tragedy that man's thoughtlessness allows him to abuse and spoil his own countryside.

I continued on to Kirkandrews and Knockbrex to get to Fleet Bay. Five miles later, and before the reception committee was ready, I walked into the picturesque village of Gatehouse of Fleet. The president of the Lions Club walked with me through the streets and we were joined by a piper playing an air. I camped on the president's lawn that night.

26.4.78

The plan for the day was to walk round the eastern side of Wigtown Bay to Creetown, and from there to walk inland to cross the river Cree to Newton Stewart. I realize now that I was very tired at this point from the mental strain of having so many people always seeking me out. While I posted some letters at the post office at Gatehouse of Fleet, a walker approached me and said he was sponsored to walk with me for the day! That was the first I had heard about it, and I am afraid that I blew up and told him that it just wasn't on. When I had calmed down, I agreed he could meet me at Creetown for the final six miles of the day.

My log records two important statements, which at the time I thought little of: 'right foot – heel sore underneath skin', and 'find can't push myself as much – cumulative effect?' I joined the sponsored walker who happened to be a doctor, but I said nothing. I felt guilty about my outburst in the morning, but after I had explained why it had happened he quite agreed that I was within my rights. I stayed with him that night as the youth hostel was closed.

27.4.78

I left Newton Stewart early so that I could get to Burrow Head, about thirty miles away, before night. Eight miles of walking on the road beside the river Cree took me to Wigtown church, and the Martyr's Grave. On the nearby marsh an obelisk marks the spot where, in 1865, two covenanters, Margaret Mclauchlan and Margaret Wilson, were tied to stakes at low tide and were drowned for their beliefs by the incoming tide. Their tombs are in the churchyard together with a third to three men who were hung without trial also for their devotion to the national covenant.

I pressed on across the river Bladnoch to the village of Garlieston. The coastline became spectacular and it was a magnificent walk past Rigg Bay, Port Allen and Portyerrock Bay to reach the Isle of Whithorn. At Rigg Bay I could see England, and Workington clearly, while out to sea was the Isle of Man. The name Whithorn is derived from Candida Casa, or

121

White House. St Ninian, who is believed to have been a British bishop, built the first Christian church in Scotland there in AD 397. The present church on the Isle of Whithorn dates from the twelfth century. After visiting the church I passed the harbour and rounded the cliffs of Burrow Head to the camp site.

28.4.78

Two miles on my way, I dropped down to the pebbled shore and visited St Ninian's cave. It is said that he used to go there for solitude, and it has since become a place of pilgrimage. Some of the best-preserved crosses made by the pilgrims are now protected. The next few miles were along pebbled shore to Monreith Bay. The main road from there runs close to the shoreline and I followed it to Port William. As I walked, I looked across Luce Bay in hazy conditions to the thin peninsula of the Mull of Galloway. Almost midway between were the rocks called Little Scares and Big Scare.

Gannets have always fascinated me. Their huge, powerful wings, which stretch to six feet, give them the support to hunt food over a very large area. One of the finest sights on the coast was to see them diving from as high as 100 feet above the sea to catch a fish. The Scares has a small gannetry of about 450 pairs and they were in evidence as I walked around Luce Bay.

Port William was formerly a smugglers' haven and regular boats crossed the sea to the Isle of Man. The small harbour with its collection of boats made a delightful picture. As I began walking out of Port William, I was hailed by the local minister who had been watching out for me.

Six miles later, I reached the ruins of Chapel Finian, named after the sixth-century Celtic saint, Findbarr. The rectangular ruin is above the site which is believed to be where the pilgrims landed their boats. The final few miles of the day took me over the cliffs of the Mull of Sinniness to Stair Haven and Glenluce, where I camped.

29.4.78

Red flags were flying on the Torrs Warren range so I could

not walk along the Luce Sands. Instead I followed the road around the range before walking the shore to Sandhead. On the way I noticed that lesser celandines, violets, blackthorn, primula and pussy willow were in full bloom. Meadow saxifrage and white deadnettle were also coming into flower. The birds were active and I saw a pair of crested tits busily building their nest. Terns flew noisily by and both male and female eider ducks floated in large rafts close to the shore.

On the long finger of the Mull of Galloway there were several beautiful bays and on one, on the way to Drummore, I saw a shipwrecked boat stranded high on the pebbled shore. Drummore itself was picturesque and I saw a water skier being towed around the bay. Even though the weather was deteriorating, I was determined to reach the lighthouse on the Mull of Galloway, the most southerly point of Scotland. I arrived in a force seven gale and sought refuge in the lighthouse. The keeper was delighted to see me, having seen my photograph in the local paper. Rather than put the tent up in the exposed conditions I slept in the occasional keeper's caravan which, although secured to the ground by heavy wire, rocked disconcertingly through the night.

30.4.78

The cliffs along the western side of the Mull are spectacular but in the continuing bad weather conditions I kept slightly inland as I headed northwards to Clanyard Bay and Port Logan. I liked Port Logan with its sunken rows of houses protected from the westerly wind. At the end of Port Logan Bay I reached a circular stone wall enclosing a fish pond. It was built in the eighteenth century and was damaged by a mine during the last war, but was restored in 1955. In the enclosed water are tame cod and bass which, when a bell is rung, surface to be fed by hand. Inland is Logan House and near the fishpond I walked through part of its woodland which included several rhododendron bushes in full bloom.

The coast from there to Portpatrick was extremely rugged and necessitated a considerable amount of ascending and descending. In good conditions it must have been quite

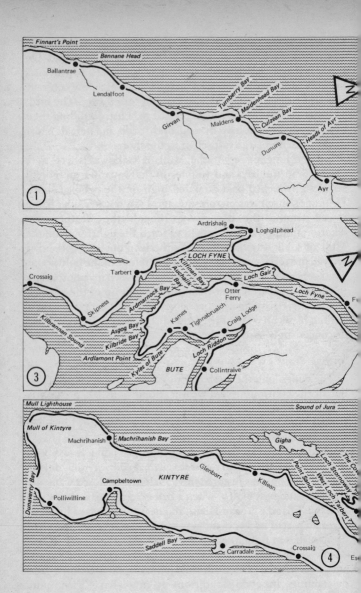

Map 1

Finnart's Point — Bennane Head — Ballantrae — Lendalfoot — Girvan — Turnberry Bay — Maidens — Maidenhead Bay — Culzean Bay — Dunure — Heads of Ayr — Ayr

Map 3

Ardrishaig — Loghgilphead — LOCH FYNE — Crossaig — Tarbert — Killman Bay — Auchalik Bay — Ardmarnock Bay — Loch Gair — Loch Fyne — Skipness — Otter Ferry — Fu... — Kilbrannan Sound — Asgog Bay — Kames — Tighnabruaich — Craig Lodge — Kilbride Bay — Ardlamont Point — Loch Riddon — Kyles of Bute — BUTE — Colintraive

Map 4

Mull Lighthouse — Sound of Jura — Mull of Kintyre — Machrihanish — Machrihanish Bay — Gigha — Dunaverty Bay — Glenbarr — Killean — Point Sands — Polliwilline — Campbeltown — KINTYRE — Loch Stornoway — West Loch Tarbert T... — The Co... — Saddell Bay — Carradale — Crossaig — Ese...

124

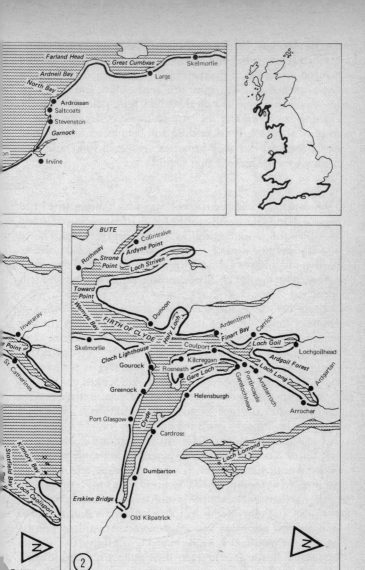

Farland Head
Ardneil Bay
North Bay
Great Cumbrae
Largs
Skelmorlie
Ardrossan
Saltcoats
Stevenston
Garnock
Irvine

BUTE
Colintraive
Rothesay
Ardyne Point
Strone Point
Loch Striven
Inveraray
Toward Point
Wemyss Bay
FIRTH OF CLYDE
Dunoon
Holy Loch
Ardentinny
Finart Bay
Carrick
Loch Goil
Lochgoilhead
St. Catherines
Point
Skelmorlie
Cloch Lighthouse
Coulport
Ardgoil Forest
Gourock
Kilcreggan
Rosneath
Loch Long
Ardgartan
Gare Loch
Portincaple
Greenock
Helensburgh
Garelochhead
Arddarroch
Arrochar
Kilmory Bay
Port Glasgow
Clyde
Loch Caolisport
Cardross
Stotfield Bay
Loch Lomond
Dumbarton
Erskine Bridge
Old Kilpatrick
Tarbert
(2)

125

spectacular, but the weather was still poor and by the time I reached Ardwell Bay the rain poured down. I pressed on and camped just south of Portpatrick. The only good point about the day was that it was light until nine o'clock and I could lie in the tent cooking my meal while I read. Before, when the evenings were dark, I used to go to sleep straight away. I finished the book I was reading and bought a science fiction novel the next day in Portpatrick; it would make a change from my usual choice of non-fiction.

1.5.78

On waking, I realized it was 1 May which meant that I had been walking continually for just under four months. I could look forward to summer and, as if to confirm that idea, I heard and saw my first cuckoo. At the end of the day I decided to lighten my load for I did not expect any more cold weather. I parcelled up my duvet, gloves and climbing breeches and sent them back home.

From the camp site I regained the cliffs at the ruins of Dunskey Castle. Half a mile of walking, partly along the line of an old railway from Stranraer, took me to Portpatrick. This was once a busy ferry port for Ireland but the severe gales that hammer this coast have meant that Stranraer at the head of Loch Ryan has taken over its business. As I walked up the coast from Portpatrick I could see the ferries making their way to Larne. Despite the loss of trade, Portpatrick is still a very busy and popular holiday centre and deservedly so.

I continued round the cliffs to Black Head and its lighthouse, and on to Knock Bay. There I saw several people gathering seaweed into sacks, which I learnt would be sent down to Swansea to be used to make lava bread. The next few miles up to the northern end of the peninsula were along gentle coastline to Corsewall Point and Milleur Point where I was delighted to find my first sea pinks and sea campion. At Milleur Point I entered the mouth of Loch Ryan and began the final few miles of the day towards Stranraer. Five miles from the town, I camped at Wig Bay camp site. The local rotary club was waiting, and Mrs Sheila Milne was also there to see how I was progressing and to finalize a lottery that would be completed on the next day's walk to Ballantrae.

2.5.78

I reached Stranraer early in the day. At the end of the pier I stood to watch a Sealink ferry with its front bows open for the cars to berth. Exactly six miles later near Cairnryan I passed another ferry operator to Larne, but their boat had already sailed. I was feeling tired; I had walked approximately thirty miles a day for the last seven days and I decided that perhaps I needed a shorter day to catch my breath. My right ankle was very painful and both my achilles tendons were tender. I tried to ignore the pain and carried on out of Cairnryan and onto the magnificent cliffs of Finnarts Hill. I saw several black guillemots on the sea and on a small rock stack were numerous shags, several of which had one or two eggs in their nests. I am always surprised at the smallness of their eggs, for the shag is such a large sea bird.

Three miles later I descended to Currarie Port, a really beautiful remote bay with a burn and lots of gorse bushes in bloom. I had originally planned to camp there and wished I had for the location was perfect, but this was the start of a lottery, so I had to begin timing myself for the walk to Ballantrae, five miles away. Two hours later I walked into Ballantrae and, feeling hungry and wanting to get out of the rain, I walked into a café. The proprietor recognized me and I had a meal on the house! I also discovered that it had been arranged that I should stay in the village, and Lady Ballantrae arrived to escort me to my lodgings. Ballantrae is known in folklore for the tribe of Sawney Bean who, in the early fifteenth century, scoured the area plundering and attacking people. Word was eventually sent to James I and he sent soldiers and bloodhounds to the area. In due course the tribe were found in a cave full of treasure and human remains. The men were burnt in Edinburgh while the women and children were made to watch. They later had their feet and hands cut off and were left to bleed to death. A gruesome tale!

To reach Girvan I had to walk along the road for much of the way. I set off at a good pace round Bennane Head to Carleton Port and Lendalfoot. I saw a fine sail-rigged ship aground on the sands and was told that it was one of the boats used in the TV series 'The Onedin Line'. Out to sea I saw the pyramid shape of Ailsa Craig, which has a very large gannetry.

Three miles from Girvan a police car drew up. The BBC were filming a programme for 'We are the Champions', and I was told they would like me to appear on it. I quickened my pace and met the producer a mile later. At two o'clock I walked into the swimming pool, as prompted, and was deafened by the sound of hundreds of cheering children. The cameras were rolling and I nervously walked through to be interviewed by Ron Pickering. Three minutes later it was all over and I walked out with the sound of clapping children in my ears.

As a startling contrast, I walked out of Girvan to the quietness of the harbour and the beach. Three miles later I noticed that the beach was covered with minute pieces of seaweed, the size of tea leaves. Above the beach was the seaweed factory which uses the weed to extract alginic acid. The industry provides a livelihood for many people in the Outer Hebrides who collect the weed for processing, but I was shocked by the waste on the beach. The extracted alginates are used for a variety of products – a stabilizer for ice-cream, the gel formation for table jellies, milk desserts and pet food and as a thickening powder for textile printing pastes.

I pressed on to Turnberry and walked round the famous golf course to Maidens. There I had very kindly been offered accommodation at Malin Court. In 1971 the Malin Housing Association was formed to provide housing and care for the elderly. They had built twenty flats and to help offset the running costs some of the rooms are made available to the public. The dining room, which had earned itself a gourmet's reputation, is open most evenings to the public.

In the evening I met the matron and mentioned that my feet had been aching. She took one look at them and strapped them up.

4.5.78

With both ankles in elastic bandages, I left Malin Court and walked round Maidenhead Bay and into Culzean Country Park. Both ankles felt even worse in the bandages so after a couple of miles I took them off.

I entered the park near the swan pond and from the top of a lookout I could see a mute swan on its nest, several mallards, some coots and moorhens and a grey heron which stood motionless in one corner. In 1945 the castle and 531 acres were given to the National Trust for Scotland by the fifth Marquis of Ailsa and the Kennedy family. Since then about £800,000 has been spent on restoration, conservation and maintenance work. The present building mainly dates from the last quarter of the eighteenth century and is built of old red sandstone. Robert Adam became involved in 1777 when he was commissioned to reconstruct the interior of the old castle and to build turreted blocks to the east and west. The feature which really caught my attention, though, was the oval staircase, where Adam had unconventionally used Corinthian capitals for the first floor. The effect was stunning, giving an impression of immense height and grandeur. One room was devoted to a display of the life of Eisenhower. In appreciation of his work, the Scots gave him a part of the castle for his use, and he stayed there on several occasions.

From the castle I walked down to the beach and round Culzean Bay before gaining the cliff tops to reach Dunure. From there I should have been able to see the Isle of Arran but the weather was very warm and hazy. To reach Ayr, nine miles away, I walked along the rocky shore beneath the Heads of Ayr and on to the spectacularly-placed ruined castle near Longhill Point, which is perched on the very lip of a rocky outcrop. Both feet felt all right and I soon forgot the trouble I had been having with them, and walked into Blacks' Ayr shop to meet the manager. I stayed that night in the youth hostel.

5.5.78

The morning brought clearer weather and as I walked to Troon, I had good views of Arran, Ailsa Craig and the Mull of

Kintyre. I walked along the beach, and as I approached Troon I was delighted to see Roger Smith waiting for me. We spent a couple of hours chatting about the walking I had done in the past month before he left me to continue along the sands to the river Garnock. My final words to him were: 'I feel in great shape and have no worries.'

As I neared the river Garnock my right foot became very painful. I dismissed it and continued walking inland to Irvine. But gradually it got more painful and I became aware that I was limping. I struggled on to Stevenston and at Saltcoats I called it a day and found a bed and breakfast. When I took my right boot and sock off I found the foot was very swollen. I put my feet up that night, not really appreciating that I was in serious trouble. I wrote in my log 'Right foot and ankle hurting – badly! Strapped up yesterday but not today. First crack in non-stop plan?'

6.5.78

In the morning my right foot was back to normal and I put my boot on and set off. I had only walked a few yards before I felt a searing pain in my right foot. I found a doctor who gave me some pain-killers. He told me that he thought I might have a fatigue fracture. I didn't understand what it was and preferred not to ask; I didn't want anything to interrupt the walk. I carried on and did another two miles through Ardrossan to North Bay. The doctor's words kept coming back to me 'Why not rest a couple of days? You are five days ahead of schedule.' At North Bay, after just three miles, I stopped at a bed and breakfast and found myself inside during the day for the first time in months. It felt very strange but I thought that perhaps a day's rest would put the matter right.

7.5.78

I felt much better and my foot seemed to have recovered. I decided to have another day resting, but by the afternoon I was restless and put my boots on and went for a walk. I felt fine and there was no pain. I resolved to carry on the next day. I informed Christine that perhaps something was wrong but told her that I was not worried.

8.5.78

I left North Bay early and began to walk to Largs. Five miles' walking brought me to Ardneil Bay and Farland Head. The view from there was particularly pleasing and I could see both Great and Little Cumbrae islands and the Isle of Bute beyond. Five years before I had walked round those three islands during a blistering week in June.

My right foot gave a slight twinge now and again but was otherwise feeling all right. I thought that perhaps I was going through a physical barrier. I pressed on to Fairlie and as I approached Largs I was surprised to see what looked like an Irish round tower. It was in fact a memorial to the Battle of Largs in 1263 at which Alexander III with a mercenary army had defeated the invasion of King Haakon of Norway.

I reached Skelmorlie and camped above the town. I was delighted with myself and felt as though I had walked through the barrier. Just to prove how fit I felt I jogged round the camp site barefoot, and was pleased when I felt no aches or pain from the foot.

9.5.78

I left early in the morning so that I could reach Blacks' works in Greenock in time for a press conference that had been arranged. I hadn't gone far when I knew all was not well. My right foot was extremely painful, but I walked on and managed to reach Wemyss Bay. There I was met by a director of Blacks and I agreed to be driven to the factory instead of walking as planned. I told no one at the press conference about my problem which I then still considered to be temporary.

When the press had gone I mentioned my foot to Norman Lamond, the managing director. He immediately suggested that I have it X-rayed. Two hours later I was in Greenock Royal Infirmary having my foot looked at. Before the specialist came to me with the results of the X-ray I knew I was in trouble. He told me that the fourth metatarsal of my right foot was fractured. I had pushed my body to the limit and by walking 3,300 miles in 126 days my bones had become so brittle that one of them, just as happens with metal fatigue, had snapped. Had I fallen and broken a bone I would have felt better. The doctor explained it all very carefully, but I was still shocked when he told me that I must stop walking and have the foot encased in plaster. I wouldn't let him do it that day and asked if I could call the next day with my decision. I needed some time to think about it.

I went back to the works for lunch and in the afternoon did an interview with Scottish Television. Later I wriggled my toes for the press photographer and still didn't mention my fracture. The Gourock Rotary Club had arranged for me to stay in a hotel and I retired there to sort out what had happened and to come to terms with it. There really was no alternative but to have it in plaster for a month. I convinced myself that it wasn't the end of the walk, but just a story of the walk, for until someone had pushed himself to this limit no one had known how the body would react. I had now found out and had created medical history.

Alone in my room I accepted the situation calmly and philosophically. I rang Christine and informed her straightaway. She reminded me of my promise that if anything like this happened I would stay where I was and recover before carrying on. Having made the decision, I had every intention of doing just that. Next I had to find somewhere to stay and I told her that I would ring Sheila Milne, who lived near Glasgow, and ask if I could stay with her. I rang and before I could even put my proposal to her, she suggested it. The specialist saw me later that night and I told him I would be at his surgery at eleven o'clock to have the plaster put on.

10.5.78

Back in hospital I lay on the couch while my right leg and foot were encased. Not being able to put any pressure on the leg I hopped from the surgery to a waiting car. As Sheila would not be arriving until late afternoon, Blacks placed an office at my disposal. I telephoned all over the country to begin dismantling my arrangements for the coming months and generally to delay everything by five or six weeks. At teatime Sheila arrived and took me back to her house.

As we drove home there was an instant rapport between us. That night we sat up talking until the small hours, both enjoying each other's company and interests. We discussed how I should cope with my immobilization. I had resolved that I would camp out, walk around in the same shirt and boot and generally hold everything in suspension. I am convinced this was the right approach. Also to help me keep tuned in to what I was doing, and to maintain my mental approach, I decided that it would be a good idea to go round local schools and clubs to lecture on the walk so far. The camping, however, proved impossible, for in a tapered sleeping bag I couldn't turn over with the plaster on my leg.

For a month I was extremely busy rushing around on one leg. I gave about thirty lectures, opened fêtes and ceilidhs and did a programme report for 'Nationwide'. After the first two weeks my right leg was in agony. Never having been restricted before my muscles wouldn't relax and kept jumping out. There was no way of pushing them back, I simply had to endure the pain. After two weeks I had had enough and went back to the hospital. My right leg was extremely painful when touched. Another plaster was put on and I was given pain-killing tablets. I felt better, but after another week my leg swelled alarmingly and pressed against the sides of the plaster. Two days later it finally calmed down and I had no further trouble.

At first I tried to get some sort of exercise but there was little I could do. I had a walking iron on the plaster and as I could get around, I tried a one and a half mile walk – it took two and a half hours to do it! The thing I really missed was observing the countryside. I had been following spring northwards for several months and just as I reached Greenock the weather changed to six weeks of continuous sun. Suddenly everything came alive – the leaves opened, fern fronds uncurled, and birds were feverishly making their nests. While I enjoyed watching what was going on around me I missed not travelling and seeing more.

Many people commented upon how calmly I was reacting to the fracture. But long distance walking makes you calm; you have to accept the weather, people, and events on such a walk. But I also have an inner strength – my faith in God. On every walk that I have undertaken I have always set off with total faith in what I was doing and that I would complete it. This is one reason why I started and ended the walk at St Paul's Cathedral. I wanted to pray for strength and guidance at the beginning, and to offer my thanks for being allowed to do it at the end. I prayed often during the walk.

After a month I returned to hospital to have the plaster removed. The specialist told me off for he had watched the 'Nationwide' film in which I was seen mowing a lawn, playing swing ball, doing keep-fit exercises and dancing the Gay Gordons! With the plaster off I was X-rayed again and the doctor said the bone had healed very well. He told me that I must only walk around the garden for the next two weeks before even contemplating setting off again. I was stunned that it should take so long and agreed to see him again in a week's time.

In the car I told Sheila I was setting off again in eight days' time, on Thursday 15 June. The thought of spending the next two weeks walking around the garden did not appeal in the least! The leg was very weak and I limped noticeably. By comparison with my left leg, my right was like a piece of cotton, as the muscles had shrunk through lack of use. I had a day's rest before Roger Smith and a mutual friend, Sydney Smith, joined me for an ascent of Conic Hill, which is about 1,500 feet high and rests above Loch Lomond. I felt in great shape and was delighted when I managed it successfully.

With renewed confidence, the next day Sheila and I climbed Ben Venue (just over 2,000 feet) in the Trossachs. The following two days saw me doing short walks along relatively level ground in Buchanan Forest and on the Whangie Hill. The sixth day out of plaster I persuaded Sheila to walk with me up Ben Lomond (over 3,000 feet). I was euphoric and knew I was right to set off again in two days' time. The following morning I was back in hospital and although the doctor did not approve, I told him I was resuming the walk the following morning. If I didn't set off then, I knew the walk would have been finished, for I could not hold everything in suspension any longer.

15.6.78

I returned to Skelmorlie where I had ended my last full day, and resumed the walk. The press and television recorded the event. I was delighted to be on the move again, but I felt very sad at leaving Sheila. Over the weeks that we had spent together we had realized that we had each found our ideal companion. We later admitted that we had realized it the first evening we had spent together. To have found a wife on the walk was a bonus I had definitely not expected! People had often asked why I hadn't married and I had always replied that I had never been in one place long enough.

I was very weak, unfit, and unaccustomed to carrying fifty pounds of equipment. I weighed almost twelve stones, the heaviest I have ever been in my life! I decided not to alter anything, I would carry all the gear as before, continue my routine and have no rest days. I set off, wearing my second pair of boots, to Wemyss Bay, Cloch Lighthouse and then to Greenock. There I camped. The fifteen-mile walk took nearly seven hours to complete. I couldn't walk fast, my foot hurt and I was limping. But I was confident and as my log records it was 'Good to be on the road again'.

16.6.78

I began walking up the Clyde to the Erskine Bridge and Old Kilpatrick. In Greenock I stopped to have a look at the replica of the paddle steamer *Comet* which was launched on 1 September 1962, the 150th anniversary of the launch from Lithgow's East Yard of the original vessel. The original boat plied across the Clyde to Helensburgh. Two miles further on I reached Port Glasgow. Many of the people who had seen me off the day before turned out to shake me by the hand or give a friendly wave. I was rather touched by their concern and continued interest in my walk. From Port Glasgow I had to

135

keep to the main road to reach the Erskine Bridge. In the final stages I left the road and walked along tracks to Kirkton. As I was crossing the bridge, Sheila appeared to see how I was doing and we walked together to Old Kilpatrick where I decided to stop. I felt very tired; I had walked seventeen miles though the doctor had advised only ten. That night I tucked into a steak followed by strawberries and cream.

17.6.78

The weather was perfect as I went through Dumbarton and Cardross and along the beach to Helensburgh. My only plan was to keep moving and to take each day as it came. I had thrown the original schedule 'out of the window', resolving to pick it up only when I was happy that I had got back into my stride again. For the moment I was content simply to walk and somehow to achieve my goal of walking the entire coastline of Britain. I completed another seventeen miles that day.

18.6.78

It was fifteen miles around Gare Loch from Helensburgh to the outskirts of Rosneath. Again the walking was excellent and the weather sunny. The trees, leaves, grass and flowers all had that clean, new look of early summer and I began re-establishing myself with the world of nature. This walk around the lochs that border the Firth of Clyde was perhaps the most tortuous part of the British coastline. Near Garelochhead I walked past the submarine base at Faslane Bay. As I neared Rosneath a car pulled up and the occupants, Bobby and Ann Gray, offered me their lawn to camp on. Ann got out and took me to their house where, much to the delight of the children, I put the tent up on their lawn.

19.6.78

With Ann carrying her youngest child in a papoose, we walked together round Rosneath Bay to Portkil Bay. I enjoyed her company and I was interested to hear her thoughts on religion and her reaction to my own. We parted firm friends, she to walk back along the road and myself to go on to

Kilcreggan and Loch Long. I hadn't intended to push myself quite so far that day, but six miles from Kilcreggan the road ended at Coulport and, as it was too early in the day to stop, I continued round the coast taking the higher ground around Loch Long to reach Portincaple. The walking was through tussocky grass and in the latter stages through woodland. I had hoped to camp at Portincaple but as there was nowhere, I carried on to Arddarroch and finally camped a mile later near the bridge over the Allt Derigan burn. It was then eight o'clock and I had walked twenty-two miles. I felt tired and weak.

20/21.6.78

I had really pushed myself too far that day, for by the time I had walked up to the head of Loch Long to Arrochar and then to the Ardgartan Forest, I felt so tired that I decided to camp, having walked only eleven miles. At the camp site I suffered my first real onslaught of midges. As I packed up the tent the next morning in the rain, they attacked my bare arms and legs mercilessly. It was one of the few times that I packed my gear while running! I walked as fast as I could through Ardgartan Forest to Ardgoil Forest and Lochgoilhead. I felt refreshed after my easy day the day before, and enjoyed the signposted walk through the trees and moorland. At Lochgoilhead I treated myself to lunch before walking a further six miles along the western side of Loch Goil to Carrick where I camped beside the castle. I had walked twenty-one miles and although I still limped, I still thought it would only be a matter of days before it got better!

22.6.78

After completing my weekly broadcast I left Carrick in high spirits for Dunoon, the half-way point of the entire walk. The first part of the day was spent walking through the forest to Knap beside the shore of Loch Long. Another two miles took me to Finart Bay and Ardentinny. As I neared the bay I was saddened to see a rabbit caught up in a snare. I managed to undo the wire from the fence but it got away before I could take it off its foot. It upset me to think that it would probably get the wire caught in something else and die anyway.

I spent a delightful hour at the Ardentinny Outdoor Centre talking with the warden about his centre and marathon walking. During the conversation, Hilary Smith, a British international orienteer, walked in and 'stole' my rucksack. When I left I discovered that she had sewn the centre's badge on to it. From the centre, I went more or less by road along the shore of the sea loch to Strone Point and the American submarine base at Holy Loch. There, it poured with rain and I got soaked. As I walked past the American houses with their large cars and barbecues outside, I began to feel tired and my foot started to ache.

I reached Dunoon just after six o'clock where the local rotary club took me to a nearby hotel to dry out and have a celebration meal. From Skelmorlie to Dunoon, on my original schedule, should have taken five days, so now I was pleased to have walked it in seven.

23.6.78

I set off along the shore of the Firth of Clyde to Toward Point where I turned due west for Loch Striven. Across the mouth of the Kyles of Bute was the Isle of Bute and its main town, Rothesay. I was amused to see that Toward's post office was a caravan! Two miles on, at Ardyne Point, I was escorted through the construction site run by Sir Robert McAlpine. At that time there was no work on, but normally some three thousand men live and work there, building cement oil rigs.

I began walking up the eastern side of Loch Striven which is a reasonably remote sea loch. It was wild, rugged and inviting. I tingled with excitement; at last I could really enjoy Scotland! I began to see more wildlife: mute swans and cygnets, an oyster-catcher with two young, grey herons, gannets, a curlew, sanderlings and an eider duck with four chicks. The flowers, too, were prolific; ragged robin, red campion, rhododendron, spotted heath orchid, bell heather, goatsbeard, germander speedwell, dog rose, vetch, stitchwort, meadow cranesbill, stonecrop, sea pinks, yellow flag iris and tormentil were all in full bloom and displaying their rich colours of early summer. Two-thirds of the way up the Loch I reached the Craig Bothy owned by the Ardentinny Outdoor Centre. I joined a party there and slept on the floor.

24.6.78

Another perfect day of remote, beautiful countryside and hot sunny weather to highlight the scenery. I walked the final three miles to the head of Loch Striven before walking down the western shore. There was no road or path and it proved quite difficult to fight my way through the six-foot tall bracken; it was also unnerving for I was never sure what I was treading on! But I really enjoyed the day: the stillness and peacefulness of the landscape made me want to cry out with joy. A cuckoo kept me company for a while and later a seal popped up. As is often their habit, he followed me for half a mile. I found several eider duck nests beautifully lined with down, and each containing four or five eggs. The hens were sitting on some of them and I was pleased that they made no move as I passed by.

Six miles down the loch I came to a track which eventually developed into a road to the second Strone Point. Across the loch I could see seven huge tankers laid up because of the over capacity of the refineries. At Strone Point I started walking up the Kyles of Bute. At Colintraive, with twenty miles walked, I camped. I was pleased that I had managed to negotiate the rough terrain on my right foot and although it still hurt and made me limp, it seemed to be no worse for the experience.

25.6.78

I continued beside the Kyles of Bute before walking round the head of Loch Riddon. From Craig Lodge, on its western side, a footpath is signposted to Port Driseach and Tighnabruaich. However, I could not find the path and so I had to fight my way through thick rhododendrons before climbing up the hillside to walk along the road. Dropping back down to the shore, I walked through long grass to Port Driseach. On the way my legs began to itch and looking down I counted

139

about twenty sheep ticks. I carefully removed them one by one, and from then on I checked my legs daily, occasionally finding some a quarter of an inch across. I stayed at Tighnabruaich Youth Hostel, where I wrote an article on coastal litter which had been commissioned by *The Sunday Times*. I wrote articles for several magazines on the walk but I found them quite a chore to do.

26.6.78

As I left Tighnabruaich, I felt in great shape and thought I was beginning to get back into my normal stride. At Kames I watched a marvellous display of about thirty gannets diving for fish. Another mile and I was watching a pair of basking sharks. The beauty of this part of Britain is that you never know what you are going to come across next. Six miles from Tighnabruaich I reached Ardlamont Point and, turning westwards, I entered Loch Fyne, the final sea loch before the Mull of Kintyre. The whole day was filled with stunning views as I made my way northwards to Otter Ferry via the five bays of Kilbride, Asgog, Ardmarnock, Auchalick and Kilfinan. After all the rocky shores of the sea lochs it was really good to see some sandy beaches. They are rarely visited and I had them all to myself. At eight o'clock, and feeling very tired having covered twenty-four miles, I camped just past Otter Ferry.

27.6.78

Loch Fyne was the longest sea loch I had to negotiate, for from its head to the open sea is seventy miles. Argyllshire has more than 2,000 miles of coastline, although much of this includes islands. From Otter Ferry I continued northwards up the eastern side of Loch Fyne to St Catherines, where I stayed with Norman Chaddock, the tower master of Inveraray Church. There had been little to see all day due to the low cloud and continuous rain. I felt extremely tired when I reached St Catherines, and I noticed that my right foot was swollen and aching. Again I had pushed myself too far.

28.6.78

I carried on in the morning to Inveraray, which, via the coast, was a walk of about sixteen miles. I had arranged with Norman that I would arrive at three o'clock. On the way I was stopped by a doctor who inquired after my progress and told me that I was not to carry on doing twenty or more miles a day. I listened and said nothing. At Inveraray I rang the bells in the church before doing three more painful miles to Battlefield camp site. The doctor reappeared and asked me to dinner. It was a sumptuous affair with a whole salmon on the table.

29.6.78

Before I left the camp site, the Duke and Duchess of Argyll came to see me, and met the two children from Inveraray school who were to walk with me that day. We set off in the rain to walk through the forest to Furnace. The whole school had turned out to greet us and I joined them for lunch. An hour later, on the way to Loch Gair, a stranger presented me with a can of anti-midge spray! I thanked him profusely, for it was a most welcome and useful gift. By the time I reached Loch Gair I was exhausted. I had walked only seventeen miles and approximately 300 from Skelmorlie, and my right foot was very painful. I was not at all happy. I retreated into myself and for the first and only time, I questioned what I was about. I decided that I would carry on to Tarbert but after that I would have an easy weekend to let the foot settle down.

30.6.78

I left Loch Gair early in the morning and, having shaken off my depression of the day before, I set off to walk the eighteen miles towards Tarbert. Seven miles brought me to Lochgilphead, and, as I crossed the burn, I stopped to watch a pair of mute swans with their twelve cygnets. They usually have between five and seven offspring and I was amazed to see so many. The parents posed proudly as I sat down opposite to take their picture. Just under two miles later, I reached Ardrishaig at the start of the Crinan Canal. The canal is eight and half miles long and was opened in 1801. Prior to its construction, the canal boats had to round the peninsula of Kintyre, a journey of about 130 miles. My walk around this same peninsula was nearer 150 miles.

1.7.78

After thirteen hours' sleep I set off to walk the seven miles into Tarbert where I stopped again. Finally accepting the advice of the doctors, I decided to ease up. It was very hard to restrict myself but as I still limped and my right foot was still swollen, I thought it would be for the best.

2.7.78

Leaving Tarbert, I planned to walk just eleven miles to Skipness. As it was not possible to walk along the shore, I moved to higher ground where I was rewarded with superb views of the high mountains of Arran: Goatfell, Cir Mhor, and Beinn Bharrain. As I crossed the rough moorland to Skipness I startled a pair of hinds. A mile from the red sandstone ruins of Skipness Castle, I camped. Taking my boots off I was delighted to see that the swelling had gone down and that for the first time I could see the bones of my feet. Perhaps the two easy days had done me some good.

3/4.7.78

The next two days I walked thirty-four miles beside Kilbrannan Sound via Carradale to Campbeltown. The weather was atrocious with continuous heavy rain. Shortly after leaving Skipness I walked through a small woodland which is well-known for its fairy legends. One tells of the story of a woman who was held by the fairies for seven years, and was only rescued when her husband lay in wait and, as she came past, threw her wedding dress over her.

Grianain Island near Carradale was full of nesting terns. Carradale itself has a small busy harbour and beautiful sandy beach. At Saddell Bay I went inland to look at the ruins of Saddell Abbey and to admire the remarkable collection of gravestones. On reaching Campbeltown I went straight to the hospital where it had been arranged that I should have my feet checked. I went in determined to carry on regardless and ready to do battle if necessary. But the wind was knocked out of my sails when the doctor asked 'If I tell you to stop walking, will you?' I said no. Respecting the fact that he had left the decision to me, I admitted that in fact both feet still hurt. I stayed in Campbeltown that night and dried out my equipment.

5.7.78

This was my last full day of heading southwards down the peninsula of Kintyre. I was then much further south than I had been on the Firth of Clyde. The weather changed dramatically from a dull, overcast and rainy day to really lovely sunshine; a strong wind made the walk invigorating. My destination was Dunaverty Bay, the penultimate bay before the Mull of Kintyre. The coastline was excellent: at first it was very rugged and rocky but from Polliwilline onwards there were good, sandy beaches. I had not expected to find such scenic beaches in this remote corner of Scotland. It was interesting to hear that the release of Paul McCartney's song 'The Mull of Kintyre' had created a boom in tourism. Putting the tent up in the galeforce winds at the exposed camp site above the beach at Dunaverty Bay was a hard task. The tent stood up remarkably well to the gales and I was delighted with its performance.

6.7.78

With 'Mull of Kintyre' in my head, I left Dunaverty Bay and began a steady climb along the cliffs to Mull Lighthouse. The weather was disappointing for early July; it was very cold, visibility was poor and there were galeforce winds. I was experiencing the worst summer for ten years. At the lighthouse I turned right and began the long trek northwards towards Oban and Cape Wrath. The first few miles to Machrihanish were along a wild and broken stretch of coastline. The easiest way of progressing was by keeping to the high ground for as long as possible. I looked across at the southern end of the Inner Hebrides and saw my favourite islands: Islay, Jura and Gigha. My crossing to Machrihanish held a few surprises for I saw several red deer, a pair of buzzards, a short-eared owl, and

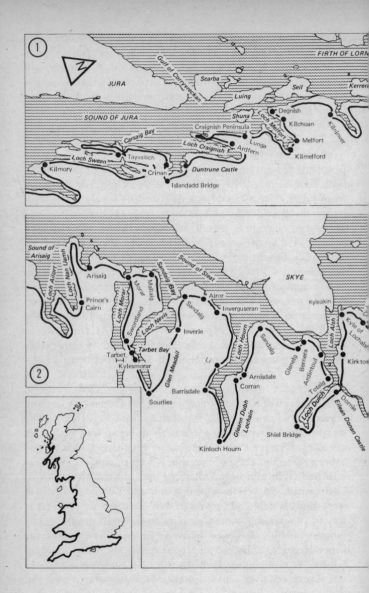

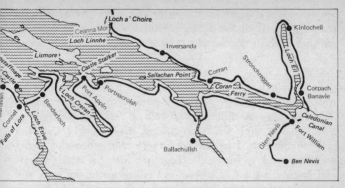

a sparrowhawk which was hovering above the ground looking for prey. Walking into Machrihanish I was recognized by another friendly doctor who invited me to camp on his lawn.

7.7.78

In galeforce winds and heavy rain I began a magnificent four-mile walk along the superb sands of Machrihanish Bay. After twenty-one miles, I was well up the peninsula and at Point Sands camp site, overlooking the island of Gigha, I pitched the tent. I hadn't been there long when the owner asked me back to his house. Together with his family we sat and enjoyed a glass of whisky as I talked about the walk and what I had seen so far. I returned to the tent and looked across at Gigha, God's island, which has one of the highest sunshine totals each year. Could it really be eight years since I was there and on my first thousand-mile walk? I couldn't believe it.

An hour later a spectacular sunset filled the sky.

8.7.78

Although my goal was to get back as near to Tarbert as possible, I only managed eighteen miles to Escart camp site. I was finding that eighteen to twenty miles a day was all I could manage. I felt in good spirits but I still limped and this worried me, for I thought that it was time to be back to normal. Perhaps it was as well that I did not know just how long it would take.

9.7.78

Rounding the head of West Loch Tarbert, and going down its western side to Ardpatrick and Loch Stornoway, was memorable. Loch Stornoway has a superb beach and Highland cattle were there enjoying the hot sun. I waded across the burn and a little over a mile later reached the cliffs known as The Coves. Looking up I saw a buzzard's nest. Leaving my rucksack behind and armed with a 300-mm lens, I scaled a rock-stack within fifty feet of them where I could look almost directly into the nest. The buzzards remained still while I took numerous pictures. Four miles further on I camped at Port Ban and witnessed a stunning sunset over the Paps of Jura. I have climbed those mountains three times and for me they are some of the finest in Britain. The last time I was on them was New Year's Day 1974, when I had seen and photographed a Brocken Spectre.

10.7.78

I woke up to find the sun streaming through the tent. For the past two weeks I had been setting off at 9.30 a.m. but because of the stunning weather I packed up and was away by 8.15. The only drawback was that good weather had brought out the flies and clegs: they were a thorough nuisance. To reach Loch Caolisport I had to walk across the small, sandy Miller's Bay and Stotfield Bay. I encountered herds of Highland cattle on both. At Miller's Bay they dispersed as I approached, but at Stotfield Bay they stood their ground and looked threateningly at me as I eased past them. At Loch Caolisport I tried to cross the sand and bars but was beaten back by the incoming tide. Taking my boots off, I paddled round which avoided the long trek inland.

My destination was Castle Sween. To get there I had to cross some very broken terrain to Kilmory. The lochs on the way were a lovely sight, all bursting with white water lilies. At Kilmory Bay I went inland to visit the ruins of Kilmory chapel, where there are several well-preserved examples of Celtic and late-medieval grave slabs and a cross, known as the McMillan cross, which dates from the fifteenth century. A little over two miles later I reached the ruins of Castle Sween. A camp site has spread all around its base and the sheltered sea loch beyond is a popular sailing ground.

11.7.78

My log records 'Very hot, hottest day so far'. My route lay up the side of Loch Sween, through Knapdale Forest and down to Tayvallich. The village was once a herring and lobster fishing community but now concerns itself with tourism. I camped near Carsaig Bay and ate an early tea, so that I could travel light and walk round the Keillbeg peninsula. I quickened my pace for there were only four hours of daylight left. The western side of the peninsula, facing the Sound of Jura, offered spectacular walking along a very broken coastline. The map at this point gave no real indication of the actual terrain, and I discovered lochs that were not even marked. On the rocks of one bay I found a bomb which I reported to the post office upon my return. When I got back to Carsaig it was dark, but I was rewarded for my effort by seeing exceptional views of Jura. I had walked twenty-six miles, the most in any one day since the fracture.

12.7.78

To reach Ardfern involved twenty-five miles of very hard walking and took almost twelve hours. From Tayvallich I had to go by compass through the forest to reach Crinan Harbour. Using the forest breaks, I worked my way through, ducking under branches and fighting through tall grass. At Crinan I was able to catch my breath and walk in open country beside the canal to Islandadd Bridge. From there I rounded the shore of Loch Crinan to Duntrune Castle, which dates back to the twelfth century and is one of the oldest inhabited castles in Scotland. More broken country took me up the side of Loch Craignish to Ardfern. The trees came right down to the loch side and the shore was a mass of tumbled boulders. Progress was very slow and my speed went down to one mile per hour. The hot weather ensured that the clegs had a field day, and a swarm of these flies swirled above my head and persistently buzzed in my ears and nose and crawled over my bare arms. I kept swatting them with a map but their numbers never seemed to diminish. By the time I reached Ardfern at ten o'clock I was exhausted. I camped on a friend's lawn.

13.7.78

Before continuing my walk northwards I had to walk round the Craignish peninsula, via the sixteenth-century Craignish Castle. From there I was able to see the Gulf of Corryvreckan which runs between Jura and the Island of Scarba. The Navy classed this gulf as unnavigable for a long while because of the speed of the tide race; close to Scarba is the second largest whirlpool in the world. I have camped near it on Jura, and it is an alarming experience to hear its thunderous roar. From Craignish Castle I began weaving my way round pebbled beaches and over the small cliffs and forestland to Lunga, where two girls were sponsored to walk with me. A wildlife park had recently been created in the area but the pair of wolves which were to be its main attraction had escaped the week before and had had to be shot. The girls went with me as far as Loch Melfort Hotel, where Katherine Lindsay-Macdougall, who had organized their walk, was waiting to give us all a meal. The views from the hotel across to the islands of Shuna and Luing were spectacular.

An hour later I was on my own again and walking around the shore of Loch Melfort. By the time I reached the head of the loch I was tired, but I couldn't find anywhere to camp and so had to continue. Three more miles took me to Kilchoan, where I asked permission to camp at the farm. The farmer's wife told to check with her husband who was baling hay in the field below. He recognized me and, after I had pitched the tent facing the view over the loch and islands, I tucked into a home-cooked meal and a can of ice cold lager given to me by his wife. A second welcome change from cooking a dehydrated meal!

14.7.78

While I borrowed their phone for my live broadcast, the farmer cooked me a huge fried breakfast. I thanked them for their kind hospitality and left soon afterwards to walk via Degnish to reach the Seil Sound. My destination was the outskirts of Oban. Five miles up Seil Sound, walking along a pebbled and rocky shore, I came to Seil Bridge which links the island of Seil to the mainland. The bridge is often referred to as the only one over the Atlantic, but I know of several more in the Orkneys and Shetlands. The bridge was designed by Thomas Telford and opened in 1792. Seeing an inn on the other side I suddenly thought it would be nice to have a pub lunch. I crossed over to Seil and enjoyed a drink and a sandwich.

Back on my route, I made my way to Loch Feochan. Rounding that, I crossed high ground to reach the Sound of

Kerrera where I camped, overlooking the sound with the island of Kerrera in the background. I was delighted to get there, for it marked the completion of my first whole month, and almost 600 miles of walking, since restarting. But my right foot was still painful and I still limped.

Two miles away was Oban which meant, for me, the start of the finest section of coastline, via the Morvern and Ardnamurchan peninsulas to the Kyles of Lochalsh, Torridon, Ullapool and Cape Wrath.

7. North-West Scotland

15.7.78
Half an hour's walking brought me into the bustling town of Oban, the gateway to the Hebrides. Dominating the largely Victorian town is McCaig's Tower. Built in the last century as a replica of the Colosseum in Rome, it had temporarily helped to ease unemployment.

It was good to be in Oban, for it had played a significant part in my first walk through the Hebrides in 1970. I had also been there a few weeks before when my leg was in plaster. A ceilidh had been organized to coincide with my original date of arrival, and, rather than cancel everything, the plans had gone ahead and I had been driven there by car to open the proceedings.

Waiting for me were a group of children from the Oban Primary School and Oban High School, sponsored to walk with me to Ganavan Bay and back – a walk of about six miles. Although it was a cool, cloudy day, there were views beyond the island of Kerrera, which shelters Oban harbour, across the Firth of Lorn to Mull, and, when we neared Ganavan, to Lismore island. Leaving the children to return to their schools, I walked round the edge of the golf course to Dunstaffnage Bay and Castle. The castle dates back to the thirteenth century but was partly burnt down in 1810. Prior to the ninth century, the Coronation stone was kept there before being moved to Scone.

On the eastern side of Dunstaffnage Bay I joined the road and crossed the Connel road bridge over the Falls of Lora and the entrance to Loch Etive. I was not walking very well and felt listless and very tired. I went a further four miles from the bridge to Benderloch and camped at Tralee Bay camp site. I had only walked fifteen miles. I was going through a bad patch and for the first time it really registered that I was not going to get into my normal walking pattern for a long while, and that my foot was going to take some time to recover. After more than a month I was still limping and in pain. Up to now I had still dreamt of reaching London in September, but I realized it was not on, and that it would be late October or even early November before I achieved my goal. It took a couple of days for me to accept this fact and so make the decision to cancel all the lectures I had planned for the winter of 1978-9. I made up my mind that the walk came first and that nothing would stop me from doing it, however long it took. Once I had sorted all this out, I walked on in an easier state of mind.

There were still times on the walk when I found it difficult to cope with the attention I was receiving and Tralee Bay camp site was one such occasion. The tent, as part of my sponsored equipment, was sign-written and I wasn't exactly inconspicuous, but that didn't excuse people's behaviour. When I was asleep people would come up and unzip the tent to see if I was inside, and at Tralee someone put a note under the tent asking for autographs! It could be fun at times but, at others, it was a strain.

16/17.7.78
My foot troubled me for the next two days and I only covered fifteen miles each day. The first day I walked around Loch Creran and camped near Port Appin, overlooking Lismore island. But it was the view beyond that fascinated me: the weather was immaculate and I could see Loch Linnhe, and the Morvern peninsula. In three days' time I would be walking round that wild, remote and rugged shore. The next day I made my way towards Ballachulish. Two miles from Port Appin I crossed a very dilapidated wooden footbridge to reach Portnacroish. In the bay is a small, rocky island which is almost completely covered by the restored sixteenth-century Castle Stalker. Feeling extremely weary, I reached Collum Beg, close

to Ballachulish, where I was recognized by a party of handicapped children who were on holiday there. They had been at the ceilidh in Oban and invited me to camp. I accepted and spent a very pleasant evening helping with the children. I left full of admiration both for the children and the people who look after them.

18.7.78

In the morning I had shaken off my despondency and in good spirits I began the walk beside Loch Linnhe to Fort William and Glen Nevis. I crossed the Ballachulish bridge and a little over four miles later reached the Corran Ferry. The far side of the loch was barely a quarter of a mile away, but the journey around the shore was sixty miles. Three miles later I stopped and spent half an hour watching and photographing seals on Black Rock. I counted twenty-one. Motorists rushed by on the A82, oblivious of the seals; a sight which could have been one of the highlights of their trip. After Fort William I camped at Glen Nevis. Roger Smith arrived later that night with a most welcome bag of strawberries from his garden.

19.7.78

To accompany Roger and myself up Ben Nevis, my third and final mountain, were the head boy of Lochaber High School and the president of Lochaber Rotary Club, plus the latter's dog! We took the normal route and soon found that the dog was racing ahead of us. The conditions were poor and we concentrated on keeping moving and getting there. At the 3,000-foot level the rain sheeted down and it was very cold. By the time we reached the summit we were frozen; just before the top we had crossed a large patch of snow. We were in cloud and so had no view, which was a pity for I would have liked to have taken a few pictures down Loch Linnhe. It had taken two and a half hours to ascend and in order to get warm and boost my morale I ran down in an hour. The president was a long way behind and so after saying goodbye to Roger and our other companions I left a note on his car and, shouldering my rucksack, set off to camp beside the Caledonian Canal at

Banavie. As I put up the tent late in the afternoon the sun broke through and for the first time I could see the summit of Ben Nevis. I sat outside the tent gazing at the view as I cooked my evening meal of shrimp curry, bananas and custard.

20.7.78

As if to confirm my good mood I walked twenty-three miles from Banavie to Stronchreggan. First I went to Corpach before walking along the northern shore of Loch Eil, and past the Outward Bound School which had recently moved there from the Moray Firth. A little past Kinlocheil at the head of the loch I turned to begin walking along the southern side of the loch, and as I did so I noticed a road sign saying 'Mallaig 30 miles'. To reach Mallaig around the coast via the Morvern and Ardnamurchan peninsulas required ten days' walking and approximately 220 miles! A question people often asked was whether I ever became dispirited at having to walk huge distances around lochs and estuaries. I didn't, because I only ever took one day at a time and never looked further ahead. At the end of the day I camped overlooking Fort William at Stronchreggan.

21.7.78

Three hours' walking brought me to the Corran Ferry. Knowing that I would reach the 4,000-mile mark that day I walked into the nearby shop and bought strawberries and cream for a celebratory tea. A mile later, near Sallachan Point, an exposed rock was festooned with seals and their pups. Highland cattle roamed the roadside at Sallachan and I also saw sheep being clipped by hand. When I crossed the river at Inversanda I had walked 4,000 miles. I felt jubilant and was at last shedding the gloom over the fracture. Eight miles later, at Ceanna Mór, I camped between the houses and gorged the strawberries.

22.7.78

It had rained hard all night and when I woke in the morning it was still streaming down and the cloud level hung around

154

the 200-foot mark. I stayed as long as I could in the tent but by nine o'clock I was impatient to be on my way and so I took down the flysheet and set off. My plan was to walk along a footpath to Glensanda from Loch a'Choire, but this proved to be another path that didn't exist. From the glen the path was supposed to cut through the mountains to Loch Aline. To try to follow the coast at this point is impossible as it is steep-sided, with no shore and in many places dense forest goes right to the water's edge. It would have been folly to attempt it and so I made a large detour on higher ground and walked along the road to Loch Aline. In the circumstances I felt totally justified. The rain didn't ease up and as I was cold and wet I just concentrated on keeping on the move and maintaining my body temperature.

Three miles from Lochaline, in the late afternoon, I passed the single row of houses of Larachbeg. It was to there in 1930 that the islanders of St Kilda were evacuated, following their decision to leave the island. I was once fortunate enough to spend two weeks on the island and, like everyone else, I was struck by its dramatic and compelling beauty. But its exposed nature must have made the struggle for survival very hard indeed. It was sad that such a unique way of life should have declined but the island retains many signs of its former occupation and is now preserved by the Scottish National Trust.

As I entered Lochaline a car passed and the lady driver gave me a look of recognition. She turned and came back. 'Would you like somewhere to stay and dry out?' she asked. I accepted and she disappeared to notify her parents before returning once more to explain that their cottage was two miles away, on my route, at Achabeg. I was most warmly received. I dried my sodden clothes, had a shower, a good meal, and slept in a caravan that was offered. I was more than grateful for their hospitality and encounters like this certainly helped to take the strain off me.

23.7.78

The rain ceased during the night and I could look across the Sound of Mull and see the island for the first time. Ploughing its way across the sound was the Lochaline car ferry. Nine miles of walking brought me to the end of the road at Drimnin, overlooking Calve Island and Tobermory, the main town of Mull. The next few miles via Auliston Point to Loch Teacuis offered excellent walking. I followed the track that curves round the headland of Auliston Point to Doirlinn. There are ruins of several villages in this area, such as Auliston and Portabhata. Walking the track, I was amused and surprised to find cast iron mile posts marking the way to Doirlinn; they must be some of the few remaining ones in Britain. Doirlinn also came as a surprise: it is a delightful house overlooking Loch Sunart and Carna Island. The house is open to visitors and, when the owners are away, they allow travellers (mostly yachtsmen) to spend the night there. It was pleasing to find people so trustworthy and, reading the log book, their generosity is obviously appreciated. I was sorely tempted to stay but I needed to find a phone for my broadcast with Richard Baker in the morning. I pressed on.

The next five miles to the head of Loch Teacuis was very enjoyable but the walking was hard. Half a mile from Doirlinn I came to a forest and spent a long time fighting my way through. I tried the shore, but it was too broken and covered with thick, slippery seaweed. In the end it was simplest to struggle through the trees. After three miles I gained a forest track and followed this to the loch head. The people I had been staying with at Achabeg the previous night knew the people who managed the Rahoy deer farm at Loch Teacuis. They had suggested that I stay there and use the phone, as it was the only one in the area. Thinking that they lived on the other side of the loch where a building marked Rahoy was shown on the map, I walked there only to find that I had actually passed the deer farm two miles back at Kinloch! I retraced my steps and was made most welcome at the farm.

After a meal the manager took me to see the three hundred red deer fawns in their pens. It was interesting to see so many tame animals. They are brought from estates all over Scotland to be bred commercially and to create a home market for venison. The scheme is partially financed by the Highlands and Islands Development Board.

24.7.78

Just after nine o'clock I did my radio piece while my hosts sat in the car and listened to the programme! I was sorry to leave this idyllic spot and to say goodbye to such a homely couple.

I moved on in dull weather to reach Loch Sunart at Glencripesdale and began walking the southern shore of the loch. I had successfully rounded the Morvern peninsula and was then approaching the Ardnamurchan peninsula. The first part was along forest tracks before joining the A884 road for the final five miles of the day to the head of the loch and Strontian on the northern shore, where I camped.

25.7.78

Much of the day was in poor weather, which turned to heavy rain all afternoon, as I followed the road beside the shore of Loch Sunart to Salen and Glenborrodale. There was little to be seen apart from a few eider ducks and their chicks, several grey herons, and some buzzards. I was soaked by the time I reached Glenborrodale but as there was no room in the hotel, I had to go a further two miles to stay at Glenmore Lodge.

26.7.78

The morning brought hot sun and clear blue skies. I left early, bound for Ardnamurchan lighthouse. People had often commented on how beautiful the peninsula was with its sandy beaches, pleasant people and remote coastline, and I was not disappointed. A little over two miles' walking took me to Camas nan Geall, a small beach. Ahead was a rocky promontory known as Maclean's Nose, which possibly takes its name from the Macleans of Duart Castle on Mull. The first part of the walk from the beach to the nose was relatively straightforward around a pebbled shore, but it gradually became steeper and boulder-strewn. According to the map the only real problem was getting round the nose. Although the slope was steep and grassy, I was able to follow sheep trails. But ahead, and not detailed on the map, was a rock face; it was not very high, but it cut straight down into the sea. The tide was going out exposing the boulders, and I thought that perhaps by using these and climbing the face at its lowest side I might be able to get round. I tried with the rucksack on but felt unstable, balancing from boulder to boulder, and so I waited half an hour for the tide to go out further before trying it without the rucksack. Having sorted out all the moves I put the rucksack on and managed it. The next little bay caused no problems, but then an even bigger face blocked my way. (Again this was not detailed on the map.) In the end I back-tracked a little way and climbed vertically up unstable rock to a grassy summit. From there I could see the way ahead was clear and after a quarter of a mile I climbed down a steep gully to the shore and walked round to the ruins of Mingary Castle where in 1493 James IV held court.

Two miles further on, I entered the picturesque village of Kilchoan. The setting was magnificent in the clear, sunny weather and the steep hills behind the village gave it an air of grandeur. After stocking up with chocolate and food I pressed on to Ardnamurchan lighthouse and camped in front of it. The view was breathtaking across to Mull and Coll to the east, while northwards were Eigg, Rhum and Soay. Lying between them the distant Cuillin hills on Skye stood out clearly. Westwards were the Outer Hebrides: Barra and South Uist. I was overjoyed to have reached the most westerly point in Britain: twenty miles further west than Land's End. Ardnamurchan means Point of the Ocean. The peninsula is made up of very hard igneous rock and formerly this was the centre of a very large volcano.

27.7.78

The weather on reaching Ardnamurchan had been excellent but when I left it was foul; it rained hard and did not let up for twenty-four hours. I walked twenty-five miles that day and my log records 'Strong galeforce winds and heavy driving rain. Soaked to the skin. No views, no birds – nothing. Walked well!

Rucksack contents soaked.' Two miles from the lighthouse, heading eastwards, I reached the rain-soaked Sanna sands. It was all a great pity for I had been looking forward to seeing these famous sands in good weather. I carried on round the coast, passing the deserted village of Plocaig. Five miles on I reached Fascadale and followed the road to Achateny to cross the swollen burn before heading directly to Kilmory and Ockle where the road ends. A largely overgrown track took me round the headland to Gortenfern and Kentra Bay. Without the track, the crossing of this jagged and broken terrain would have been a nightmare, especially in the atrocious conditions.

At Kentra Bay I wanted somewhere to stay to dry out, but as it was so remote there was nowhere. The rain lashed down and I pressed on, eventually heading south towards Loch Shiel and to Ardshealach. After trying various hotels and farms which were full, I found a farm where, because the lady had heard me on the radio, I was allowed to stay. I was too late for a meal but I had noticed a tea room a little way back along the road. Leaving my rucksack behind I walked back and bought myself the cheapest meal possible, as I was short of money.

28.7.78

My equipment was still soaked when I set off in bright conditions to retrace my steps to Shiel Bridge. There I crossed the river before walking along its eastern banks to Loch Moidart. At the mouth of the loch I crossed some delightful sands close to a rocky island, the summit of which was adorned by Castle Tioram. From there a path climbs through the trees and rhododendrons, then along the shore to the head of the loch and the road at Ardmolich. Eight miles later I camped at Forsay caravan site overlooking the Sound of Arisaig. I had only covered sixteen miles but I felt extremely tired, partly from lack of food and partly from the extremely hard terrain of the last two days.

29.7.78

I realized I must ease off and not walk quite as far over the next two days because I did not want to get to Mallaig, forty miles away, until Monday morning – I had to pick up my next parcel of maps and dehydrated food from the post office there. Rounding Loch Ailort and the northern shore of Loch Nan Uamh, I reached Prince's Cairn, which marks the spot from where Bonnie Prince Charlie is believed to have left for France on 20 September 1746. Having walked twenty-two miles, I camped near Arisaig so that I could walk round the peninsula just south of the village next morning, without carrying my rucksack.

30.7.78

The day proved excellent, being hot and sunny with clear views over to the Small Isles of Eigg, Rhum, Soay and Canna. The Sgurr on Eigg was particularly clear. On the northern shore of the peninsula I stopped to watch a herd of about a hundred red deer. Over the course of the next two hours I saw the rare sight of several of the stags getting up on their hind legs and boxing each other.

After a leisurely day of only twelve miles I reached Garramor Youth Hostel, close to the Morar Sands, and stayed there. A little over four miles would take me to Mallaig and, beyond that, some of the remotest coastline in Britain. I slept well that night.

31.7.78

Mallaig is always a busy place with its large fishing fleet and ferries to the Small Isles and to Armadale on Skye. The holiday season was at its peak and the place was bursting with people; as soon as I had picked up my parcel and bought some chocolate I left.

The coast around the sides of Loch Nevis is very hard to walk and in many places it is quite impossible to follow. The only way to make progress is to keep to high ground. I spoke to people in Mallaig who advised me to retrace my steps to Morar and from there walk along the northern shore of Loch Morar to Swordland, from where I could head northwards to Tarbet. From there the shore along Loch Nevis is still hard to walk, but at least it was feasible.

160

Along the shore of Loch Morar I met up with the Loch Morar Expedition who had been searching the loch for monsters for six years. Several have been sighted, notably by the occupants of Swordland, and it is believed there could be as many as thirty in the loch. By obtaining a core sample they had established that the loch was once connected to the sea and while I was there they were attempting to obtain a sample from the deepest part of the loch, which at 1,017 feet, is the deepest freshwater loch in Britain.

At Tarbet Bay I met the one and only postman and his son who were raking hay on their small croft. They see few people, and then only when the mailboat calls or when the owners of nearby houses at Kylesmorar come for a holiday. I followed the path to the houses and camped beside a burn. While cooking a dehydrated meal I really felt the isolation and remoteness of the area. The stillness was remarkable: a few sheep nibbled the grass nearby, but there were no other sounds or signs of activity.

1.8.78

I headed along the coast to the head of the loch and Sourlies bothy. The going was very hard for there was no path, just broken ground, tall wet grass, bog, rocky shore and expanses of wet, slippery seaweed. I passed several ruined houses (some had been blown up by the army), outside which, standing forlornly, were old beds and cast-iron cooking pots. As I fought my way along, barely walking two miles an hour, I kept looking at the northern shore of the loch and soon realized it was going to be impossible to get round it except by keeping to the high mountains. At Sourlies bothy I brewed a cup of tea while I read the visitors' book and recorded that I had walked more than 4,220 miles.

Low cloud was still clinging to the mountains and obliterating the summits as I climbed a steep hill, just across the river Carnach beyond the bothy, to Glen Meadail, which would take me to Inverie. Arriving in the late afternoon, I joined a couple of backpackers and we camped on the edge of the Inverie river. Typically, the clouds dispersed and a crystal clear evening unfolded. Inverie with its whitewashed houses and high mountain behind was a beautiful example of remote and wild Scotland. The village has a minor tarmac road which runs from Inverie House to Airor, but does not link up with any other road. The only way to reach these places is either on foot or by boat. The area is part of Knoydart, the wildest and most remote area of Britain – long may it remain so.

2.8.78

Packing the tent up was made an ordeal by the midges which descended in droves. I rushed back to the village to do my weekly broadcast for Radio Sheffield and after considerable difficulty I finally got through to the studio and awaited my cue. I heard the presenter say, 'As always at this time we have John Merrill on the phone. Are you there John? Where are you and how far have you walked?' I replied, but they could not hear me. We tried four times but to no avail; it was the only time I failed to make a link up with them. My two friends departed for the hills and I continued round to Airor, disturbing several red deer hinds as I went.

Nearing Airor, I reached Sandaig Bay and thought I had found the location of Gavin Maxwell's house where he had kept his famous otters. Finding a ruined house I was convinced this was Maxwell's and I photographed the area. The setting was right and there was a waterfall nearby where Edal could have played. But the bay was a total disgrace; it was covered with plastic bottles of every size, and plastic and wood fish boxes – I assume this debris comes from Mallaig which is just across the mouth of Loch Nevis.

For six miles from Airor to Croulin and the mouth of Loch Hourn, I was able to follow a track around the shore. After two miles I approached Inverguseran only to find the bridge down. The river is wide there and because of the poor weather it was quite swollen. There was no other way across and so I had to take off my socks and walk through in my boots. On the other side, I tipped the water out of my boots and put my socks back on – a ritual I was to perform often as I continued up the west coast. From the bothy at Croulin I was once more in very remote country. Walking around the mouth of Loch Hourn proved very hard but exciting walking. I realized that I was totally on my own and that if anything happened it could be a week before anyone began to search for me. Near a croft at Li, I had to ascend the steep sides of a rock face and traverse diagonally through a wood. I just hoped there was a way out at the top. There was.

At this particular stage of the walk I felt very close to God. The remoteness and peacefulness of the surroundings perhaps heightened my senses. I prayed often for help and guidance and, as I walked round Loch Hourn, I could lift my mind out of myself and think of other things while I walked on mechanically. It was in some ways a strange experience but one I feel can only be appreciated after you have been alone for many days. It is not something that can be forced; it has to be allowed to come naturally. It is only in remote country that my awareness is sharpened and my mind ready to accept very deep spiritual feelings.

Just beyond Li I camped and a small herd of goats nibbled the grass close to the tent.

3.8.78

Midges descended in the morning and attacked me ferociously as I packed the tent away. The coastline from Li to Barrisdale Bay is extremely rugged and it took me two and a half hours to walk four miles; overall that day it took eleven hours to walk twenty-one miles. At Barrisdale the walking became more straightforward when I followed a track to the head of Loch Hourn. The weather was poor, there were no views and several sharp rainstorms thundered down. I couldn't help but marvel at the beauty of the area: rugged mountains dropped steeply to the loch, outcrops of rock tiered the steep grass slopes and Scots pines were everywhere.

Two miles from the head of the loch I passed a small croft and continued on around the shore. A few minutes later a small boat with a lady at the helm approached me. 'Are you the walker?' she asked. I confirmed that I was and she pulled into the seaweed. It transpired that she had heard me talking to Richard Baker from Rahoy Deer Farm and had therefore been able to work out when I would pass her croft. We sat on the seaweed and ate some cheese sandwiches while she told me about four killer whales that had been seen near Li a few days before. Before we parted she presented me with a two-pound Christmas cake! I was extremely grateful, and especially so because I had not seen a shop for four days and it would make a welcome change from my dehydrated food. I ate half of it for tea that night.

Near the head of the loch at Kinloch Hourn, I watched a pair of otters through the binoculars as they played in the water. It was impossible to walk along the northern shore of Loch Hourn to Corran, so I followed the old postman's route past Dubh Lochain and through Glen Arnisdale where I camped on a villager's lawn.

4.8.78

I took down the tent in the rain and with the clouds lying at two or three hundred feet there was little to be seen all day. Seven miles from Arnisdale I reached a second Sandaig and discovered that this was where Gavin Maxwell had actually lived. Beside a fir tree was a memorial to the otter Edal. The plaque records: 'Edal, The otter of Ring of Bright Water 1958–68, Whatsoever joy she gave to you, give back to nature. Gavin Maxwell.' Close by was the waterfall which features so strongly in the book.

Eight miles further on I came to Glenelg, one of the few place names that spells the same both ways. As I approached the village I was within a couple of miles of the Glenelg brochs and I was sorely tempted to visit them. But I felt extremely listless and very tired. I wrote in my log that night, 'Is this the start of the cumulative effect or the result of the last four days hard walking?' Entering Glenelg I was recognized by a caravan owner who immediately invited me to join him in a cup of tea and some homemade cakes. Before I left he presented me with some miniature bottles of whisky. Half an hour later, near the eighteenth-century ruins of Bernera Barracks, I found a bed and breakfast where I could dry out.

5.8.78

The morning brought no improvement in the weather but as I walked round the side of Loch Alsh the sun finally broke through. I passed the Glenelg ferry which was unusually busy because the ferrymen at the Kyle of Lochalsh were on strike and it was the only ferry operating to Skye. From there I took the path to Ardintoul which after a mile offered splendid walking along a pebbled shore.

At Ardintoul I cut slightly inland to find the path through Letterfearn forest, for the way along the shore was blocked by several vertical cliffs. Passing a cottage I inquired whether I would be able to get through and the owner told me the way was marked with white posts and that I would be all right. He asked me in for a snack, and I spent a very pleasant hour, learning as we talked that he was related to my doctor who lives opposite me in Winster!

I left feeling pleasurably full and began to pick up the path behind the cottage. I followed the posts along the top of the cliffs and, as I began to climb down to Totaig, I passed the ruins of Letterfearn broch. These tall circular towers, once seventy feet high with a single entrance, a well in the centre and rooms and spiral stairs in the fifteen-foot thick walls, are believed to have been built by the Picts, two thousand years ago. Within two minutes of leaving the ruins I stopped in my tracks at the sight of a pine marten, our rarest mammal. It was the only one I have ever seen and it was only a fleeting glance for after a second or two he vanished. At Totaig I joined the road which runs along the southern shore of Loch Duich and camped at Shiel Bridge, at the base of the Five Sisters of Kintail.

6.8.78

The weather was still poor when I began walking up the northern shore of Loch Duich to the beautifully restored Eilean Donan Castle. The castle was built by Alexander II of Scotland in 1220. It was badly damaged in 1719 by an English warship when it was being held by the Jacobites, but was restored in 1932 at a cost of £230,000. From Dornie my route lay along the shore of Loch Alsh to the Kyle of Lochalsh. I was about to run out of food and even though it was Sunday I hoped to find a shop, knowing that it was a major ferry point for Skye. When I arrived I could find only the fish and chip shop open. It was obviously popular for the mound of litter outside the shop and neighbouring car park was an absolute disgrace. As I walked up the coast through the quiet months into the holiday months I could have told the time of the year just by the litter. In the peak months all the lay-bys and litter bins were over-flowing with refuse left by carefree holiday makers.

I moved on to the youth hostel only to find it was full. I searched in vain for a bed and breakfast establishment but all were full or closed. In the end I gave up and got on the Skye ferry to Kyleakin to find somewhere there. After five attempts I eventually found a lodging, and a restaurant where I was able to have a meal and buy some chocolate.

7.8.78

I crossed back to the mainland and continued heading northwards around the Inner Sound to Duirnish, Plockton and Loch Carron. Plockton is regarded by many as the most picturesque village in Scotland. It occupies a sheltered position, palm trees grow along the main street, and it is a popular sailing centre and an artist's paradise. It must be one of the few villages with its own airstrip. The village was established in the eighteenth century and the houses are built from large blocks of red and brown sandstone. I was seeing it in poor weather, but given some sunshine I could readily appreciate that the village and its setting would combine to make it very picturesque.

From Plockton I walked along the shore past Duncraig Castle, built in the nineteenth century and now converted into a school, to Loch Carron and Stromeferry. I had only walked fourteen miles but already I felt very tired, just as I had done for the past four days. To make me even more despondent I looked at my feet and saw that both were badly swollen. I went to the post office at Stromeferry, where the postmistress very kindly offered to put me up for the night. I wrote in my log

'What now?' I had walked just over 1,000 miles since restarting at Skelmorlie and I still limped. It was most disappointing but in order to keep going I had to put it to the back of my mind and simply concentrate on finishing the walk.

From then onwards my performance began to improve as I started to walk more than eighteen miles every day, gradually increasing to thirty or more miles a day.

8.8.78

I walked twenty-one miles around Loch Carron to Loch Kishorn. Until quite recently there was a ferry from Stromeferry (as the name suggests), to Loch Carron. The road signs for the ferry still exist at Stromemore, on the other side of the loch, and in a small inlet I found the ferry boats.

Five miles from Stromeferry I walked through an Avalanche Shelter, which was built not for snow, but to safeguard the road from being submerged under stone and trees. The loch side is extremely steep at this point. Two miles later I had walked through Attadale and was nearing Strathcarron railway station at the head of the loch when a young girl cycled up to me and presented me with a box of fudge, biscuits and a ten-pound note for the charity. Her parents had seen me pass by and had sent her to catch me up. I never ceased to be amazed by people's generosity.

Just past Strathcarron I got onto the northern side of Loch Carron and walked along it to Lochcarron, the village with the longest main street in Britain – it is about one and a half miles long. Beyond the village I walked through the trees to Stromemore and back into forestland to reach Achintraid on Loch Kishorn. I had planned to stay at the youth hostel there but discovered that it had been closed up. I pressed on to Ardarroch and was told to inquire at the post office for a place to camp. As soon as I went in I was recognized and offered the use of a caravan plus a meal and a bath! How could I refuse? I spent a pleasant evening feeling clean and full while I recounted the walk to date. That night I put on the twenty-fourth pair of socks since leaving London.

9.8.78

At the head of Loch Kishorn I passed close to the Rassal Ashwood Nature Reserve, which is the most northerly natural ash woodland in Britain. I headed around the head of the loch to gain the northern shore, and as I did so I came across the road sign for the single track road to Applecross, over Bealach na Ba. It stated: 'This road rises to a height of 2,053 feet with gradients of 1 in 5 and hairpin bends. Not advised for learner drivers, very large vehicles or caravans after first mile.' From the shore the road through the mountains looked very impressive.

Two miles later I came to the gates of an oil rig construction company. Just over two months before (May 1978), they had produced the largest cement oil rig ever made. It weighed 600,000 tons and was towed to the North Sea. The security officer let me in and, as he walked with me through the site, showed me the coffin path to Toscaig, so called because the dead used to be carried along it. The path has long ceased to exist and it proved to be a hard walk over jumbled terrain to reach Airigh-drishaig. From there a clearer path led to Toscaig. Along it I found bell heather in full bloom and large expanses of the pretty yellow bog asphodel. Numerous eider ducks hovered close to the shore, cormorants stood on rocks spreading their wings out to dry and an occasional black guillemot could be seen further out to sea, while overhead a couple of buzzards soared on the thermals. As I walked, I munched my way through my thousandth bar of chocolate!

From Toscaig I went along the shore of Inner Sound to Applecross, and camped there. I was told that the royal yacht, *Britannia*, was to anchor off shore the next day and the Queen and Queen Mother were to stay at Applecross House for the night – I had just missed royalty again!

10.8.78

There is now a road from Applecross around the coast to Loch Torridon. Part of it follows the old postman's route, and I walked it in perfect weather; it proved to be one of the best days for a long while. Four miles from Applecross I reached the dazzling white sands of Sand. Another four miles brought me to the almost deserted village of Kalnakill where one of the crofters was busy patching the thatch of his barn. Five miles later, at Fearnmore, I reached Loch Torridon. Across the loch I could see the red sands of Red Point, while eastwards I enjoyed looking at the dramatic scenery of the Torridon hills. I stared at them for a while and felt it was worth walking 4,400 miles just to see that view. I then headed eastwards along Loch Torridon to Shieldaig.

I had seen a variety of birds during the day: a red-throated diver, a golden eagle, a red-breasted merganser with seven chicks, cormorants, buzzards, a merlin, a wren, gannets and eider ducks. I erected the tent on the unofficial site overlooking the houses of Shieldaig and lay in it witnessing a magnificent sunset.

11.8.78

It was another glorious day as I walked around the shore of Upper Loch Torridon to Torridon and on to Torridon House and Alligin Shuas. I had to concentrate hard on where I was walking because my eyes kept straining upwards to admire the Torridon hills. It took considerable willpower not to camp at Torridon and climb some of the mountains: Liathach, Beinn Alligin and Beinn Eighe. These red sandstone mountains are topped with white quartzite believed to be 750 million years old. Much of the area is owned by the National Trust for Scotland.

At Alligin Shuas I searched for the path which was marked on the map and which went through extremely rocky country to Loch Diabaig. I was relieved when I picked it up, for without it a crossing of the area would have been exceedingly awkward. As I wove my way through the outcrops I suddenly noticed a boat ahead in Loch Torridon. Looking through the binoculars I saw it was the royal yacht departing for the Orkneys.

From Lower Diabaig I picked up the path to Craig Youth Hostel, four miles away. This is my idea of what a hostel should be, far from civilization and the only way to reach it is by foot. All supplies have to be carried in. There is one problem – the

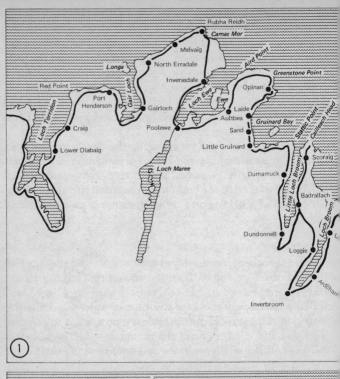

①

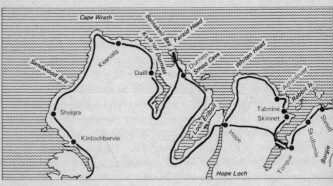

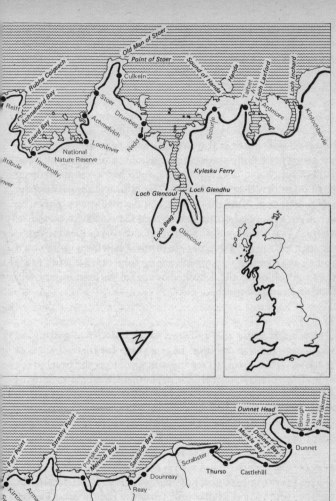

Reiff
Rubha Coigeach
Old Man of Stoer
Point of Stoer
Sound of Handa
Handa
Tarbet
Loch Laxford
Loch Inchard
Achnahaird Bay
Culkein
Stoer
Enard Bay
Drumbeg
Scourie
Ardmore
Kinlochbervie
Achmelvich
Lochinver
Nedd
National
Nature Reserve
Inverpolly
iltibuie
nver
Kylesku Ferry
Loch Glencoul
Loch Glendhu
Loch Beag
Glencoul

N

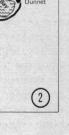

Dunnet Head
Brough
Ham
Skarfskerry
Farr Point
Strathy Point
Portskerra
Melvich Bay
Sandside Bay
Dunnet Bay
Muckle Bay
Dunnet
Swordly
Kirtomy
Armadale
Reay
Dounreay
Scrabster
Thurso
Castlehill
Halladale

N

②

midges. I don't think I have ever seen them so thick in the air. Still more alarming was that even inside in the room where people were cooking, midges lay five deep on the inside window sills! Naturally the hostel log is full of stories about the ubiquitous midge.

12.8.78

The weather broke during the night and as I set off from the hostel to Red Point and its sands, the rain poured down. On the sands is a fishing station and a whole complex of poles and pulleys supported dozens of nets which had presumably been put out to dry! I trudged on, in the rain, to Port Henderson and Gair Loch. Nine miles later and decidedly wet, although it had now stopped raining, I reached Gairloch. As I was low on food I visited a small supermarket and was quite shocked to see such a large crowd of people inside. I had been on my own and away from people for such a long time that I couldn't face the shop full of people. I walked out again without buying any food and camped nearby.

13.8.78

Sheila arrived in the morning to see how I was getting on and also to finalize the fund-raising plans for the east coast of Scotland. It was good to see her and we sat on the beach, four miles from Gairloch, overlooking Longa Island. After lunch I continued on alone to walk via North Erradale and Melvaig to Rubha Reidh lighthouse. The views as I walked were extensive with Skye and the Outer Hebrides lying on my left. I camped near the lighthouse.

14.8.78

The morning brought rain but as the day progressed the weather brightened. Half a mile from the lighthouse I walked along the top of steep cliffs past several very impressive rock-stacks to the sandy beach of Camas Mór. I doubt if many people know that such a beautiful slice of coastline exists there.

Just inland are a couple of ruined crofts, one of which was being restored and inhabited by a young local. He had been

172

living off the land for the past three months. As he saw few people, I was warmly welcomed in and we sat on fish boxes in his one-roomed dwelling and sipped mugs of tea. I envied, in a way, his capacity to be self-sufficient and content in one place. I am a restless individual and cannot stay in one place too long.

Feeling refreshed, I left to follow the line of an old path to Loch Ewe. Part way along the western shore of Loch Ewe, I reached the outskirts of Inverasdale where a huge notice reminded the inhabitants that the Sabbath should only be for rest.

At the head of the loch I entered Poolewe, a popular angling base for Loch Maree which is just inland. The other attraction of the village, the Inverewe Gardens, lies a little under a mile away. I have visited these gardens often in early and late summer and have always been staggered at the variety of colourful flowers that blossom there. Because of the Gulf Stream the area is relatively mild and can support a thriving range of semi-tropical plants and trees from the Americas, Australia and Japan. Work began in 1865 when the area was basically grass and bog. The gardens are now cared for by the National Trust for Scotland. After a brief look and seeing my favourite flower, the Himalayan Poppy, I headed due north to Aultbea and its youth hostel overlooking the Isle of Ewe. The island makes the bay sheltered and during the two World Wars the home fleet frequently anchored in the harbour. The hostel is a large wooden building on Aird Point, a relic of the naval presence. The warden, a single woman, was a character who rarely wore her false teeth. If she took a liking to you you were all right, if she didn't, she was abusive!

15.8.78

Leaving the hostel early the next morning I was greeted by the sight of the hot sun shining on the sea. It was a still, warm day so the midges were out in force. One of the hostellers joined me for the next seventeen miles as we walked around Greenstone Point to Laide and Gruinard Bay. The walking via Slaggan Bay and Opinan was good, over rugged terrain with small but impressive cliffs and a whole string of freshwater

173

lochs close to the western side. At Laide we parted, he to return to Aultbea hostel, four miles away, and I to continue round the shore of Gruinard Bay to Gruinard House.

A mile from Laide I reached the caves of Sand. The main cave was used as a Free Church of Scotland from 1843 to the end of the century, and the last christening known to have taken place there was in 1898. The smaller cave was once lived in by two women, one of whom was aged seventy, in 1885. The southern end of Gruinard Bay is a beautiful expanse of sand and in the warm weather was proving to be a popular spot. Two miles out to sea is Gruinard Island, a place that is barred to the general public. During the Second World War the island was contaminated with anthrax as part of germ warfare experiments. A little over a mile from the beach I camped near the only telephone box for several miles, near Gruinard House, ready for my weekly radio link. The midges descended in swarms, and I was forced to cook inside the tent though the heat often became quite unbearable.

16.8.78

The morning brought rain and wind – and relief from the midges. After my broadcast I shouldered the rucksack once more and headed to Stattic Point and the mouth of Little Loch Broom. I was still only walking about twenty miles a day and my feet still complained, but mentally I was improving and at least I knew the worst was over. From then on I expected gradually to increase my daily mileage. The realization that I had walked more than 4,500 miles also acted as a psychological boost, for it meant two-thirds of the walk were completed.

As I rounded Little Loch Broom I called into the post office at Durnamuck to post another exposed film for processing. The postmistress invited me in for lunch, which I accepted gratefully although I declined her offer of a bath. Half an hour later, in brighter conditions, I continued around the shore of the loch to Dundonnell and up the northern shore of Badrallach. There I camped on the lawn of a potter's croft.

17.8.78

It was absolutely gorgeous weather and I was particularly pleased for I was about to enter one of my favourite areas of Scotland, the country north of Ullapool. First I headed round the shore of Little Loch Broom to Scoraig using the postman's route; there is no road to the village, and the only access is on foot or by boat. Beyond the village I reached Cailleach Head, the furthest extremity of the peninsula. Rounding the mouth of Loch Broom I was rewarded by a sight I shall never forget. In front of me were my favourite places: Achiltibuie and the Summer Isles. With renewed vigour I pressed on and about six miles later I gazed down across the water to Ullapool, my last pick-up point on the west coast of Britain. Crowding the loch were more than a dozen Russian and Bulgarian fish factory ships. Because the crews could not go ashore to purchase fish, all the local boats were taking their catch direct to the boats and from all accounts were doing a roaring trade.

The next two-mile section of coast from my vantage point overlooking Ullapool was through exceedingly difficult terrain. I don't think I have ever waded through such thick or high heather in my life. Often I was completely submerged and it took considerable floundering around to make any progress at all. After an hour of hot, sticky work I finally reached the road at Loggie. I continued on along the shore of Loch Broom and at its head, near Inverbroom Lodge, walked up a magnificent avenue of trees. Two miles further on, near Ardcharnich, I camped in a small caravan site with twenty-two miles walked that day.

18.8.78

The good weather held as I walked the final seven miles to Ullapool. I have always liked this northern outpost because it is the gateway to north-west Scotland and Stornoway on Lewis, in the Outer Hebrides, and also because of its location and its white-painted houses. I headed straight for the post office and collected a couple of parcels and several cards. Suddenly I realized that the following day was my thirty-fifth birthday. After stacking away the food and maps, I put in the other mail ready for opening the next morning. As I was eager to get away from the milling crowds and make full use of the exceptional weather, I hurried out of Ullapool to Loch Kanaird. Before me were the steep, craggy mountains of Coigach and I wondered whether the path marked on the map around their base to Acheninver existed. After searching around I found it and began following a truly beautiful route which went through deep gorges and around rocky outcrops with only the occasional post or cairn to indicate its line. All the time the Summer Isles stood out clearly ahead. I thoroughly enjoyed that walk in those incomparable conditions and by early evening I had reached the youth hostel at Acheninver. The hostel was full but the warden willingly allowed me to sleep on the floor.

19.8.78

At breakfast everyone joined in singing 'Happy Birthday'. An American girl asked if she could walk with me: apparently I had 'the right vibes, man'. I agreed and in overcast conditions we headed round the bay to Achiltibuie and eventually on to Reiff. Offshore I could still see the Summer Isles which can be visited by boat; it was four years since I had been there. At Loch of Reiff my companion and I sat in the pouring rain beside the loch and I opened my birthday mail. I unwrapped the parcel first and found a birthday cake made by Sheila. What a wonderful surprise! I opened the birthday cards; there were eleven and, strangely, I had to rack my brains to try to recall all the people who had sent them. I had been away for so long and was so out of touch and involved with what I was doing that my own private life had shrunk into the distant past.

Leaving the loch, the rain poured even harder and for the next three hours as we walked around Rubha Coigeach to Enard Bay and the sands of Achnahaird Bay, we got soaked and could see nothing. We kept our heads down and just watched the rain beating down on to the puddles. At the sands of Achnahaird Bay we parted company. We had walked about seventeen miles around a peninsula but were then only four miles away from the hostel. Seven miles further on I reached the salmon farm in the Inverpolly Nature Reserve. I had walked twenty-five miles and had had enough, but there was nowhere to stay. Lochinver was another nine miles away and I was just wondering what to do and whether to push my foot that far when a couple of birdwatchers from the hostel drove up. They confirmed there was nowhere to stay or even camp and offered to take me back to the hostel and return me the following day. I agreed.

Twenty minutes later and much to everyone's surprise I walked back into the hostel and was given a meal immediately by the warden. To celebrate my birthday, several of us then walked two miles to the pub. As we strolled along, the sun was setting, lighting up the clouds into the richest orange sunset I have ever witnessed. It was absolutely stunning. I had also been fortunate enough to witness a remarkable sunset on my three previous visits to Achiltibuie.

20.8.78

I was taken back to the salmon farm and walked the nine miles to Lochinver. To the south-east of this small fishing community is Suilven mountain. At about 2,300 feet high it is not even a Munro (which is 3,000-feet high), but its attraction lies in the situation, being on its own and rising up very steeply from the surrounding countryside. I have climbed it several times from Lochinver and I always marvel at its beauty, with its dome end and pointed ridge. The view from the summit over the area to the neighbouring mountains of Canisp, Cul Mor and Stac Pollaidh, is one of the grandest mountain sights in Britain. I felt the urge to climb it but, resisting the temptation, I pressed on towards the Stoer peninsula. The youth hostel at nearby Achmelvich was full which was a pity for the location beside a sandy beach couldn't be bettered. I went on to Stoer and stopped at a guest house, where my log records I had my 'first wash for ten days!'

21.8.78

The coastal walking from Ullapool to Stoer was magnificent, but the walking from there to Cape Wrath must be the very finest in Britain. The rugged coast, indented with lochs, offshore islands, sandy beaches and high mountains inland – all largely inaccessible — combined to make my final few days on the west coast of Britain a source of never-ending joy. I was in high spirits mentally and physically, and at last knew I was starting to hold myself back. Rather than press on harder and move up to an average of twenty-five miles a day, I tried to restrict myself to about twenty to soak up the final few miles of the west coast. When I reached John o'Groats I planned to really open up and pick up speed. For the moment I headed northwards to Stoer and on to the Point of Stoer, six miles away. Near the point I came along the cliff tops overlooking the hundred-foot rock-stack, the Old Man of Stoer. As I headed eastwards to Culkein, rain began to fall. At the Bay of Culkein I searched around for birds but found none. It was there four years ago that I had photographed a pair of shelducks and their eleven chicks. One was lost the next day when a black-backed gull took it for breakfast.

A good seven miles later at Loch Drumbeg, near Drumbeg village, I spotted my first black-throated diver. Two miles earlier I had been bombed by a great skua. As soon as I entered its territory it took to the air and dive-bombed from behind, tapping my head with its feet. At first the attacks were rather alarming, but in the end I faced the bird and watched it swoop at me. They are a pirate bird and will chase any other bird with food, harassing it until the food is disgorged. The nearby cliffs, even though it was late August, still had shag, kittiwake and fulmars on their nests attending to their young. In the shop at Drumberg I bought my usual dozen bars of chocolate and asked if there was anywhere to stay. A couple who had just walked into the shop heard me and suggested I stayed with them in their cottage at Nedd, a mile along my route from the village. I was extremely grateful for I needed a phone.

22.8.78

I only walked eighteen miles during the day, not because my foot was hurting, but because of the rugged terrain and some of the worst rain I have ever experienced. It simply streamed down, and the ground was soon waterlogged. The first part of the walk was reasonably straightforward towards the Kylesku Ferry, and from there around the Lochs Glencoul and Glendhu. To reach the head of Loch Glencoul I had to use the path to the summit of Eas a Chuál Aluinn waterfall (the highest waterfall in Britain at 670 feet) to avoid the rock faces that blocked the way. By this time I was absolutely soaked but I wouldn't stop early and so I pressed on along the path which in fact had become a continuous stream. Low cloud obliterated the mountains.

Two hours of wet, slippery walking brought me to the summit of the fall. The river that fed it was a raging torrent and somehow I had to cross it. Nowhere seemed feasible, and so I went upstream a little way and just waded through. From that side of the fall I could really appreciate its grandeur and watch the huge volume of water pouring over its lip to fall several hundred feet onto the rocks below. Down there it joined more streams which were equally swollen, and through which I knew I would eventually have to wade. In time I got to the glen floor and made my way to the bottom of the fall, where I again stopped to admire its beauty. To reach Loch Beag, I waded across three more rivers. At times it was quite alarming for the power of the water could easily have swept me under.

A mile later I reached an empty house at Glencoul and, finding the door open, walked inside. There were two rooms, one with a bed and fireplace and the other full of wood. I could hardly believe my luck and took advantage of the find by getting a roaring fire going. My boots and all my clothes and gear were sodden and so I laid them out to dry. I slept on a single divan in my sleeping bag.

23.8.78

It was still overcast but at least it wasn't raining. I carried on round the cliffs of the loch to Loch Glendhu and at its head joined a track which took me along the shore of the loch to the northern side of the Kylesku Ferry. I knew there was a telephone there and thought I had better use it to make contact with Christine. It was just as well that I did, for I discovered that everyone was rather concerned as to my whereabouts. Also I learnt that John Lloyd, the editor of *Practical Camper*, was looking for me either by boat, or on foot, or, as I learnt later, he was even contemplating hiring a helicopter! As he had travelled some 800 miles I began to make inquiries as to *his* whereabouts. The ferryman told me that someone on the other side was looking for me. Having walked twenty extremely wet miles to avoid using the ferry, it was rather ironic that I then had to use it to get back to the other side to find him. I searched around at first without success, but finally found his car. I left a note on it and as a last resort tried the pub. As I walked in John was speaking on the phone; he turned and I heard him say, 'I don't believe it, here he is!' We sat and enjoyed a round of sandwiches while I recalled my walk and the adventures of the day before. We had met just in time for he was at the point of giving up because he had to be back in London the next day for a meeting. We adjourned to his car and did a taped interview which later appeared in his magazine. Leaving him to return to London, I boarded the ferry once more and set off for Scourie, which I reached in the early evening just as the rain started again.

24.8.78

This was to be my last full day on the west coast of Britain, and I was disappointed to find it cold, overcast and raining, with galeforce winds. Just north of Scourie, as I made my way to Tarbet, I passed the two most northerly palm trees in the world. Across the Sound of Handa was Handa Island, a nature reserve belonging to the Royal Society for the Protection of Birds. Four years before I had spent five days alone on the island, staying in the hut to watch and film the sea birds. The cliff ledges are covered with guillemots, razorbills, puffins, shags, fulmars, numerous gulls and both arctic and great skuas nest on the island. On the sandy shores are sanderlings, ringed plovers and oyster-catchers. I know of no finer place for observing sea birds amidst dramatic cliffs and a massive rock stack.

In worsening weather I rounded Loch Laxford, past John

Ridgway's Adventure School near Ardmore, to Loch Inchard and Kinlochbervie. Five miles later, at Sheigra Beach, I camped for the last time on the west coast of Britain. I had walked twenty-five miles and felt tired, but knowing that Cape Wrath was just ahead I had pushed myself. That night as I lay in the tent I let my mind roll back to some of the 3,600 miles of coastline since Land's End. It all seemed unreal and long ago: Devon and the blizzards, the river Severn, Wales and the ascent of Snowdon, Liverpool, Cumbria and Scafell Pike, the Solway Firth, the Mull of Kintyre, the fracture, and the stunning west coast of Scotland. I couldn't take it in.

25.8.78

It was sunny – I couldn't believe it! Quickly I packed up and set off for the Cape. I was delighted, for the coast to the Cape is very broken, with spectacular high cliffs, and to have had to walk it in rain would have been very disappointing, especially as it was to be a major highlight of the walk – my reward for the months of toil.

Five miles from Sheigra Beach I descended the cliffs to Sandwood Bay, a massive expanse of golden sands, and the most northwesterly beach of the mainland. I strolled around, unhurried and determined to enjoy every step. I stopped to watch the waves crash on the sand, the fulmars gliding around, and I gazed across at Am Buachaille, the rock-stack I had walked past a mile previously.

Then, in an instant, I climbed off the sand, up the cliff and began the walk along the very high and impressive cliffs to the Cape. In the clear, hot, sunny conditions, all I wanted was to absorb the beauty. After two hours I could see the lighthouse, barely a mile away. I shuddered inside as the enormity of what I had achieved so far became clear. Tears began to stream down my face, as much from a sense of total joy as from a feeling of intense gratitude and humbleness. I walked on slowly towards the lighthouse hoping that I would not meet anyone. The lighthouse keepers were there but I didn't linger because of my need to be alone. I climbed the hill nearby and sat down; I just wanted a few minutes' peace to say a prayer before turning right once more and walking away from the west coast of Britain along the north coast to John o'Groats and Duncansby Head. Ten minutes later I set off.

Ahead were the cliffs of Clò Mór, the highest sheer cliffs (about 860 feet) in Britain. Just before them I dropped down to a lovely little beach near Kearvaig before climbing back up the cliffs again. It was late afternoon and the clarity was perfect as I again took my time walking the cliffs. I saw only fulmars; the other sea birds had flown. In the early evening, glowing with happiness and joy, I camped at Daill at the mouth of the Kyle of Durness. A family who were camping nearby very obligingly swopped some of their food for a few bars of Dextrosol, and this was particularly welcome as I hadn't found a shop for a few days and my stocks were low. I cooked a meal in silence. Behind me was the west coast of Britain; London was only two months away. The thought seemed unreal. By 8.30 p.m. I was fast asleep, a very contented person. What, I wondered, would the north and east coasts of Britain hold in store?

8. Turning the Final Corner

26.8.78

As I woke, I heard the familiar sound of rain beating down upon the tent. I had been very fortunate in having such an exceptional day to round Cape Wrath. I packed the tent up in the rain and left Daill to walk southwards along the western shore of the Kyle of Durness. After about three miles and as the tide was out, I set off to cross the large expanse of sand, wading through the river channels. I had no trouble with the first river, but the second channel, half a mile later, was more awkward and surprisingly wide and deep. Part of the way across, I suddenly caught sight of an otter playing with a piece of seaweed, only thirty feet away. He hadn't noticed me so I froze and, resisting the temptation to photograph him in case the movement would scare him, I stood and watched for five minutes before he finally tired of his game and swam away.

I carried on walking beside the Kyle of Durness to Balnakeil Bay. It was a shame that the weather was so bad, for the sands of the bay to Faraid Head are very beautiful. I rounded the headland in gloomy conditions as the wind lashed the heavy rain against me. Just east of Durness, I stayed at the youth hostel above the Cave of Smoo.

27.8.78

I had a look around the limestone cave. Only the first of the three chambers is accessible, the other two require potholing equipment. The Smoo burn descends through holes in the roof of the first cave which, according to a legend, were made by the Devil and three witches; they were trapped there by the Wizard of Reay (the first Lord Reay in the seventeenth century), and had to blow the holes through the limestone in order to escape from him.

Five miles from the cave, in cool cloudy weather, I reached the mouth of Loch Eriboll which, being a safe, sheltered and deep loch, was used by the home fleet during the two World Wars.

All the time I was walking round the loch, I was aware of someone following behind me wearing a kilt and pushing a pram! I met him later that night and learnt he was on a 'Round Britain Walk' to raise money for a hospital. The pram which carried his equipment was known as Betsy. It had taken him thirty-seven days to get there from London by road but, as he told me, he was not doing the 'nooks and crannies' that I was!

On the north-eastern side of Loch Eriboll I had to cross the river Hope. I would have liked to camp there, but I was extremely short of money and had very little food, so I decided to cut inland and head straight for Tongue Youth Hostel. On the way across I spotted eight red-throated divers on Loch Maovally. By the time I reached the hostel, I had walked twenty-eight miles – the first time I had done more than twenty-five miles in one day since the fracture. I felt tired and hungry and was most grateful when the warden allowed me to buy a huge meal on credit.

28.8.78

I walked into Tongue to visit the bank, and shop for food and chocolate. Returning to the hostel I left my rucksack and, carrying only waterproofs, set off to retrace the eight miles back to Hope and so back to Tongue via the coast and Whiten Head. The weather was good at first but by lunchtime there were high winds and rain. I trudged on along the cliff tops looking down 500 feet to the sea. On a good day the walk round the headland must be superb but in those conditions I wasn't encouraged to stop and admire the scenery! By late afternoon I reached Achininver and joined the road to Talmine and Skinnet. Offshore the Rabbit Islands were largely obliterated by cloud; at low tide it is possible to walk across the sand to them. I pressed on to Tongue Hostel and stayed there a second night after having walked twenty-four miles.

29.8.78

As I left the hostel the rain was still streaming down. I had managed to dry my clothes again but my boots were still very wet. The first part of the day's walk was along the eastern side of Tongue Bay to Skullomie and the ruined croft at Sletell. In good conditions this, too, would have been a superb walk along an exciting coastline but for much of the time everything was submerged in cloud. Beyond Sletell I reached the magnificent sands of Airdtorrisdale and, with the wind whipping up the sand I walked round its edge and inland to cross the river Borgie. Back out to the bay, I rounded the dunes and walked up the river Naver to use the road bridge and get to Bettyhill.

At this point I realized that in the last twelve months I had walked 7,000 miles: 4,780 of them on the coastal walk and the rest on the Land's End to John o' Groats walk and the various training walks that I had done prior to beginning the coastal walk.

For the remainder of the day I walked along a rugged coast to Farr Point, Swordly and Kirtomy to Armadale where I arrived soaked through. I needed somewhere to dry out with a phone for my radio link-up. Armadale House was the only possibility but when I arrived they were full. Feeling despondent, I was just setting off down the drive when someone called me. They had remembered they had a caravan and I could use that! So there I slept while my clothes and equipment dried out. I had my first bath for ten days and put on my first clean pair of underpants for five weeks! I had then worn through twenty-four pairs of socks and the hotel owner very kindly offered to wash eight pairs of them for me, because they were wet from the continuous rain.

30.8.78

The rain had ceased but it was extremely cold and for the

first time since April, on the Cumbria coast, I wore both my pullover and anorak. Already the seasons were changing and I began to notice autumn colours and shorter daylight hours; it was then dark by 9.30 p.m. The early part of the day was spent walking almost due north to Strathy Point where one of the newest lighthouses in Scotland (built in 1958) operates. Six miles later I walked through Portskerra to the golden sands of Melvich Bay. The Halladale river is crossed by a magnificent swingbridge near Melvich. I got to the middle and couldn't resist rocking it like a naughty schoolboy!

The next section of coast is very rugged with several small but deep geos (coves). From this section I could see the Dounreay Nuclear Power Experimental Station ahead. The dominant feature was its 135-foot diameter metal sphere housing the reactor. It seemed strange to find such a building on the remote sands of Sandside Bay. Since I would obviously not get permission to walk through, I negotiated both the station and an American base before gaining the coast once more to get to Scrabster. The last time I had been there was in 1971 when it was my starting point for a 1000-mile walk through the Orkneys and Shetlands. Waiting for me at Scrabster House was Donald Mackay, the local representative of RCSB, and a most likeable character – I stayed with him that night at Dunnet, nine miles away.

31.8.78

Donald took me back to Scrabster in the pouring rain. Two miles along I came to Thurso, the most northerly town on the British mainland. The street names such as Haakon and Magnus reminded me that this was formerly a Viking settlement. In the past twenty years, because of the growth of Dounreay, the town has trebled in size and now has a population of nine thousand. Keeping close to the shore I went round the harbour. In the nineteenth century it used to be a hive of industry, for flagstones made from nearby quarries were shipped from there all over the world. A little way on were the ruins of Thurso Castle. It is said that the original castle was built so close to the sea that it was possible to fish from its windows.

186

It was easy going round the coast from Thurso, for the cliffs are very small, and six miles of walking took me to Castlehill via Murkle Bay. Remains of the once prolific flagstone industry lay scattered around. Half a mile later, in streaming rain, I began walking the sands of Dunnet Bay. At Dunnet, feeling exceedingly wet, I called on Donald Mackay for lunch. In view of the weather conditions I decided to stay for I knew that the next day I would be able to reach John o' Groats comfortably. I also knew that some reporters from the London *Evening News* would be there and so I was anxious not to get ahead of schedule.

1.9.78

The rain ceased during the night and as I set off I had a very good view of Dunnet Head, the most northerly point of the British mainland. Although it was very cold, I could at least enjoy this spectacular section of coastline in dry weather and actually see some views. I left early, agreeing to meet up again with Donald at about five o'clock at John o' Groats. I hadn't walked more than a mile and a half when I heard someone calling me. I turned to see two people running towards me, a reporter and photographer from the *Daily Express*! Half an hour later I carried on to enjoy the coastal scenery of Dunnet Head. The cliffs are beautifully vertical and in the right season are the home of a wide variety of nesting sea birds. Only a great skua was to be seen and as I approached his territory even he took to the air and flew out of sight.

The lighthouse at Dunnet Head stands on top of 300-foot cliffs. The view over the Pentland Firth to Scapa Flow and the Orkneys was very impressive. Hoy stood out clearly and through binoculars I could see the 450-foot rock stack of the Old Man of Hoy. Looking due west on a really clear day it is possible to see Cape Wrath, but although I searched through the binoculars I found nothing. I continued on round the eastern side of the headland through the heather to Brough, Ham and Scarfskerry. Two miles later I walked past the Queen Mother's Scottish home, the Castle of Mey. Built at the end of the sixteenth century, it was known as Barrogill Castle and was

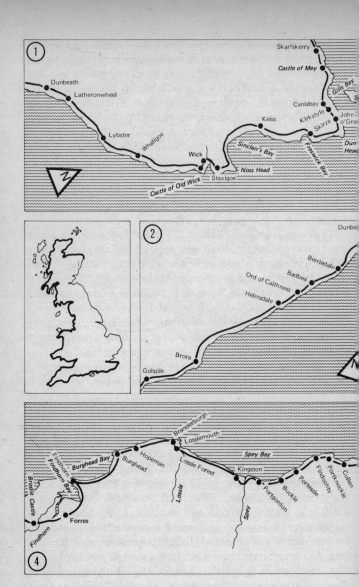

1

Skarfskerry
Castle of Mey
Gills Bay
Dunbeath
Latheronwheel
Canisbay
Lybster
Whaligoe
Keiss
Kirkstyle
Skirza
John o'Groats
Wick
Sinclair's Bay
Freswick Bay
Dun Head
Noss Head
Castle of Old Wick
Staxigoe

N

2

Dunbe
Berriedale
Badbea
Ord of Caithness
Helmsdale
Brora
Golspie
N

Brangerburgh
Lossiemouth
Spey Bay
Hopeman
Findhorn
Findhorn Bay
Burghead Bay
Burghead
Lossie Forest
Kingston
Portknockie
Findochty
Portessie
Cullen
Brodie Castle
Lossie
Spey
Portgordon
Buckie
Forres
Findhorn

4

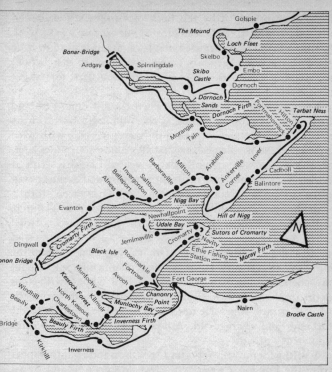

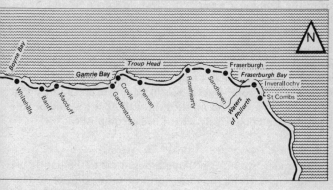

for 350 years owned by the Earls of Caithness. I had been invited to tea with the Queen Mother but because I was a week behind schedule I had missed her. I was asked instead to have tea with the housekeeper but I had to decline so that I could reach John o' Groats before it became too dark for taking photographs.

I pressed on to St John's Point. There the notorious Pentland Firth is at its most ferocious, as the Admiralty warns on its notice: 'The extreme violence of the race, especially with W or NW gales, can hardly be exaggerated'. Almost four miles later, on the eastern side of Gills Bay, I visited Canisbay Kirk at Kirkstyle. The church is thirteenth century and is the resting place of John de Groot who died in 1568. The Queen Mother, when holidaying at the Castle of Mey, worships in this church.

Barely three miles later I reached the John o' Groats Hotel where I was given a room free of charge. Close by is the spot where John de Groot built his famous octagonal house in the late fifteenth century. His seven descendants quarrelled about precedence, and so to overcome this he built a house with eight doors, and inside placed an eight-sided table to avoid the trouble at meal times. He ran a ferry service from there to the Orkneys and charged 4d. A fourpenny coin later became known as a groat.

Waiting for me were reporter Lee Wilson and a photographer from the London *Evening News*. Donald joined us and we sat down to a celebrative meal while I tried to recall the walk from Lyme Regis (where I had first seen Lee) to Land's End, and along the whole of the west coast of Britain to Cape Wrath. At times I became emotional, but at others I talked almost mechanically – I couldn't really appreciate or grasp what I had done so far. In some ways it was like a dream and I knew that it was only when I had finished the walk that I would be able to understand objectively what I had accomplished.

2.9.78

Just under two miles walking brought me to the lighthouse at Duncansby Head, the most north-easterly point of Britain. I have never understood why John o' Groats is so designated for Duncansby is the correct point and has an extremely dramatic coastline as well. It took me a while to register that from there, not only would I turn right for the last time, but that I would also be heading properly southwards to begin the walk down the east coast of Britain to London. I had to keep a tight grip on myself for in theory it was downhill all the way! This was my second visit to Duncansby in twelve months. On the first occasion I had walked 1,608 miles from Land's End, but this time, walking the coast, I had walked 3,715 miles from Land's End and 4,853 miles from London.

Heading south, I walked along the impressive cliffs and past the beautifully shaped rock stacks of Duncansby. The place is alive with sea birds during the summer but only the odd fulmar and great skua remained. As if to give blessing to my 'turning the corner', the sun came out and for the next four days I had exceedingly good, hot, sunny weather. After four miles I entered Skirza village and descended to the white sands of Freswick Bay. From there, more rocky coast took me past several ruined brochs to Keiss where I crossed the beach of Sinclair's Bay, the longest sandy beach in Caithness. At its southern end I climbed back onto the cliff tops near the fifteenth-century Ackergill Tower, which is still lived in. A further three miles took me to Noss Head where I tried to find the cliff path to Staxigoe and Wick. On the ground it hardly existed but by eight o'clock I entered Wick and camped, almost in the dark, at the camp site beside the river. That night I slept in my third sleeping bag, having changed from my lightweight summer one back to a heavier, down-filled bag for the colder weather of autumn.

3.9.78

The rotary club, who had visited me the previous evening, had arranged for me to have breakfast in the nearby hotel. I broke camp early and walked there. Inside was a large coach party waiting for breakfast and, in between eating mouthfuls of bacon and eggs, I found myself signing autographs, rather embarrassed by all the attention I was receiving. After breakfast I hurried out to walk round Wick harbour which was busy with several small cargo boats being loaded and unloaded. Two miles from the harbour, I reached the ruins of the Castle of Old Wick, known to sailors as the Old Man of Wick. I was very impressed by the next piece of coastline with its high cliffs and numerous rock archways. A small islet, known as the Brough, has been worn through in the middle by pounding waves. Nearby was another archway known as Brig of Trams.

Eight miles along very beautiful cliffs brought me to Whaligoe. There I discovered a total of 365 steps down a steep cliff to a very small harbour. They are beautifully preserved and are a remarkable relic of yesteryear, for they were once used by the fishermen's wives in the nineteenth century to carry baskets of fish from the boats to Wick market, six miles away. I left my rucksack at the top and climbed down them. In bright, sunny conditions the steps looked perfect and I spent a lot of time photographing them from various angles.

The next few miles to Latheronwheel were along more fine coastline. At Lybster I bought chocolate, for now that I was walking more than twenty miles every day, my chocolate consumption had risen and I was regularly eating six or more bars a day. Nearing Latheronwheel Hotel (where I stayed), I met a cyclist who, to mark the centenary of the Cyclists' Touring Club, was attempting to cycle from John o' Groats to Land's End in seven days, thereby becoming eligible for a special meal. I wished him luck and thought that perhaps next time I would do it by bicycle, too!

4.9.78

I left Latheronwheel early for it had been arranged for me to meet the Duchess of Portland at Berriedale, eleven miles down the coast. I passed through Dunbeath revelling in the glorious weather; it was one of the hottest days of the whole walk. The clarity was amazing, with rich blue seas and a cloudless sky. A steep descent took me to Berriedale and the estate office. I was looking forward to my visit, for the Portland family have strong connections with my own county of Derbyshire where they gave the impressive Bolsover Castle to the then Ministry of Works in the 1930s.

I was taken to see the Duchess at her home, Langwell House, by the factor. The Duchess, then in her early nineties, was a remarkable woman, very fit looking, articulate and with a great sense of fun. She gave me some money for the charity and insisted on taking my photograph. Afterwards I had lunch with the factor before having a brief look round the 54,300-acre estate. The gardens, one of the most northerly 'English' gardens in Britain, were beautifully laid out and, because everything was late in coming out, were a riot of colour. Leaving the gardens (which are open twice a year to the general public), we made our way down to the deer park. On the estate there are estimated to be three thousand red deer and in 1977 twenty tons of venison was shot. The deer, which were reasonably tame, were kept in the fenced enclosure and I was able to get several photographs of the stags with their impressive antlers.

Seeing the estate in such good condition I couldn't help but admire everyone's enthusiasm to maintain it in good order. There was one thing that puzzled me as I walked round and, as I was about to leave, I suddenly realized that it was the abundance of trees! The west coast of Scotland is bare and I had become used to not seeing any. With regret I said goodbye to the factor, and left for Caithness and the outskirts of Helmsdale where I stayed at the youth hostel. I had had a most enjoyable day.

5.9.78

I wanted to reach Brora before one o'clock to collect my third pair of boots from the post office. The ones that I was wearing, although not fully worn out, had walked 2,100 miles and with under 2,000 miles left to go I felt it would be a good time to change. I left Helmsdale in very cold weather. Before I left, I spoke to a local about the previous day's walk, telling him that I had followed the cliff tops from Berriedale to Badbea. He told me that along there was a former site of a crofting community who were driven off their land in the early nineteenth century. Because the cliffs were so steep both cattle and children used to be tethered to safeguard them from falling into the sea! He also told me a little about the Ord of Caithness. In 1513 the Earl of Caithness and 300 soldiers had passed through there en route for the Battle of Flodden. They never returned, and it is said that anyone walking through the Ord on a Monday would be unlucky. I am very superstitious, and realizing that I had actually done just that, I started to worry about the bad luck I might have!

The final three miles to Brora were along a beautiful stretch of beach beside the golf course, designed by Scottish golfer James Braid in 1924. At the post office I was alarmed to learn that my boot parcel had not arrived. It was the first time the coordinating had gone awry; it seemed quite a coincidence that it should happen just after I'd heard about the legend. I asked them to redirect it to Inverness for I would be there in about seven days' time.

I was walking an average twenty-five miles every day and for the first time since the fracture I began consulting my original schedule. I felt very fit, my foot had settled down and no longer complained or made me limp, and I even started to project that I would reach London in early November.

From Brora I hugged the shore to Golspie, passing close to Dunrobin Castle. The castle was the former seat of the Dukes of Sutherland and dates from the sixteenth century, but much of it was built in the 1920s. The building has the air of a French château, but with a strong Scottish influence. It is now a boys' school. Close to the castle on the shore I found an unexploded shell which I reported to the police when I reached Golspie. High above the village on the summit of Beinn a' Bhragaidh is a large monument to the first Duke of Sutherland.

I continued along the beach before heading inland through Balblair Wood to The Mound, a road embankment built by Thomas Telford in 1815. This then took me across Loch Fleet. As I walked along The Mound, cars stopped and their occupants grabbed cameras to photograph me – there had been a piece about me in the local newspaper that day. It amused me that most of them didn't bother to ask if I minded before they took their photographs, jumped back into their cars and drove off again!

Shortly after crossing The Mound I left the A9 road and walked along the southern shore of Loch Fleet, past the ruins of fourteenth-century Skelbo Castle. Near there I left the muddy shore and walked through the sand dunes to Embo, where I camped on a deserted site, having walked twenty-eight miles. I had been travelling southwards for four days in perfect weather and this had meant the one inconvenience of having the sun in my eyes.

6.9.78

During the night the weather changed to rain and wind which battered the tent. By nine o'clock it was still pouring, but I took the tent down and set off for Dornoch. To reach the small town I walked beside the golf course which, as it was first written of in 1616, is said to be the third oldest in Britain and therefore in the world. I was impressed by the wide streets of Dornoch and the yellow sandstone houses. The cathedral was built in 1224 and, for a population of just a thousand, it is a handsome building of which they are justly proud.

It was Sheila's birthday in two days' time so I stopped and bought her a long tartan skirt which the shop very kindly parcelled up for me.

Leaving the town I reached the spot where the last witch in Scotland was burnt to death in 1722, apparently for changing her daughter into a pony. A mile later I was walking along the side of Dornoch Sands, on the shores of Dornoch Firth before heading inland past Loch Evelix to Loch Ospisdale in front of Skibo Castle. There were several mute swans on the loch, one with six cygnets. Four miles on I reached Spinningdale, which I assume was named after the cotton mill which was built there in 1790. It was gutted by fire in 1808 though the ruins can still be seen.

I pressed on to Bonar-Bridge which spans the Kyle of Sutherland. It was designed by Thomas Telford and built in 1812. At Ardgay, a mile later, it was still raining and so I decided to stay at a guest house, where I could at least dry some of my equipment. I was coming down the east coast fast, but the daylight hours were noticeably shrinking for it was now dark by eight o'clock.

7.9.78

Much of the day was spent walking in the rain along the road which runs next to the southern shore of Dornoch Firth to Tain. A mile before Tain I passed the Morangie distillery, established in 1943, where the ten-year-old malt whisky is made. At Tain I crossed the swing bridge and visited the ruins of the thirteenth-century St Duthus chapel. St Duthus was born in Tain in about AD 1000 and his remains were brought back from Ireland in 1253.

I had to retrace my steps to join the minor road which runs along the southern side of an RAF base. Morrich More to the north is a bombing range and all the red flags were flying. As I walked the range perimeter I saw the jets flying overhead to 'bomb' targets which erupted into smoke and flames when they scored a direct hit.

Once past the range, I got back to the coast and walked into Inver, a delightful little village of single-storey whitewashed houses. The rain had ceased, a rainbow glowed, and occasionally a double one flickered into brilliance. The final four miles of the day along the shoreline from Inver to Portmahomack were very pleasant, with oyster-catchers and gulls as constant companions. I was surprised to find several wild pansies growing so late in the season. Portmahomack, so I was told, has the unique distinction of being the only village on the east coast of Scotland to face west. Finding a caravan site but no owner I camped on the grass just above the village beach.

8.9.78

The following morning saw the return of the rain as I headed northwards for four miles to the lighthouse at Tarbat Ness. The cliffs around the lighthouse are home, during the summer, to a large number of guillemots and razorbills; but then only the odd oyster-catcher was to be seen. From the lighthouse I enjoyed the walk beside the cliffs to Rockfield, four miles to the south. This hamlet is a remarkable cluster of buildings and huts and is well off the beaten track. I rang Sheila to wish her a happy birthday and learnt that the skirt had arrived and, much to my relief, it fitted her.

Still walking close to the shore, I pressed on to Hilton of Cadboll eight miles away. In the next village, Balintore, I made my fifth pub visit of the walk and ate two rounds of sandwiches. My appetite was increasing with my mileage but there was another reason for breaking my usual routine. I had just walked more than 5,000 miles! I felt very pleased with myself – it was also 1,700 miles since the fracture and I was at last walking quite normally. Half an hour later I was back walking in the rain along the top of the 500-foot cliffs of the Hill of Nigg. From there I could look down on the oil rig platform construction site at the entrance to Nigg Bay. Looking south, across the mile of water, I could see Cromarty quite clearly but to get there would involve about fifty miles of walking around Cromarty Firth.

I rounded Nigg Bay via Ankerville Corner and Arabella to Milton where, as it was well past six o'clock, I tried to find somewhere to camp or stay. I was out of luck and so pressed on to Barbaraville. There was nothing there either, so I walked on in the growing dusk to Saltburn.

Saltburn has grown dramatically since 1969 when a large aluminium smelter was built there at a cost of £37 million. Cromarty Firth is a deep sea loch and as a result ships of up to 50,000 tons can draw up at the three-quarter-mile-long jetty and unload their cargo of aluminium oxide from the Caribbean.

A mile further on, at Invergordon, after trying several guest houses, I finally found a room at a small hotel.

9.9.78

The day was cool and cloudy, but dry, and I walked only seventeen miles, the last easy day of the entire walk. As I left Invergordon I noticed the fuel tanks which are used by the navy and tankers. Because of its sheltered and deep waters, during the two World Wars the Firth served as a base for both seaplanes and boats, and it was only in 1956 that it was closed down. Today the Firth has become a major base for North Sea oil operations.

Two miles later at Belleport I moved inland to cross the Alness river at Alness. Five miles further on, past Evanton, I had no option but to follow the busy A9 road along the shore to Dingwall. On the exposed mud flats a curlew, oyster-catchers and the occasional grey heron could be seen, while out in the Firth three dolphins swam past. At Dingwall I learnt that the local rotary club were looking for me; three miles later we met up and I stopped for the day at Conon Bridge. Inverness, at this point, was only about sixteen miles away but my walk there was seventy-three miles – a three-day journey around the Black Isle.

10.9.78

Bad weather approached again with rain and galeforce winds as I made my way northwards from Conon Bridge, along the eastern shore of Cromarty Firth, heading for Cromarty.

Black Isle is principally farming country and I could tell that autumn had arrived as the harvest was already in. Out of everything that I saw right through the seasons, the finest sight in my opinion was the farmers harvesting. At Newhall-point I could look across the Firth and see Invergordon less than a mile away. Close by were the 210-foot chimneys of the aluminium smelting works. From Newhallpoint I followed the track beside Udale Bay past the remains of a chapel to the road which runs along the shore to Jemimaville and eventually to Cromarty.

Cromarty is a delightfully unspoilt village, full of character. The nineteenth-century geologist, Hugh Miller, was born there and his home has since been converted to a museum of his life's work by the National Trust for Scotland. Regrettably it was closed when I arrived. I found a tea room and was pleasantly surprised to discover I could stay the night there. Later that evening one of the organizers of Greenpeace, the conservation group who were protesting against the seal culls, came in and also stayed the night. Unfortunately, as I was too tired to stay up late I did not get to talk with her.

11.9.78

I left Cromarty early so that I could reach Inverness by the following night. I was slightly worried about my left knee as it had been complaining for the last week and was quite tender, but the pain disappeared during the day and I had no more trouble with it. A little over a mile from Cromarty I stood on the cliffs at Sutors of Cromarty and looked over to the Hill of Nigg where I had been three days before, just three miles away across the water! I headed south again as I began walking down the eastern side of the Black Isle beside the Moray Firth. About three miles from the tip of the peninsula I reached the farm called Navity. According to the map there was a path from the top of the steep cliffs down to the shore. On the ground I found nothing except a stile; everything was hopelessly overgrown and making progress proved a nightmare. Added to these difficulties was the fact that the ground was sodden and the earth stuck like glue to my boots. The map gave no indication of the steepness of the cliffs or that there were small rock faces. After floundering around for a considerable time, I just forced my way down, hanging on to bracken stems and gorse bushes and hoping for the best. Scratched and muddy I reached the shore in one piece.

It was easy enough to follow the shore to the Ethie Fishing Station but beyond that it proved awkward. However, it was rewarding to see the views across the mouth of the Moray Firth to Fort George, where there was another oil rig platform construction yard. In time I reached the delightfully-named town of Rosemarkie where I stocked up with chocolate, before continuing along the golf links to Chanonry Point and westwards to Fortrose. The ruined cathedral dates back to the twelfth century and was founded by David I of Scotland. It is ruined because Cromwell's troops used the stone to build Inverness Castle.

A little over a mile of road walking took me to Avoch with its colourful houses and busy harbour. A mile later I had to move inland to round Munlochy Bay via the village of Munlochy. Late in the day I went through Kessock Forest to Kilmuir and round the coast to the mouth of the Beauly Firth

199

to North Kessock. Inverness was just a mile across the Firth, but for me twenty-four miles away. I had walked twenty-seven miles; I felt tired and needed a phone for the radio link-up. Looking in the post office window in North Kessock I could see a notice for accommodation. That one was full, but after several recommendations and four phone calls, I secured a bed a mile away at Charlestown. The couple there had planned to go out for the night but when I gave them my name they kindly changed their plans and invited me to stay.

12.9.78

It rained as I left Charlestown and began the long haul along the northern shore and lanes to Windhill and the A9 road to Beauly. Beauly is a busy, prosperous town with the ruins of a priory on its northern side, which was founded by Sir John Bisset of Lovat in 1230. It is a major stopping point for coach parties and several were there as I walked through. I pressed on to the Lovat bridge and Kirkhill before regaining the A9 which I followed to Inverness. This was the worst main road I had walked along; it was narrow and often when two cars passed the one on my side would not give way, and so I had to jump out of its path. To make the walk even more unpleasant, the rain got heavier and so I was drenched as well by jets of spray from the passing cars.

I reached Inverness at four o'clock and made my way to the post office. Fortunately my boots had arrived and so I changed into them and sent the old ones back. Jeremy Smith from Blacks met up with me and together we tried to find somewhere for me to stay. The youth hostel was full, as was everywhere else, and so, as Jeremy was already booked into the Station Hotel, we decided that I should sleep on his bedroom floor.

I ate a steak that night by way of celebration for I felt confident that nothing would now stop me from reaching London. Ahead of me was the remainder of the east coast of Scotland and the whole of England. On paper it was exactly seven weeks' walking. I committed myself to reach London on Wednesday, 8 November, at one o'clock. Would I make it?

9. Return to the Border

13.9.78

Wearing my third pair of boots and walking under a brightening sky, I left Inverness and headed along the shore of the Moray Firth. At Fort George I spent a pleasant hour exploring the fort which is one of the finest eighteenth-century forts in Europe. An earlier fort occupied the site but was sacked by Bonnie Prince Charlie's troops in 1746 shortly before the Battle of Culloden. The present fort was built in the years 1748–69. Today it is garrisoned by the Gordon Highlanders, and among the buildings is a comprehensive museum with a wide range of exhibits from the Queen's Own Highlanders.

I passed the oil rig construction site I had seen across the Firth a few days earlier and reached Nairn. The next section of coastline from Nairn to Forres is the most densely forested in Britain. To walk the shore is not straightfoward; the area is renowned for its dangerous marshes. I had been advised by the police not to attempt it. Taking their advice I walked along a minor road beside the forest to a camp site near Brodie Castle. The castle is the home of the Brodies of Brodie, whose clan have lived in the area for centuries. The building was gutted by fire in 1645 but was rebuilt and now contains some exceptional plasterwork. It has recently been acquired by the National Trust for Scotland.

As I neared the camp site eating my 1,189th bar of chocolate, I felt something snap in my mouth. A large filling had broken in half, and I knew that I would have to find a dentist in the next town. Waiting for me at the camp site were members of the Forres Rotary Club. The ground was waterlogged but one member, who is a caravan salesman, had brought one to the site for me to use. I was very grateful and more so when I found inside a basket of fruit, two dozen bars of chocolate and a half bottle of whisky! It was indeed very kind of them and it provided rather an apt celebration; it was three months and 2,000 miles after setting off from Skelmorlie, and I had walked thirty miles for the first time since the fracture. After arranging to meet the club the next day at the road bridge over the Findhorn river, I unrolled my sleeping bag and cooked a meal.

14.9.78
Before leaving I weighed myself and was reassured to find that I was back to my normal weight of 10 stone 12 lb. I tidied up the caravan and started to pack some of the gifts. I took most of the chocolate, all the fresh fruit, but left the bottle of whisky. I met a dozen club members at the bridge and they escorted me to Forres. Fortunately, one of the members was a dentist and it had been arranged that he should have a look at my tooth. Feeling rather guilty at bypassing the waiting queue, I was ushered in and told to sit in the chair. Within twenty minutes he had filled the tooth properly (without giving me the injection I normally need), and had given me a thorough check-up. Despite eating so much chocolate, there was no sign of decay.

Walking along the shores of Findhorn Bay was a noisy experience as the planes on Kinloss aerodrome were constantly revving up. The present Findhorn village is the third on this site. In the seventeenth century the first village was buried during several savage sandstorms, and in 1701 a great flood devastated the second village. As bad fortune is said to come in threes, I hope that the present village is safe.

At Findhorn I reached the magnificent beach of Burghead Bay, which offers some seven miles of beautiful sands fringed with pine trees. It gave me a foretaste of some of the beach walking I would be doing over the next two weeks. I was becoming increasingly impressed with this section of coastline;

the west coast is the most popular side, yet on the east coast are beaches that match anything the west coast can offer. From Burghead, which is a largely nineteenth-century village, I walked along the cliff tops to Hopeman. There waiting for me was a master from nearby Gordonstoun School. I was delighted for, having been to a school that similarly laid much emphasis on outward bound training, I was very keen to see Gordonstoun at first hand. I stayed with the master that night, who very kindly showed me round. Unfortunately the autumn term had not yet started, but I was able to see the facilities and get a feel of the atmosphere; I was most impressed. I also met the headmaster, John Kempe, who was retiring at the end of the year. Pupils in his charge included Prince Charles and Prince Andrew who, like their father, spent several of their school years here.

15.9.78

The first seven miles from Hopeman were along the cliffs to Branderburgh. Lossiemouth aerodrome was just inland and the scream of jets taking off and flying overhead was a constant interruption on this sunny but windy day. Branderburgh and Lossiemouth now join together as one town. Lossiemouth is the earlier; it was founded in the seventeenth century and today is an important fishing base. (It was there in 1921 that the Danish seine net was introduced to Britain.) Branderburgh was founded in 1830 and is the birthplace of Ramsay Macdonald, the first Labour Prime Minister.

At Lossiemouth I crossed a long wooden bridge over the mouth of the Lossie river to reach the sandy beach, which I followed for the next eight miles to Kingston and Spey Bay. It was a marvellous walk in perfect solitude: I saw no one, and heard nothing except the sound of the waves breaking on the beach. In order to get across the Spey, Scotland's fastest flowing river, I walked inland for a mile and used the old railway bridge. Back down on the shore again I continued along the sands to Portgordon. From there onwards the coast followed the two-mile-long township of Buckie, which is really five towns in one (with Buckpool, Seatown, Gordonsburgh and

Portessie). Fishing is still a major industry and during the herring boom at the end of the last century, the sheltered harbour could accommodate four hundred fishing boats.

Near Portessie, the last town of the five, I came upon the Gollachy ice house that was still in use as recently as 1966; it was primarily used to store salmon. A mile later I camped and because of the galeforce winds I erected the tent behind some caravans, in order to gain a reasonable amount of shelter.

In the last three days I had walked seventy-six miles from Inverness in my 'new' boots, but I had no blisters. This can be attributed to my rule of walking 500 miles in a pair of boots in order to break them in. I could certainly not have walked this distance if I hadn't done the preparation.

16.9.78

The gales still blew as I made my way to Banff. My first town was Findochty where in the olden days people were summoned to church by a foghorn. Two miles later I came to Portknockie, a former fishing town, and the small but beautiful sweep of Cullen Bay which took me to Cullen town, past several remarkable rock stacks. From Cullen I left habitation and walked along some fine cliffs, past the ruins of Findlater Castle (abandoned in about AD 1600), to the village and beach of Sandend. Continuing along the cliffs I reached Portsoy and a further six miles took me to Boyne Bay and Whitehills. The wind made the walking very hard, and I learnt later that it was a force nine gale. At Banff, with only twenty-one miles walked, I called it a day and stayed in the luxury of the Banff Springs Hotel as a guest of the manager.

17.9.78

The gales continued to batter the coast through the night and they had not abated when I left. Banff is a large and imposing town with several interesting buildings which resulted from the herring boom of the last century. A little over a mile further on, across Banff Bay and the river Deveron, I reached Macduff, where the fishing boats in the sheltered harbour bobbed up and down on the heaving swell. The next few miles to Gardenstown were along a very rugged coastline which in the windy conditions was even more impressive. Two miles from Macduff I reached a field full of cows and one bull. Remembering my last encounter I entered the field cautiously. I had reached the half-way point when the bull charged. I ran for the barbed wire fence and leapt over it only to find myself staring straight down to the sea some two hundred feet below. The bull reached the fence and snorted several times, kicking up the dust. My heart was pounding. Keeping my eye on the cliff edge, I walked round the field and climbed down a gully, out of sight. When I re-emerged some way on he charged again. Luckily, this time there was a barbed wire fence between us. It took me a good three miles to calm down.

Gardenstown, situated half way round Gamrie Bay, came as rather a surprise, for it is very close to the sea with a steep hillside behind. In the heavy gales I could appreciate how vulnerable the village was, for at high tide the sea swept in and crashed over the sea wall. The first part of the path around the cliffs to Crovie was made more exciting by the gale and it was a struggle to get through. Crovie looked even more vulnerable than Gardenstown; it was situated on a very small piece of flat ground, again close to the sea and with 350-foot grass slopes towering behind it. The houses do not face the sea but are at right-angles to it, with their gable ends taking the brunt of the gales. The sea often crashed on to them, right against the gable ends. A steep climb out of the village towards Troup Head was worth the effort just to look back down on to the bay and these two villages.

Three miles from Troup Head I reached another attractive village, Pennan. To many it is the most picturesque village on the east coast of Scotland. Pennan Head, like Troup Head, is a popular sea bird nesting area especially for razorbills and guillemots. Eight miles later, in the dark, I reached Rosehearty. At first I couldn't find anywhere to stay but eventually a local shopkeeper kindly arranged for me to stay in the hotel.

18.9.78

I left at nine o'clock having been unable to find anyone to

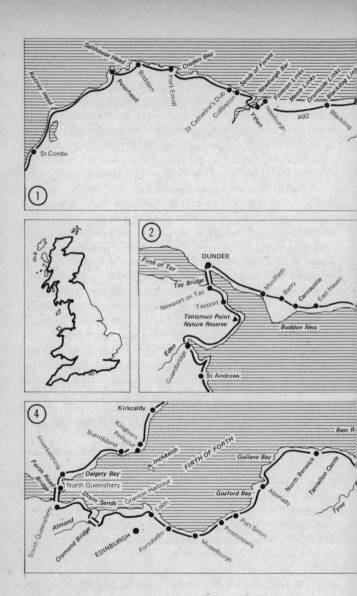

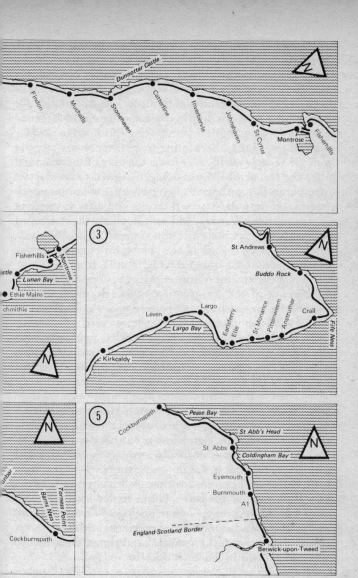

Findon
Muchalls
Stonehaven
Dunnottar Castle
Catterline
Inverbervie
Johnshaven
St Cyrus
Montrose
Fisherhills

③

Fisherhills
Montrose
Castle
Lunan Bay
Ethie Mains
chmithie

St Andrews
Buddo Rock
Largo
Leven
Largo Bay
Earlsferry
Elie
St Monance
Pittenweem
Anstruther
Crail
Kirkcaldy
Fife Ness

⑤
Cockburnspath
Pease Bay
St Abb's Head
St Abbs
Coldingham Bay
Eyemouth
Burnmouth
A1
England-Scotland Border
Berwick-upon-Tweed

unbar
Torness Point
Barns Ness
Cockburnspath

pay and so left a note for them to send the bill on. From Rosehearty I followed the B9031 beside the shore to Sandhaven and Fraserburgh. The town gets its name from Sir Alexander Fraser who founded it in the sixteenth century. It is still one of the principal fishing centres of Scotland. I headed straight for the post office to collect my parcel of maps, films and dehydrated food. The local rotary club were waiting and we adjourned for coffee in the bank! Also waiting to meet me was a reporter from the *Sunday Post*. In order to get the story of the walk, and to get the feel of what I was doing, he agreed to walk across Fraserburgh Bay with me to Inverallochy. I found him good company as we walked over the sands and after a couple of miles reached the Waters of Philorth. Recalling the crossing of Duddon Sands in Cumbria, I announced that I would walk across without boots. Not to be outdone, my companion took his suit trousers off and waded across in his Y-fronts!

Inverallochy and the nearby village of St Combs were places of ill-repute in the nineteenth century. Huge amounts of money were earned from the herring boom and, instead of using it wisely, most of the fishermen squandered it on whisky. They earned the reputation of being brawlers and their houses of being hovels. Following two cholera epidemics in the 1850s, most of the houses were demolished. Today the past is forgotten and many of the remaining houses are holiday homes.

The coast to Peterhead was one long beach – a good fifteen miles via the sixty-foot dunes of Rattray Head. It really was a magnificent walk and for five hours I had the sea and shore to myself. Just beyond the lighthouse at Rattray Head I found an oiled guillemot. It was unable to move away from me as I photographed it, but it was the only example of oil pollution that I found on the entire coastline of Britain. A mile later I saw a young seal on the beach, but he moved back to the sea before I could get near enough to photograph him. The birds I saw on these beaches included cormorants, curlews, lapwings, large rafts of eider ducks, gannets, sanderlings, black-headed gulls, common gulls, and lesser black-backed gulls.

A little after seven o'clock, as it began to get dark, I walked into the centre of Peterhead. I noticed a man get out of a white, sleek car, and a couple of minutes later he approached me. He asked if I was John Merrill and introduced himself as Ron Ferrari from the rotary club. I made the obvious remark 'I suppose you drive a Ferrari?' but was more than surprised when he announced that he did! We walked across to one of his hotels, the Caledonian, and I stayed there as his guest. An hour later after a good wash I joined him in the dining room and sat down to the biggest T-bone steak I have ever eaten. I enjoyed his company very much and was extremely touched that this busy man should spend time waiting for me and then be so generous as to place his hotel at my service.

19.9.78

Peterhead is the most easterly point of Scotland and its harbour bustled with activity, the reason being that because of the oil boom the town now plays a major part in servicing the oil rigs. In the early nineteenth century it was an important whaling centre while in the early twentieth century huge catches of herrings were landed. It is recorded that in 1820 fifteen ships landed 103 arctic whales and in 1907 that 520 million herring were caught by local boats.

Leaving Peterhead in perfect hot, sunny and still weather, I watched an oil rig being towed into harbour. The front two tugs guided it in and the back two kept everything in tension.

At Salthouse Head on the southern side of Peterhead Bay I walked beneath the prison and looked along the breakwaters which were built by the inmates between 1886 and 1958. Another mile of walking took me towards Boddam and from there I walked for seven miles along the cliff tops to Port Erroll. There I descended to the shore once more and walked round the beautiful, curved sweep of sand of the Bay of Cruden. The view eastwards was immaculate and exceptionally clear. I could see two oil rigs far out to sea, and a multitude of large and small boats. Meanwhile, the helicopters overhead were busy ferrying stores to the oil rigs.

At the end of the bay I climbed back on to the cliff tops to head for Collieston, six miles away. I passed the ruins of Old Slains Castle, which was destroyed by James VI in 1594, but still has two cannons which were taken from a shipwrecked Spanish boat. Further along the coast the small cove of St Catherine's Dub is named after a Spanish galleon, *Santa Caterina*, which was wrecked there in 1594. At the southern end of Collieston I walked into the Sands of Forvie Nature Reserve. The area is an impressive mass of sand dunes, some of which are up to two hundred feet high. It is a popular nesting area and has the largest single concentration of eider ducks in the country. Terns breed at Newburgh Bar, at the southern end of the reserve, and as I walked along I saw several shelduck, too. The sands started to build up about two thousand years ago and over the years the village of Forvie has been covered to such a depth that only the church remains visible. Inland from Newburgh Bar I reached the roadbridge over the river Ythan and a mile later I camped on the outskirts of Newburgh village.

20.9.78

I left Newburgh early in perfect weather, aiming to be at Aberdeen by three o'clock where I had arranged to go to Blacks' shop. In front of me was perhaps the longest stretch of uninterrupted sandy beach in Britain – the Foveran, Menie, Pettens, Drumside, Eigie, Millden and Blackdog links. With the tide out I could walk on firm sand much of the way, but when I had to walk on soft sand my progress became extremely slow and laborious.

After about ten miles, I came to Blackdog firing range and noticed that all the red flags were flying. As I approached the boundary, two sentries, armed with guns, came down to prevent me from walking through, but I argued and stood my ground. Whereas before I had accepted this sort of restriction, now that I had walked 5,300 miles I did not feel like doing a two-mile detour around the range when to cross it meant a distance of only a quarter of a mile. While the sentries went back to check with their CO I set off. Having realized that I was 'the person walking the coast' they ceased firing and let me through!

A couple of miles on I reached an old abandoned fishing boat. It had obviously been there for a long time and seeing a piece of rope dangling over the side, I scaled up it to look around. Unfortunately it had been stripped of anything interesting or valuable and was just a rusting shell.

Three miles later I was walking along the promenade at Aberdeen. This was my first city for several months and it seemed very strange. I walked into the centre, and the sight of such a large number of people and cars sent me into a state of shock. I was totally disorientated and I found myself walking up the centre of roads as though still on a remote stretch of beach. The cars swerved and hooted and people dragged me out of the way. I was almost knocked down. I stared unbelievingly at the tall buildings. For months I had been walking on lonely shores, seeing only wildlife and crofts, and for a while the contrast was just too savage.

After visiting Blacks' shop and obtaining a pair of socks, I headed for Aberdeen Youth Hostel for the night. I have always enjoyed hostelling, although I feel today the Association has 'lost its way' slightly by creating super hostels with carpets and plush surroundings and by allowing car drivers to use them. The number of walkers or cyclists who use such hostels now is comparatively small. The Aberdeen hostel was full and seemed to be mainly used by the oil rig workers; it didn't seem right at all.

I spent a lot of time ambling around Aberdeen's docks watching the boats arriving and leaving, and being unloaded or loaded with cargo. Aberdeen is not only one of Scotland's principal seaside resorts, but is the third largest fishing port in Britain; it is also a major base for North Sea oil.

21.9.78

I left Aberdeen in beautiful, hot, sunny weather. I walked only twenty-two miles to Stonehaven, but from then onwards, until I reached London, I averaged thirty miles a day for much of the way walking better than I have ever done before in my life. Much of the walk from Aberdeen to Stonehaven was along the cliff tops and past smugglers' villages; Muchalls even has a secret passage. The walking was awkward as the railway line often ran close to the cliff tops. I passed through the little village of Findon where in the nineteenth century the 'Finnan Haddie' was smoked over cottage fires. The Factory Act put paid to this cottage industry and as a result the village almost died. Two miles south of Muchalls I reached the A92 road where, because the railway line and road run so close to the cliff edge, I had to walk along the latter into Stonehaven. There I found the caravan site but I was not allowed to use it and so I moved on to an alternative site.

22.9.78

The following morning brought the return of the sun and it proved to be a really warm day. Stonehaven was formerly a fishing town but has recently developed into a popular seaside resort. As I climbed away from the town, I looked back on to the harbour and buildings; the view was stunning. The perfect weather coupled with the remarkable clarity made the setting breathtaking, and I would rate it as one of the most picturesque sights of the entire walk. A little over a mile from Stonehaven I came to the fascinating ruins of Dunnottar Castle, perched on top of the 160-foot cliffs. The castle dates from the fourteenth and sixteenth centuries and during the mid-seventeenth century was one of the places where the Scottish crown, sceptre and sword of state were hidden. Because of the impregnability of the castle, Cromwell's troops were thwarted in their attempt to get the state jewels.

For much of the day I kept to the cliff tops through delightful scenery, watching the odd sea bird fly by, ships going out to sea and an oil rig being towed out to its location. I passed through the village of Catterline and pressed on to Inverbervie, Johnshaven and St Cyrus. There, in the late afternoon, I at last reached sandy beaches and walked round the edge of the St Cyrus National Nature Reserve. The present village of St Cyrus is situated above the cliffs but the earlier village was near the mouth of the North Esk River and was lost during storms in 1795. The nature reserve covers 227 acres and is famous for its huge variety of flowers (more than three hundred species have been recorded there).

I moved inland to Fisherhills to cross the river before

reaching Montrose in the dark. A campsite was marked on the map at the southern end of the town so I headed for it. On arrival I found all the taps had been disconnected from the water supply, and so I had to find another site where I could get water. It was my first real indication that the summer season was over, and it was now dark by 7.45 p.m.

23.9.78

After leaving Montrose via the main road bridge over the neck of the Montrose Basin, I came to the sands of Lunan Bay. Just beyond the Lunan Water estuary, the ruins of the sixteenth-century Red Castle look out to sea. I made for the beach again and it was good to see the waves breaking and listen to the cry of the gulls. At the southern end of the beach I was surprised to find a cluster of houses at Ethie Haven, near Ethie Mains, tucked away at the base of the cliffs. It was a delightful little community and the views from the houses must have been stunning. I climbed up on to the 250-foot high cliffs and walked along the top to Auchmithie and finally to Arbroath. About twelve miles out to sea is the Inchcape lighthouse, the oldest rock lighthouse off the coast of Britain. It was built by Robert Stevenson in 1811 and stands 115 feet high.

Arbroath is famous for its smell of 'smokies' or smoked haddock. Unfortunately I didn't have a chance to sample any as the local rotary club were waiting and walked with me past the harbour and along the sands towards Carnoustie. At East Haven, two miles from the town, they left having completed their sponsored walk, and headed for home. Golf has been played at Carnoustie for more than four hundred years and it has one of the finest courses in the world. Even if you had no prior knowledge of the town's connection, you would be able to guess just by walking through it and looking at the shop windows which are full of every conceivable article of golfing attire and equipment. Even the locals walked round in chequered trousers and bright sweaters! I moved on a mile and camped at the campsite in Barry. Officially it was closed and there was no water, but fortunately a shop was open and I was able to buy some tinned food.

24.9.78

I inquired whether I could walk around Buddon Ness but unfortunately, since it is part of Barry Camp and the area was out of bounds that day, I had to walk along the road to Monifieth. From Monifieth I was able to walk close to the shore all the way to Dundee. At Dundee I had to decide whether I should use the Tay Road Bridge or go on to Perth. I was encouraged to use the bridge as it is the first road bridge, but I only finally decided when I saw it had a footpath sign. The path across is rather novel, for instead of being on one side of the bridge it was in the middle, with traffic passing on either side. To get a better view of the bridge and of Dundee there are several observation platforms. The other enjoyable aspect of the bridge is that from north to south the bridge rises and I was thus walking uphill. Since I was still having the problem of thinking that because I was walking south – psychologically downhill – I could race home, this little hill acted as a brake!

Down on the southern shore of the Tay I made my way to Tayport and the Tentsmuir Point Nature Reserve. The first part of the walk around these sands was along good clean sand but the further I walked southwards to the mouth of the river Eden, so it gradually deteriorated into dangerous, soft, glutinous mud. Rather than retrace my steps, I decided to struggle round. Just inland was Leuchars airfield, and nearby I could see discarded parts of planes and tyres strewn all over the area. I struggled through, often alarmed at the power of the mud as it sucked my boots down. I was relieved to reach Guardbridge and, after crossing the river Eden, I walked along the firm shoreline and the golf course of St Andrews. I arrived in the dark after thirty-four miles, my longest day for many months. I was tired, but very pleased at my performance. I doubt that many people have walked from the turf of Carnoustie to St Andrews in one day!

25.9.78

St Andrews is a most attractive town and has the ruins of a Norman castle and twelfth-century cathedral. I regretted that I couldn't linger but I had arranged to meet Roger Smith later in the day and had to make an early start. As it was, because I was making rather slow progress, we missed each other.

The walk along the rocky and sometimes sandy shore to Fife Ness is extremely pleasant and, most of the time, I had it all to myself. Part way along I came to Buddo Rock, a large soft sandstone rock with a fine vertical archway. I was surprised to find such a delightful piece of coast this far down the east coast of Scotland, even more so when I discovered a string of towns, each with an attractive harbour. The first of these was Crail, followed by Anstruther Easter, Anstruther Wester, Pittenweem and St Monance, with its fourteenth-century church just above the coastline.

At Elie I sought somewhere to stay and update my notes. Noticing a guest house sign I knocked on the door and was instantly recognized. The owner was a local rotarian and couldn't believe that I had unknowingly knocked on his door for a bed that night.

26.9.78

I left just after 8.30 a.m., with my mind filled with items of interest to look out for during the day. Two miles from Elie, and beyond Earlsferry, I found my first feature which was the Chain Path. Although I knew of its existence, I didn't quite know what to expect. The path winds around the cliffs and, to help you scrabble down, sometimes twenty feet at a time, there is a heavy chain firmly fixed onto the cliffs. As the tide was in it made the descent all the more exciting and, out of sheer devilment, I dumped my rucksack and repeated the course all over again!

Largo Bay made an enjoyable walk across two miles of sand to Lower Largo. I called in at a shop to buy some stocks of chocolate – I was now consuming seven or eight bars a day. Near the shop was a monument to Alexander Selkirk, who was born there in 1676. He went to sea but after an argument with

215

the ship's captain was put down on the island of Juan Fernandez off the coast of Chile. There he led a spartan life, living off the land for four years, and his story was the inspiration for Daniel Defoe's *Robinson Crusoe*. I carried on to Leven and the abandoned coal mines of East and West Wemyss. Three miles later I reached Kirkcaldy.

One of my plans before setting out from London was to take a skiing holiday at the end of the walk. I had always wanted to ski but had never found the time to try. I decided at Kirkcaldy that now was the time to make some arrangements. I walked into a travel agents and was given several brochures to look at. I found a guest house nearby, which quite coincidentally had the apt name 'Everest', and sat down to select a holiday. First thing the following morning I booked an eight-day cross-country ski-ing holiday in Norway for the latter half of December.

27.9.78

As I left Kirkcaldy I saw further evidence of the advancing season. Shops were already stocking Christmas cards and advertising Christmas clubs. The leaves were changing colour and were beginning to fall and starlings gathered in the trees. From Kirkcaldy I kept close to the shoreline to Kinghorn and Pettycur at the mouth of the Firth of Forth. Out in the middle of the Firth was the small island of Inchkeith. For the first time it dawned on me that there wasn't much of the coast of Scotland left.

I walked over the sands to Burntisland, where the first rail ferry had begun operating across the Firth in 1850. Ahead I could see the Forth rail and road bridges. To reach the latter entailed walking round Dalgety and Donibristle Bays to Inverkeitning. From there I joined the footpath across the bridge to South Queensferry. As I crossed, I could look down on Rosyth Naval dockyard which was founded in 1909; a few naval boats were secured to the jetties.

At Queensferry I continued on in the gathering dusk to walk round the Drum Sands to the Almond river. It was arranged that I should stay nearby with David Flatman, a

216

friend of Sheila and a colleague of Roger Smith. I would then be well placed and ready for a sponsored walk from Leith to Prestonpans the next day. It was dark as I left the sands and by sheer good fortune I located the track in the woods beside the river Almond to head inland to Cramond Bridge. Part of the way along the track I saw a hedgehog. Normally when you touch them they curl up into a defensive ball, but this one didn't, it simply stood its ground and spat at me! At Cramond Bridge I met my host and at his house I had a bath for the first time for several days.

28.9.78

From Cramond I went along the shore to Granton harbour and at Leith headed inland to central Edinburgh to do a radio interview. Roger Smith worked nearby and we met for lunch. Afterwards I rushed to Portobello for 2.15 p.m. to join up with twenty pupils from ten Edinburgh schools. While I had been laid up in Drymen I had been to Edinburgh twice to talk to several schools about the walk. As a result ten schools had been organized to do a sponsored walk with me to Prestonpans. As we set off from Portobello the clouds began to darken and after a mile it began to rain. In no time everyone was soaked. No one complained and we trudged on to Musselburgh and so to the market cross at Prestonpans. There the children were met by a minibus and were taken home. They collected nearly £1,000 for their efforts.

I continued on alone, feeling tired and wet. To make matters worse, I could find nowhere to stay. I carried on to Port Seton and around Gosford Bay to Aberlady, where I was eventually able to find a bed for the night.

29.9.78

The sun came out as I headed northwards for a while around Aberlady Bay. The bay is a nature reserve and I saw a lot of oyster-catchers, eider ducks and plovers. As many as two hundred species have been recorded there, but it was too late in the year to see an enormous variety. I was also back in golfing country for, to reach Gullane Bay, I walked round three courses, one of which was Muirfield. The next six miles of coast to North Berwick were simply perfect with good sandy beaches, no people, and good views ahead to several small islands including Bass Rock.

I had visited Bass Rock four years previously to see the gannetry. About 17,000 pairs cover this large rock and the sight of so many fully mature birds with their fluffy chicks and absurdly small eggs was unforgettable. There are also colonies of other sea birds on the island: guillemots, razorbills and kittiwakes. Two miles from North Berwick and with Bass Rock lying due north, I reached the ruins of Tantallon Castle. Standing about a hundred feet above the sea, the castle dates from the fourteenth century and over the years has withstood many sieges. Half a mile later I reached one of the most beautiful beaches I have ever seen; it was just tucked out of the way and was totally unspoilt.

On the way to Peffer Sands the heavens opened and for the next three hours I suffered a torrential downpour. In no time the ground was awash and my clothes were completely soaked. Rather than cross the river Tyne, three miles on, I decided to use a bridge that was marked on the map. When I reached it I found a padlocked gate across the middle with six-inch metal spikes around it. Using the spikes as hand and foot holds I climbed over. My fifty-pound load made me unsteady and the bridge swayed alarmingly but with great relief I made it to the other side safely.

At Dunbar I tried several guest houses but all were either full or closed. I then tried some hotels, without success, and was just beginning to get a bit desperate and look for a bus shelter, when I found two more. I tried the smaller and as though a prayer had been answered the owners recognized me and welcomed me in. They were members of the rotary club and only that day had been asked if they knew where I was! I was very grateful for the night's lodging and to be able to dry my equipment out.

30.9.78
This was to be my last full day in Scotland. I left Dunbar in

dry conditions but for the first time I noticed that it was getting cooler. The coast was relatively flat as I passed the lighthouse at Barns Ness and two miles later at Torness Point I came upon a group of people who were protesting against the proposed nuclear power station planned for the site. Beyond Torness the cliffs began to rise past Pease Bay to St Abb's Head. The area, about 240 acres in extent, is managed by the Scottish Wildlife Trust. The cliffs reach a height of over 500 feet which makes them the highest on the east coast of Scotland. They normally support a large variety of sea birds, but because it was so late I saw none. Just beyond was the attractive village of St Abbs with its small harbour. I stayed at Coldingham Bay for my last night on Scottish soil.

1.10.78

I took it easy in the morning, for I had agreed to reach the Scotland–England border at three o'clock. I walked slowly around the cliffs to the busy harbour of Eyemouth. Three miles later I descended the hill to Burnmouth. From there I had no option but to take the A1 to the border, as it runs so close to the cliff edge. So far I had seen no one and to complete the final mile and a half to the border I followed a minor road. Five hundred yards from the border I turned back on to the main road and was greatly surprised to discover such a huge crowd waiting to greet me, with police lining the road! A piper joined me and played various Scottish airs as I covered the last few yards to the border. Before I left Scotland I had one small task to perform and that was to draw three raffle tickets. Each winner would receive a cheque for £250. A huge raffle had been held throughout Scotland which raised just over £4,500 for RCSB; a magnificent effort.

This done, I stepped into England for the first time for almost six months. I headed back to the cliff tops to follow a right of way to Berwick-upon-Tweed. With almost 5,600 miles completed, and after the crowd and clicking cameras at the border, I was glad to be alone with my thoughts. Scotland had been magnificent. I will never forget the west coast; it was a walk of never-ending joy. The east coast was more gentle, but

219

I will remember it for the unexpectedly beautiful beaches and the picturesque villages.

Five miles later I stopped in Berwick-upon-Tweed and was joined by Sheila for dinner. In a little over a month's time I would be in London. In front of me was the Northumberland coast which I knew only vaguely, the Yorkshire coast which I knew well (having walked the Cleveland Way four times before), and the Humber which was all new ground. My only fear was the weather. Would it be a good autumn or would I walk in rain and wind?

10. North-East England

2.10.78
Waiting for me at the old road bridge across the Tweed at Berwick was Neville Rigby from the *Northern Echo*. He is an experienced walker and wanted to join me to get material for a feature. For the first few miles we were accompanied by an ITV cameraman as we followed the track from Berwick-upon-Tweed beside the shore towards Cheswick Sands. Now that I was back in England, I had to learn to restrict myself to walking on rights of way only again. I found this very hard, for after the months in Scotland walking where I wanted, I didn't take kindly to being restricted. In practice, I often trespassed in order to keep as close to the coast as possible.

From Cheswick Sands, Neville and I kept to the edges of fields and went round the sands which overlook Holy Island. The weather was most uninviting; it was overcast and grey with continuous drizzle. The island, formerly known as Lindisfarne, was the first English diocese, founded by St Aidan in AD 635. Following the murder of his very close friend King Oswin at Gilling in 651, Aidan died of grief two weeks later and was buried on Lindisfarne. Bede wrote that St Aidan 'was a man of remarkable gentleness, goodness and moderation, zealous for God'. From the shore we could see the ruins of the priory and the prominent castle which dates back to the mid-sixteenth century. I have driven across the two miles of causeway on several occasions just to see the waders that live there in large numbers.

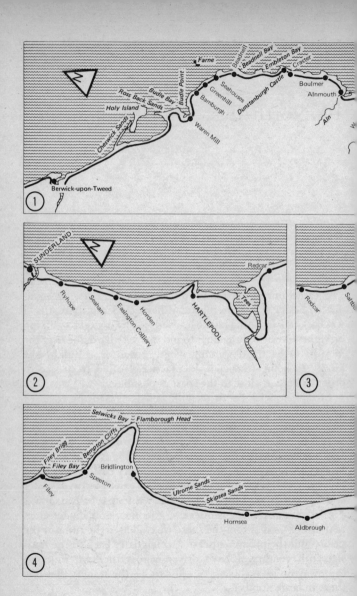

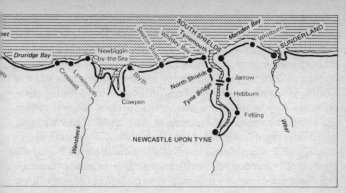

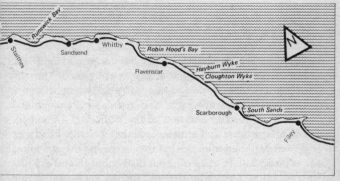

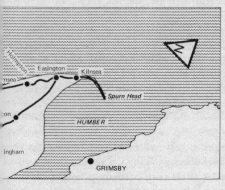

223

In the worsening weather we continued round the Ross Back Sands and Budle Bay to Waren Mill. Neville turned for home, having enjoyed his twenty-four mile walk. I carried on to Budle Point and into Bamburgh. I wanted to arrive before it got too dark to photograph the most impressive castle, and I only just made it in time. Much of the present building dates from the eighteenth and nineteenth centuries and was at that time used as a base for training servant girls. I had wrongly assumed that Northumberland had just the one attractive castle, but I was soon to learn that its coastline had a whole string of remarkable fortifications. One cannot describe Bamburgh without mentioning Grace Darling. She was born in 1815 but died of tuberculosis at the age of twenty-six. Her fame is due to an incident in 1838 when during a savage storm she helped her father row a twenty-one-foot boat out to rescue five sailors from the steamer *Forfarshire*.

I needed somewhere to stay to dry out and use a phone for my radio report. All the guest houses were closed, and the hotels took one look at me and said 'sorry'! My hair was now very long and my beard, which 'Nationwide' had encouraged me not to trim for the duration of the walk, was a good six inches long. Fortunately I remembered that a couple I had met near Waren Mill had told me that they were staying at a guest house at Greenhill. It was a mile out of Bamburgh and as I had an 'introduction' I was admitted and spent a very comfortable night.

I was now walking at full stretch, covering between twenty-eight and thirty-nine miles every day. I felt in great shape and knew London was now well within my grasp. Many people commented upon the speed with which I came down the east coast but I always work best under pressure and having set my target nothing would make me ease off.

3.10.78

The morning brought a very warm early October day. I followed the sands to Seahouses with the Farne Islands just off-shore. One of the finest coastal trips in Britain is to go from Seahouses by boat to the Farne Islands. In early summer, the cliffs are bursting with a whole variety of sea birds, while in late summer the sea is full of grey seals, I pressed on to Beadnell and along the sandy shore of Beadnell Bay. It was extremely good walking; parts of the coastline even equalled the west coast of Scotland. A further two bays took me to Embleton Bay and Dunstanburgh Castle.

Dunstanburgh is an imposing ruin which dates from the beginning of the fourteenth century. During the Wars of the Roses the castle took a considerable amount of punishment and since 1538 has been in a ruinous state. Below are the remains of a small harbour which once held Henry VIII's navy.

The footpath I had been following continued southwards to Craster which is renowned for its kippers. I was making for the post office, to send another film for processing, when a shopkeeper recognized me. He told me he had only just been saying that I ought to be passing through, and so he was amazed that I'd turned up just then. He rushed off to tell anyone he could find that I had arrived with the result that I was invited for a welcome cup of tea in a house opposite!

After spending almost an hour in the village I left to follow the shore to Boulmer. At low tide it is possible to walk across the mouth of the river Aln but I was too late and the tide was coming in fast. I had to walk inland a little way to cross before gaining the sandy shore again for an uninterrupted walk along it for almost three miles towards Warkworth. I reached Warkworth in the dark, but the character of the place was still evident as I approached the town by the fourteenth-century fortified bridge across the river Coquet. Warkworth is situated in the middle of a loop of the river, which acts as a boundary on three sides. I walked up the main street past the ruined castle and found a lodging near by.

4.10.78

Before leaving Warkworth I had a look round the town. The weather was again exceptionally good and the ruined sandstone castle glistened in the sun. The castle was built between the twelfth and fourteenth centuries and was used by Shakespeare as a setting for his play *Henry IV*. Leaving the town I walked on beside the river Coquet towards Amble and the coast, frequently turning to admire the view back to Warkworth. A mile off-shore from Amble was Coquet Island which until the sixteenth century was a refuge for hermits and monks. A cell still remains on the island, while half a mile up river from Warkworth Castle is a hermit's cave. A little way beyond Amble I reached the five-mile sweep of beach round Druridge Bay to Cresswell and Lynemouth. This was my last good beach on the Northumbrian coast before reaching the industry round Newcastle.

North of Lynemouth the cliffs fell dramatically to a black beach below. The contrast of the immaculate beaches to this disgraceful abuse of coastline was shattering. Coal is the main culprit and from the nearby power station, coal waste was literally dumped into the sea by dumper trucks. The entire beach was covered with small particles of coal, and a small industry has even sprung up to scoop the coal waste into sacks for sale. I walked across the beach and through the filthiest black stream I have ever seen. My boots remained stained for days. Near Newbiggin-by-the-Sea, a local told me that as recently as twenty years ago there had been golden sands. I was to follow coal-scarred beaches right down the Yorkshire coast, even as far as Lincolnshire.

Two miles south of Newbiggin-by-the-Sea I crossed the river Wansbeck by the main road bridge and from there took the road round an industrial complex to the river Blyth and so to Blyth itself. I pressed on via Seaton Sluice to Whitley Bay, arriving in the dark after walking thirty-four miles.

5.10.78

I left early and began to make my way through the housing estates and industry of Tynemouth and North Shields to Newcastle. The contrast was not as much of a shock as it had been at Aberdeen and I made sure I walked on the pavements! I visited Blacks' shop, collected my mail from the post office and, just after two o'clock, crossed the famous Tyne Bridge and began the long haul via Felling, Hebburn and Jarrow to South Shields. Back across the river by Tynemouth north pier I could see the ruins of the eleventh-century priory I had passed earlier in the day. I was only three miles further south than when I had started in the morning, despite walking twenty-seven miles. Before putting up for the night in South Shields I saw the Tyne lifeboat. Built in 1833 and used for sixty years, this lifeboat was responsible for saving a staggering 1,028 lives.

6.10.78

I awoke to a fine morning: 'Hot and sunny – a lovely October day', my log recorded. Having suffered poor weather throughout much of the walk I was concerned it might get worse as autumn approached, but it turned out to be one of the warmest and loveliest autumns we have had for many years. Perhaps there was some justice in this; I had suffered the harshest winter for thirty years in Cornwall, and one of the wettest summers we have known for a long time.

From South Shields I walked along the cliff tops to Marsden Bay and its rock stack and on to Whitburn and Sunderland. Much of the way was on the road through built up areas. I don't actually mind this kind of walking; it adds to the variety. In fact, looking back, there was nowhere on the coast that I did not derive some pleasure from; everywhere had its own character and beauty. You have to be adaptable and just accept the variety of the coastline in all its facets.

After crossing the river Wear at Sunderland I headed straight back to the cliffs and from Hendon followed a right of way along them. The first part, to Seaham, was fine, but beyond that the paths became involved with the coal mines. While I had been appalled at the tipping of coal waste into the sea north of Newcastle, the sight of Easington Colliery was even worse. A continuous line of buckets stretched out to sea disgorging their loads of coal waste, and a large black mound stood up out of the waves. It was a hideous sight and hardly surprising that the beaches were lined with black filth to the high tide mark. At one time there were no fewer than seven of these bucket conveyor belts tipping out their waste.

Near Horden I met up with a local rambling club who had been following my progress. We arranged that they would collect me at the end of the day and provide me with a meal and a bed in return for which I would present some prizes that night. The event made £60 for the charity. On re-entering England I had stopped my involvement with RCSB and had agreed to partake in only three events as I came down the east coast.

7.10.78

I was returned to Horden and set off to reach the Yorkshire coast at Redcar, thirty miles away. I was now regularly walking thirty or more miles a day and approximately 210 miles per week, but weighing myself the previous night I noticed that I had lost weight and was now 10 stone 3 lb. The weather was glorious and my log records 'warmer than the summer'. I negotiated several more collieries before reaching the docks of Hartlepool. Part of the way through I saw the ocean research ship I had seen nine months before near Dartmouth. It seemed an incredibly long time ago and it brought home to me just what I had achieved in all those months.

Three miles south of Hartlepool I left the coast to begin walking along the road, past several industrial complexes and oil refineries, to the transporter bridge over the river Tees and into Yorkshire. Again my mind flashed back to Newport in South Wales where in early March I had used the only other transporter bridge in the country. The next eight miles to the outskirts of Redcar were along the most unusual right of way I have ever used, through the very centre of the British Steel works. The right of way is alongside the railway line and is fenced off all the way; it was as near as I could get to the coast. The red hot slag was being dumped into railway wagons and a massive pall of thick black smoke exploded into the air. The train pushed the trucks to a water cooler where water was sprayed on to the hot slag. Great fountains of steam shot out in all directions. A little further along I passed a huge electro-magnet that was loading steel off-cuts into a large melting pot. The magnet was so powerful that it was almost lifting the wagon off the tracks. With the sun setting behind the chimneys of the ICI Wilton Chemical Works, I reached Redcar and stopped there.

8.10.78

I was away early for I was looking forward to walking the coastal section of the Cleveland Way, from Saltburn-by-the-Sea to Filey, which I had enjoyed many times before. The tide was out so I could walk all the way to Saltburn along the sands. It was a hot sunny Sunday and fishermen were out in their boats. Along the sands were dozens of tractors of varying vintage, which are used to launch their boats. Two hours' walking took me to the pier at Saltburn. Just beyond it I left the sand and climbed up the cliffs to begin the twenty-mile walk to Whitby.

The Cleveland Way is a magnificent 100-mile walk and is one of the official long distance paths of England. The walk begins at Helmsley on the North Yorkshire Moors, loops north to Saltburn-by-the-Sea and ends at Filey, on the coast. The beauty of the walk lies in the contrast between the splendid mountain and moorland country and the equally impressive coastal section. The weather was incredible: clear, warm and sunny. The only problem was the swarm of flies that buzzed round my head. Every other time I have been here, I have either had bad weather or experienced the infamous Cleveland Roak (fog).

Four miles of cliff walking took me to Skinningrove. Little remains of the steel works, and the Kilton Beck that used to run red into the sea was noticeably cleaner. A steady climb out of Skinningrove took me onto the Boulby Cliffs which at 666 feet are the highest cliffs on the east coast of Britain. The cliffs are of soft clay and sandstone which makes them unstable and less spectacular to look at than, say, the solid granite cliffs of Cornwall.

From the top of Boulby Cliffs I could see down towards Staithes two miles away. The village, situated at the base of a narrow cove, is a popular haunt, especially for artists. For a while Captain James Cook was apprenticed there to a general dealer, going to sea in 1746 at the age of eighteen as a servant to a Whitby ship owner. A further three miles took me to the sands and crowds of Runswick Bay. Crossing the beach I passed Hob Holes. In years past a dwarf named Hob lived there in a small cavern and was said to be able to cure whooping-cough. Any child suffering from the complaint was taken to the cave and it is said that if their parents recited 'Hob-hole Hob! My bairn's gotten t'kink cough, Tak't off! Tak't off!' then he would be cured.

Three miles later I descended the cliffs for the last time that day and reached Sandsend. As the tide was out I walked the three miles along the sands to Whitby. All the time I could see evidence of coal dust on the sand. Two years previously I had walked along this beach and I could not recall seeing any then.

Whitby is a pretty town with a busy fishing fleet, and is a popular seaside resort. To a lone traveller it again came as rather a shock to find huge crowds, and to hear bingo numbers being called, slot machines rattling and pinging, and the loud shots of the target shooting games. Rather than linger with the milling crowds eating ice cream and candyfloss and wearing Kiss me Quick hats, I pressed on quickly around the harbour and over the swing bridge, to the base of the 199 steps which lead up to the church. At the top I stopped and admired the view down onto the red tiled houses, the harbour and the lights. The parish church was opposite me and although the exterior is not remarkable, the interior is interesting with a three-decker pulpit and box pews. I could easily imagine the eighteenth-century 'sluggard waker' walking around during the three-hour service and prodding anyone who had fallen asleep!

I went on to the youth hostel where I stayed the night.

9.10.78

The good weather held and, for the first time, on this stretch of the Cleveland Way, I was able to admire the ruins of Whitby Abbey in clear conditions. At the base of the cliffs are found ammonite fossils. The story of how they came to be here is based on a thousand-year-old legend which relates how the abbess, St Hilda, wanted to rid Eskdale of its snakes and so drove them over the cliffs, cutting their heads off with a whip as they fell. The ammonites are their remains. A hundred years ago Whitby jet, a very hard black stone, was extracted from these same cliffs, and was fashioned into jewellery. In the last century there were as many as two hundred workshops, but today there are only a handful left.

I pressed on along the cliff path, soaking up the hot sun as I made my way past the lighthouse and on to Robin Hood's Bay. The descent into the old smugglers' village is steep and despite it being a Monday in mid-October, a lot of people were about. Its setting, with its sandy beach which at low tide exposes the lower lias (limestone) beds, is very attractive. Considerable work has been carried out to halt the cliff erosion which began to threaten the village.

I was looking forward to meeting my secretary, Christine, and another great friend from home, Lewis, who were due to meet up with me sometime during that day. I thought that Ravenscar would be a likely place and so pressed on across the sand to Boggle Hole and so to Ravenscar.

When I arrived I couldn't see anyone and so I stopped at the café for a cup of tea and a sandwich. Suddenly I noticed Lewis's car go past. I rushed out but was too late and set off to catch them up. As I got over the brow of the hill I could see Lewis in the distance and his wife, Barbara, and Christine, on a park bench close by. Walking as quietly as possible I crept up behind them and startled them by suddenly sitting down as though I had appeared from nowhere! It was very good to see them and I tucked into home-made cakes which they had brought for me. By sheer chance Yorkshire Television caught up with us and did a film interview. It was then early afternoon and as I wanted to reach Scarborough that night, I agreed to meet everyone later, and carried on along the cliffs to Hayburn Wyke and Cloughton Wyke. Lewis walked the final few miles with me to Scarborough. There was little time to go through everything with Christine, but in the space of half an hour, the arrangements for my arrival in London, then under a month away, were finalized. I agreed to reach St Paul's Cathedral on

Wednesday, 8 November at one o'clock. I was now totally committed.

10.10.78

I left Scarborough early, in warm, hazy conditions. I was still walking well, feeling exceedingly fit, and thoroughly enjoying the walk. Rounding the South Sands of Scarborough I looked back to the impressive castle. I have always liked this town with its twin bays and Castle Cliff.

The eight-mile walk to Filey Brigg was marred by numerous caravan sites, but once I reached Filey and was able to walk along the clear sands it was better, even though the view round Filey Bay towards the Bempton Cliffs was lost in thick sea mist. To get to Bempton Cliffs and Flamborough Head I planned to go along the beach, but I knew that I had to be careful not to be trapped by the tide at a point where I couldn't reach the cliff tops. The most likely place to leave the beach seemed to be near Speeton, and this proved to be right. The mist had become very thick which was a pity as I had never been there before and was looking forward to walking these cliffs and perhaps seeing a little of the sea bird population. What I could see of the vertical chalk cliffs from the viewing platforms was impressive and I made a mental note to return one day. The cliffs reach a maximum height of 420 feet and are an RSPB reserve. During the summer months the ledges are full of guillemots, razorbills, puffins, kittiwakes, gannets and rock doves, but because it was late, I saw only a few gannets and their young. It is estimated that as many as 40,000 pairs of kittiwakes occupy the cliff. They are a very clean sea bird and instead of making do with a ledge for their nest, they build a mud nest onto the vertical cliff face. It is made deep enough so that the two or three chicks which stay inside for about forty days do not fall out.

As I continued along the cliffs, the sound of the Flamborough Head foghorn became more noticeable. Darkness descended as I passed Selwicks Bay, but I was still determined to get to Bridlington even though I estimated it would take me another two hours to get there. Fortunately the footpath was clear and very well maintained, with hand rails and steps for all the uphill sections. At 8.30 p.m. I reached the town centre and found somewhere to stay before dashing out to eat a fish supper.

11.10.78

I left Bridlington in very hot sunshine; in fact the temperature rose to over 70°F that day. We were enjoying a remarkable Indian summer and I couldn't help but smile when I saw people sunbathing; it seemed ridiculous so late in the year. I was still wearing my shorts (the same pair that I had worn since March) and was walking in shirt sleeves.

From Bridlington the coast changed dramatically. The tall rugged cliffs and undulating ground gave way to flat coastline with low cliffs of soil which crumbled away at every high tide. Erosion is a major problem on this section of the coastline and I learnt that in some places as much as sixty feet of land has been lost in the last six years. But the beaches were marvellous, offering mile after mile of sand. A right of way runs along the cliffs and I followed it to Ulrome Sands, Skipsea Sands and on to Hornsea. In this small resort, made famous by its pottery, I called on the coastguard to see whether the Cowden Sands range was being used. Regrettably it was, and so I had to walk round it to Aldbrough. While I was in the station a policeman came in and joined us for a mug of tea. As we were talking a yellow RAF rescue helicopter hovered overhead and the policeman popped his head out to have a look. 'It's that bionic budgie again!' he remarked.

I walked round the ranges to the sound of gunfire, and by six o'clock reached Aldbrough. I needed somewhere to stay for I had a lot of telephoning to do, including my weekly radio broadcast. I couldn't find anywhere and eventually asked at the post office. After much thought they got in touch with some people near by and managed to fix me up with somewhere to stay. I was very grateful to everyone in the village for being so helpful. The problem of finding new accommodation every night was one of the things I just had to accept on the walk, but I couldn't have prearranged everything even if I had wanted to. At this stage I had to move inside and not camp because with London not far away, there was a lot of planning to be done which wasn't possible in a cramped tent in the dark. (It was now getting dark by 6.30.) I was also aware that with the end of the walk in sight staying indoors would help me begin to adjust back to normal life. But unfortunately it proved to have hazards of its own, for after moving into centrally heated houses I caught my one and only cold of the walk!

12.10.78

I went back to the shore from Aldbrough near Mount Pleasant Farm, and continued along the straight coastlines of the Yorkshire coast to Spurn Head. For four hours I saw no one as I enjoyed the hot sun and walked to Withernsea. As I entered the town there were numerous people about in summer dresses and others sitting on the beach enjoying the remarkable weather. Waiting for me was Tim Brown from my local newspaper, the *Morning Telegraph*. He walked with me for three miles while I traced the story of the walk for him. Near Holmpton we parted company and I raced on towards Spurn Head. Because the peninsula is so narrow I knew that I would virtually have to come back to the same point and so at Easington I looked for somewhere to stay and deposited the rucksack. Easington is one of the places where north sea gas comes in to be purified before going under the Humber to link in with the National Grid system. I found a guest house and the owners kindly offered to prepare a meal for me at 8.30 p.m. I had four hours in which to walk the fourteen miles to Spurn Head and back. I bought four bars of chocolate and set off.

Spurn Head is a remarkable spit of land. Often no more than 150 feet wide, it stretches three miles out into the mouth of the river Humber. It is a very popular bird observation point where many rare birds are sighted and passing migrants are watched. Much of the area is looked after by the Yorkshire Naturalists' Trust. Close to the point is the only full-time lifeboat crew in the country. I reached the point in the growing dusk and looked across the Humber to Grimsby and Cleethorpes, five miles away. To get there would actually involve the longest detour inland of the entire walk: to cross the Humber at

Boothferry Bridge and get back to the coast I calculated to be a distance of about 120 miles!

Turning back from the Head I reached the single track road and began to walk up the Humber to Kilnsea and back to Easington. I arrived at the guest house just after 8.30 p.m. and sat down to a delicious meal.

13.10.78

From Easington to Hull was mostly along the road and through the small villages of Patrington, Keyingham and Hedon. It was warm and misty, so there were no views and I could not even see across the Humber. As I walked through Hull I noticed the city's most well-known feature, the white and green telephone boxes of its own telephone system. I reached Blacks' shop a little after four o'clock and there waiting for me were a couple of friends who had walked with me on the Peakland Way. I accepted their kind offer of a bed for the night.

14.10.78

I left Hull in misty weather and began the long walk up the Humber to Boothferry Bridge and the river Ouse. A cat-walk was strung across the partly-built Humber Bridge and I tried to get permission to walk across. It would have been a sensational walk, several hundred feet above the river, but permission was denied. I carried on along the banks of the river to Brough, Faxfleet, and Blacktoft. From there, as there was no right of way, I had to move slightly inland to Yokefleet and Laxton. As I passed through the villages I learnt that the Boothferry Bridge was closed for repairs. Traffic was being escorted across the M62 road bridge, and foot passengers were being taken across by bus. The only way that I could get across the river on foot seemed to be by taking the rail bridge. So from Laxton I made my way along road and track to the Goole rail bridge. It was now dark, and it was a bit eerie walking through the fields and woodland, not knowing what might be lurking. I climbed up onto the railway line and approached the bridge. Hearing a train coming, I hid to let it pass. Along the bridge I could see an overhead signal box. I was glad it was dark for I

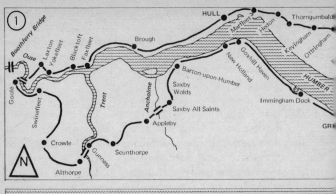

Map 1 labels:
- Boothferry Bridge
- HULL
- Marfleet
- Hedon
- Thorngumbald
- Keyingham
- Ottringham
- Brough
- Laxton
- Yokefleet
- Blacktoft
- Faxfleet
- Ouse
- New Holland
- Goxhill Haven
- Barton-upon-Humber
- Saxby Wolds
- Ancholme
- Saxby All Saints
- Immingham Dock
- HUMBER
- GRI
- Goole
- Swinefleet
- Trent
- Appleby
- Crowle
- Gunness
- Scunthorpe
- Althorpe
- N

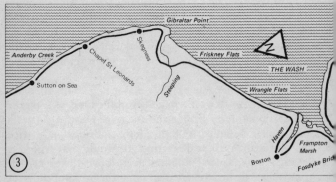

Map 3 labels:
- Gibraltar Point
- Anderby Creek
- Skegness
- Chapel St Leonards
- Friskney Flats
- THE WASH
- Sutton on Sea
- Steeping
- Wrangle Flats
- Haven
- Frampton Marsh
- Boston
- Fosdyke Brid
- N

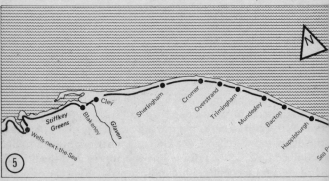

Map 5 labels:
- Cley
- Sheringham
- Cromer
- Overstrand
- Trimingham
- Mundesley
- Bacton
- Happisburgh
- Blakeney
- Stiffkey Greens
- Glaven
- Wells-next-the-Sea
- Sea Pa
- N

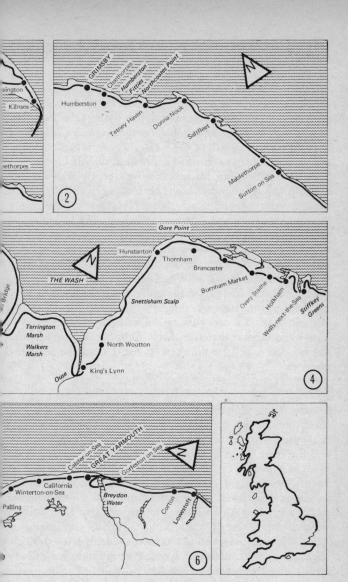

Map 2

sington
Kilsea
eethorpes

GRIMSBY
Cleethorpes
Humberston Fitties
Humberston
Northcoates Point
Tetney Haven
Donna Nook
Saltfleet
Mablethorpe
Sutton on Sea

②

Map 4

Gore Point
Hunstanton
Thornham
Brancaster
THE WASH
Burnham Market
Overy Staithe
Holkham
Wells-next-the-Sea
Stiffkey Greens
Snettisham Scalp
n Bridge
Terrington Marsh
Walkers Marsh
North Wootton
Ouse
King's Lynn

④

Map 6

Caister-on-Sea
GREAT YARMOUTH
Gorleston on Sea
California
Winterton-on-Sea
Breydon Water
Corton
Lowestoft
Palling

⑥

237

did not want to be caught. When the operator wasn't looking I quickly crossed the bridge and stopped under the signal box. Luckily, instinct told me not to continue, for seconds later I heard another train coming, and only just had time to take the rucksack off and press myself hard against the bridge before the train rushed past me. Then, hoping that the signal man would be watching its progress, I shouldered the rucksack and hurried over the remaining half of the bridge. My heart was thumping as I dropped down to the road and walked on into Goole.

By 8.30 p.m. I had reached the town centre and was just crossing the main roundabout when a police car pulled up. Feeling guilty about using the rail bridge, I immediately thought that they had somehow found out and had come to question me about it. But fortunately I was wrong. The sergeant had been following my progress through *The Great Outdoors* and wanted to introduce himself. I asked him if there was anywhere to stay and he replied immediately, 'Of course, my house!' As I had passed his house two miles back, he took me there by car. After spending an enjoyable evening looking at the magazine and discussing the walk, he finally asked me how I had crossed the river. I told him that it wasn't by the normal route, and he didn't press me. I think he probably guessed.

15.10.78

After saying goodbye to my hosts and thanking them for their spontaneous hospitality, I set off for Scunthorpe. The route was a hard one for I had to cross several drainage channels and the river Trent in order to get there. It is about twelve miles as the crow flies but on the ground it meant a walk of twenty-two miles. I crossed the Swinefleet Warping Drain, two miles from Goole, and headed southwards across marshland to Crowle. I had last been there in the spring of 1975 when I walked from Norwich Cathedral to Durham Cathedral, via York Minster. Just south of Crowle I suddenly felt extremely tired, though I couldn't understand why. Finding a railway arch, I fell asleep beside the road and woke up half an hour later to find it pouring with rain. I pressed on over Hatfield Waste

Drain and the Three Rivers to the road and rail bridge at Gunness across the Trent. Four miles later I was in Scunthorpe.

Soaked through, I decided I had better find somewhere to stay. Although I was given several addresses, I drew a blank each time. In the end I was told of a place opposite the police station, which I then discovered was the local doss house! About twenty-five of us were staying there, ranging from down-and-outs to the rather more well-off with a Jaguar outside. The three-course meal cost just 50p. It was all very strange, but I was thankful to have found somewhere to stay.

16.10.78

I was away early in the morning for I planned to get to Immingham Dock by nightfall, thirty-six miles away. From Scunthorpe I walked through British Steel's Frodingham works to Appleby. There I followed a lane, which later developed into a farm track, to cross the New River Ancholme to get to Saxby All Saints. The area is intensively farmed and everyone was out in the fields getting in the sugar beet crops; the harvesting would last for several weeks. The machines used were very efficient, since they not only dug up a couple of rows at a time, but cut off the stalks and leaves and deposited the beet into an attendant wagon, too. From Saxby All Saints I crossed over the Saxby Wolds – it was strange to find a small ridge of land in so flat an area of countryside – and reached Barton-upon-Humber. With the drains and river of Humberside behind me, I could at last get onto the sea wall and begin the walk to Immingham Dock and Grimsby.

Soon after leaving Barton-upon-Humber it began to rain and got much colder. Had the fine spell gone? After fifteen miles of walking along the sea wall, with virtually no view, except the surrounding mud flats of the Humber, I neared Immingham Dock. Walking towards me was Ray Swinburn, whom I had narrowly missed meeting at Sourlies Bothy at Loch Nevis, and we walked together to the docks. Just as we arrived the lock gates opened, and so we had to do a three-mile detour to reach his car. I stayed with Ray that night and we spent an enjoyable evening sharing our interest in camping and walking.

I was particularly delighted to have completed my last major detour, up the Humber. I had now walked 6,014 miles and in three weeks' time I would be in London. It seemed unreal.

11. The Final Miles

17.10.78

The weather had not improved: there was low cloud, rain and wind ahead. I left busy Immingham Dock and continued round the sea wall to Grimsby and on to Cleethorpes. I was due to pick up my parcel of maps and dehydrated food from Cleethorpes post office, but when I rang to check, they hadn't come. Ray said he would check again and if there was a problem, would obtain the maps necessary to complete the walk. I met up with him in Cleethorpes and as the parcel still hadn't arrived, he had bought all the maps for me. He refused to accept any money and this generous act was indeed one of the nicest offers of help that I received. Without the maps I would have been in trouble.

After an hour with Ray I left to walk down the Lincolnshire coast to Saltfleet, where some old friends were waiting to see me. On the outskirts of Cleethorpes I walked across the north – south zero longitudinal line (the Greenwich Meridian). A sign stated that the South Pole was 9,895 miles away and the North Pole, 2,513 miles. Nearby I found sea buckthorn covered with both red and yellow berries. Two miles from Cleethorpes I passed the houses of Humberston Fitties, the last houses I saw that day.

I was walking around marshy ground with the exposed mud and sand stretching out to sea a mile away. From now on, apart from the Norfolk and Suffolk coasts, I would be walking beside a distant sea. No high cliffs, no breaking waves and no picturesque villages.

Two miles from Humberston Fitties, I crossed Tetney Haven in the pouring rain and followed the sea wall around Northcoates Point. This was not a right of way but to follow the coast as closely as possible I decided to risk it. The earth dyke was overgrown and I soon got very wet fighting my way through the tall grass. Signs read 'Danger keep out'. I pressed on and walked round the edge of a rocket range. About twenty rockets were on the launching pads, all facing east. I didn't take any photographs as I was rather worried about being seen and possibly being arrested. Just over an hour later I reached the sands of the Donna Nook bombing range. Fortunately there was no practice that day and I walked along its edge for six miles before leaving the shore and walking inland to Saltfleet to cross the river and meet my friends. They were a little worried as I was rather late, but I explained that I had long since ceased to worry about time and that there had been no need to worry. That night I sat down to a delicious meal while I chatted non-stop about my adventures so far.

18.10.78

I set off from Saltfleet to regain the coast down the eight-mile stretch of sands to Mablethorpe where I would see my friends again. It was a delightful walk, and as the warm, sunny weather had returned, I shed my anorak and walked in my pullover. My friends ventured a mile along the promenade with me and just before they left gave me a present – several days' supply of chocolate!

This area of the coast is very popular with Sheffield people and I met several from this, my favourite city. The sands are good and firm but they are broken up by rows of wooden boarded posts, or groynes, going out into the sea to restrict the movement of sand. This made the walking awkward as I had to keep striding over them, so I moved inland slightly to avoid them. From Mablethorpe I walked on to Sutton on Sea, Anderby Creek and Chapel St Leonards.

I carried on along the beach, heading for Skegness. I knew

that people from my own Dronfield Rotary Club should be there, together with the District Governor and representatives from the Skegness and Clay Cross clubs. They had set up a lottery on the time that I would arrive at Skegness Pier. I had given a time of five o'clock. I learnt later that by 4.45 p.m. they had begun driving up and down the road to find me. They hadn't realized that I wouldn't be walking on the road, and at just after five o'clock I reached the pier and, walking up from the sand to the front of it, startled the waiting crowd by 'appearing like magic'! The District Governor welcomed me and immediately asked if I would address the annual conference later in the year. I agreed but the idea seemed unreal and remote. It was lovely to see everyone after so long, and I stayed with a good friend that night after having dinner with them all.

19.10.78

Leaving Skegness, I headed southwards into the Gibraltar Point nature reserve, renowned for its sightings of migratory birds, from where I had to walk inland to cross the Steeping river near Clough Farm. The weather was mild but very misty and I had no views as I walked round this strange corner of Britain with its extensive mud flats. I saw very few people and didn't see the sea for three days. It was simply a matter of walking mile after mile of earth-built sea wall. The map was not always accurate as each year more and more land is reclaimed, but all the time I walked as near the shoreline as possible. I saw the odd grey heron and occasionally a farmer working in the fields. About fifteen miles from Skegness as I was walking beside the Friskney Flats, a farmer spotted me and left his tractor to come over for a chat. He was full of enthusiasm for what I had achieved and seemed delighted to have seen me. It was quite a relief to talk to someone!

I pressed on along the wall past Wrangle Flats and nine miles later reached the mouth of the Haven. There I had to make the first of several long walks inland around The Wash to cross a river – in this case a six-mile walk to Boston. The final three miles were completed in the dark and I meandered through the docks not really knowing if I could get out at the far end or whether I was trespassing. I had walked thirty-one miles by the time I reached the centre of Boston. The rotary club were waiting and took me to the Berni Inn, where they had arranged a room for the night. Things were looking up, this was my second steak in two days! Everyone kept saying 'well done, you are nearly there', but I tried to keep such thoughts out of my head, for I still had about five hundred miles to go.

20.10.78

As I left Boston I could admire the town with its well preserved character, attractive warehouses and busy river. Crowning it all is the famous Boston Stump, 272 feet high, and part of St Botolph's church. From the tower you can look down onto the site where St Botolph founded his monastery in AD 654. In 1620 people from Boston landed in America and founded Boston, Massachusetts. I was very taken with this market town, and made a mental note to come back and explore at leisure. I crossed the river Haven and travelled along the sea wall, past Frampton Marsh, and up the river Welland to Fosdyke Bridge.

Now that I was approaching the final stages of the walk, media interest was revitalized and people were coming out to interview me again. Waiting for me at Fosdyke Bridge was Richard Else from BBC Radio Derby; I had been phoning him every week with my progress report, and it was good to see him again (the last time we had met was near Llandudno in March). I felt in good form; stories of the walk just flowed out and in the end we recorded a thirty-minute programme. An hour later we parted, and I pressed on over the Fosdyke Bridge and back along the sea wall. In front of me was a twenty-mile section to the Nene Outfall Cut, which would lead me to Sutton Bridge where I could cross the river Nene. It was now one o'clock and I knew that it would be dark before I got there.

I plodded on along the walls; there were no views as mist still carpeted the area and the monotony was only relieved by the chocolate I was eating. After about nine miles a press photographer emerged with a rotarian who told me they had arranged for me to stay at the Sutton Bridge Hotel; at least I didn't have to look for somewhere to stay. By the time I approached the river Nene it was dark, which made walking the sea walls quite alarming for I had to struggle to see where I was going. After a while I heard some cattle and found I was walking through a very restless bunch of cows! By dropping off the top of the wall I could see their silhouettes and was able to walk through without bumping into them. Two miles from the bridge, just when I felt I was over the worst, I came to another herd. It was pitch black and I couldn't see a thing. I walked straight into a cow lying on the ground and am not sure which of us was more startled. Remembering my previous experiences I ran away fast. I reached the hotel at 8.30 p.m. after walking thirty-three miles. They very kindly cooked a meal for me and an hour later I was fast asleep.

21.10.78

I was up early, and as I could find no one about I left without seeing anyone, or having any breakfast though fortunately I still had a few bars of chocolate left. After crossing the Sutton Bridge I walked down the bank of the river Nene with a reporter from the *Eastern Daily Press*. Three miles later we reached the old lighthouse where Peter Scott used to live. Here he kept and made paintings of wildfowl and geese. As we stood there a runner appeared; he was running from Wisbech to the lighthouse and back – a distance of twenty-four miles. The three of us continued our separate ways and I began walking the sea wall around Terrington Marsh, and the aptly named Walkers Marsh, to the Great Ouse river and King's Lynn. There were still no views and so I saw nothing of the 300 square miles of shallow sea that make up The Wash. I reached King's Lynn in the late afternoon.

The town has always been a busy port and until the late eighteenth century it was the fifth largest port in Britain. Ships of up to 2,200 tons still dock there. The town is also famous for its Tuesday Market. In the north-west corner of the Market Place, set into a house wall, is a carved heart. According to legend a witch named Margaret Read was burnt to death close by and her heart is said to have burst from her body and hit this house wall.

It was a Saturday and the town was busy, so after looking round some of the older buildings, and walking through the new shopping precinct, I left to find somewhere to stay. That settled, I went along the road to a Chinese take-away and back at the guest house I sat down to a splendid meal of sweet and sour chicken.

22.10.78

A little before nine o'clock I was on my way down the Great Ouse and back onto the sea wall. I had never been in this area before and I was looking forward to getting to the Norfolk coast. First I had to negotiate the ten miles of sea wall which surround the eastern side of The Wash to Snettisham Scalp. There the mud flats gave way to shingle. Six miles later I entered Hunstanton and was greatly impressed with this resort, which is the only one on the east coast of England to face west. The sandy beach was excellent and from near the lighthouse I could admire the cliffs banded with chalk and red sandstone. Several hang gliders were getting ready to take off into the light wind. In front of me was a magnificent expanse of sand round which I walked to Gore Point and into Thornham.

By the time I reached Brancaster I had walked twenty-nine miles from King's Lynn, and wanted somewhere to stay. I had been told there would be several places, and as I had agreed to go out live with Richard Baker in the morning on 'Start the Week' I was particularly anxious to find somewhere with a phone. I continued following the footpath beside the marsh, and at Overy Marsh I was told that I would find somewhere to stay in Burnham Market. Again, my inquiries led to nothing. I made my way to Overy Staithe but had no luck there either. Feeling desperate, I headed for Wells-next-the-Sea. At ten o'clock, two miles from Wells, I reached Holkham, and saw the lights of the Victoria Hotel. They had a room! I had walked thirty-nine miles and after eating a round of sandwiches I went straight to bed.

23.10.78

I made my radio link-up and by 9.30 a.m. I was back down on the sands near Holkham Gap. The sun was out and blue sky appeared; it turned out to be a really fine autumn day. I walked round the sands and up the creek to Wells-next-the-Sea, a beautiful place with a small quay, an old granary and narrow streets. One of the main industries of the town is whelks and the town is the principal supplier to Britain. I continued on in my shirt sleeves, beside the creek and along the edge of the marsh, to Stiffkey Greens and Blakeney. Blakeney has always been a favourite Norfolk village of mine ever since I first saw it in December 1977 when I gave a lecture at a nearby school.

The weather was perfect and added to the charm of the scene: the boats in the creek, the flintstone houses and the narrow streets. The place was busy with bird watchers, all making for Blakeney Point to see the passing migrants.

Three miles later I reached Cley next the Sea. By the creek was the finest windmill I have ever seen; it was built in 1713 and is now a private house. I crossed the Glaven at Cley and made my way beside the marsh, and back to the sea. The sand had now given way to a shingle bank and I began the final seven miles of the day to Sheringham where I stayed in the youth hostel. On the way I passed the following notice in a field 'Entrance to this field is free, the bull will charge later'!

24.10.78

I left Sheringham in hot, sunny weather and continued along the cliffs to Cromer, five miles away. Cromer is a busy and attractive resort with many fine buildings and an imposing church. Its perpendicular tower, at 160 feet high, is the tallest in Norfolk. The beaches are extensive and, looking down from the cliffs, I could admire the pier which was badly damaged during the last war and has been completely restored. On the cliffs between Cromer and Overstrand, I came to the monument to lifeboatman Henry Blogg, 'one of the bravest men who ever lived', who died on 13 June 1954. I remember my headmaster reading a book about him and the work of the Cromer lifeboat, of which Henry was coxswain between 1909 and 1947. His array of medals for gallantry and devotion to service is unparalleled: three RNLI gold medals and four silver medals. During fifty-three years of service he and his crew saved 873 lives.

From Overstrand there is no official right of way but I pressed on along the cliff tops, looking down on the sandy beaches, as I headed towards Trimingham. From Mundesley I could have dropped down to the beach but opted instead to keep on the cliff as I hoped to squeeze past the Bacton North Sea gas terminal, where the smell of gas lingered in the air. At Bacton I abandoned my plans of walking any further that day as a film crew from BBC TV's 'Look East' appeared. Suzanne Hall, the interviewer, and I stood around the beach being filmed before doing a lengthy interview. We also did one for radio. By the time we had finished it was 5.30 p.m. and dark. I had walked only twenty miles, but seeing a guest house nearby, I called it a day.

25.10.78

I left Bacton early for I was determined to reach Great Yarmouth, about twenty-five miles away, by nightfall. The first part of the walk to Happisburgh was straightforward, beside the beach and groynes. Off-shore are numerous wrecks and many interesting items have been washed ashore. I continued towards Sea Palling and along an eight-mile stretch of sand to Winterton-on-Sea. The village of Winterton is slightly inland and was built in the eighteenth century, largely from ship timbers. It is reputed that in one gale about two hundred coal ships were lost just off-shore. It was very pleasant walking through the dunes to the north of the village, which now forms part of a National Nature Reserve, even though the weather was drizzly and miserable.

Three miles from Winterton I walked into California, a large shanty town of wooden holiday houses, before returning to the sands of Caister-on-Sea and Great Yarmouth. As the name implies, Caister was originally a Roman fort and town. It also boasts the first brick castle in Britain which was built by Sir John Falstaff in 1432. An hour later I walked in from the golden sands to Great Yarmouth, one of the most popular seaside resorts in Britain. I was glad to be there in late October for I had worried about walking through such well known resorts in the summer months. I went to the entrance to the Britannia Pier where I recorded my arrival time for another lottery. I noticed that I was beginning to feel tired; I had walked 3,000 miles without a rest since the fracture. I found the nearby youth hostel and stayed there.

26.10.78

It was still overcast but mild. After walking down the south beach of Great Yarmouth I had to double back on myself beside Breydon Water in order to cross it near the town hall, and so get to Gorleston on Sea. A good cliff path then took me past a holiday camp to Corton. Waiting for me there were a film crew from Anglia TV; London was now only twelve days ahead and I began to feel the pressure building up again. It took two hours to complete the filming and then I left for Lowestoft.

As I went into Lowestoft, I walked round the Ness, the most easterly point of Britain. The town has always been a busy fishing port and is now a major base for North Sea oil. Just inside the harbour part of an oil rig was being constructed. I couldn't linger because of the time lost filming, so after buying a few provisions I headed on down the Suffolk coast, having left Norfolk just north of Corton.

Two hours' walking took me to Kessingland Beach, a small but popular resort. It was late afternoon and I knew that if I carried on I would be stuck for somewhere to stay, for there was no village for eight miles. After searching unsuccessfully I inquired at the post office and they gave me an address to try near the church. On the way there, however, I was hailed by a local rambling group and fortunately one of them offered me accommodation.

27.10.78

The walking, as I headed for Southwold, was very pleasant. It was mainly along a shingle beach and I passed several small

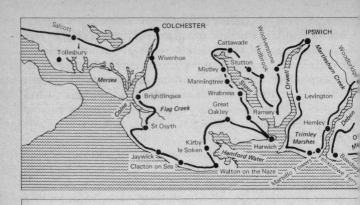

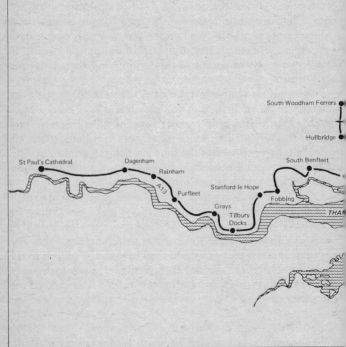

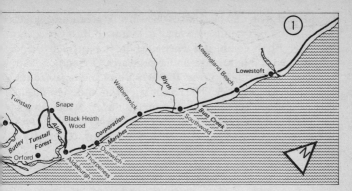

Broads and areas of woodland. At Southwold there were sands. The town in fact stands on a small island, with Buss Creek and the river Blyth completely encircling it. It is attractive and unspoilt, with a lighthouse and a large area of common land. I used the footbridge to cross the river Blyth and regained the coast near Walberswick. The recent televison interview meant that people were once more recognizing me. At Walberswick, I stopped to enjoy a cup of coffee with the owner of the Potter's Wheel tea room, who had been following my progress via 'Start the Week'.

From Walberswick I had to cross Corporation and Reedland marshes to reach the village of Dunwich, nearly four miles away. Just south of Dunwich I walked beside the 1,500-acre Minsmere Nature Reserve run by the Royal Society for the Protection of Birds. Although a Friday there were numerous bird watchers about. The reserve had a colony of avocets, the symbol of the RSPB. Bearded tits nest there and in March the booming sound of the elusive bittern can be heard. Access to the reserve was closed and all the lookouts were full, so I pressed on. Three miles later, I reached a direct contrast in coastal scenery, at the site of the huge Sizewell atomic power station, built in 1958. Another two miles took me through Thorpeness and, as darkness fell, I passed the well-preserved Moot Hall and went into the attractive town of Aldeburgh. Aldeburgh is famous for its musical festival, which was founded by Benjamin Britten, who spent many years of his life there. I thought I would have no difficulty finding somewhere to stay, but I couldn't have been more wrong; it took over an hour.

28.10.78

South of Aldeburgh is a thin spit of land, about eight miles long, which is owned by the Ministry of Defence. Entrance is prohibited and so I walked inland, following the Sailor's Path through Black Heath Wood, to the Maltings at Snape where many of the Aldeburgh Musical Festival concerts are held. The autumn woodland was lovely; the bracken was a burnt brown colour and the leaves on the trees were varying shades of yellow. Observing this, my fourth season, made me realize that I had come a very long way and that I was tired.

From the Maltings I headed through Tunstall Forest and Chillesford. There seemed no point in going to Orford, when I would have to retrace my steps to get to where I could cross the Butley river. Once across this river, I could at last reach the coastline again at Oxley Marshes. For the next few days I had to do large distances inland and only walked a small section of coastline. As I approached Bawdsey en route for the river Deben, I met a couple of bird watchers who told me they had been following my progress. I mentioned that I planned to reach Woodbridge that night and they promptly invited me to stay at their home nearby. It was such a relief to know that I could finish the day's walk and not have to search for somewhere! I was entering built-up coastline and, with the short daylight hours, had to walk long distances in the hope of reaching London on time.

Two miles from Bawdsey, just past the manor, at the mouth of the Deben, I headed up river to the bridge ten miles away. I reached it in the dark just after seven o'clock, after walking thirty-two miles. That night I weighed myself and was concerned to discover that I only weighed 9 stone 13 lb. I had lost 2½ stone in four months. This was the first time I had lost a significant amount of weight on a major walk, and I had certainly never dropped below ten stone.

29.10.78

I left my hosts after an enjoyable stay to walk through Woodbridge. On the quay was one of only three tide mills left in the country. At high tide a 7½-acre pond was filled with water, which, as the tide receded, was let out slowly to drive a sixty-foot wheel. Records show that a mill has been situated there since the twelfth century, though the present one ceased working in 1957. After Martlesham Creek, I could at last start heading down the bank of the river Deben to Felixstowe Ferry, opposite Bawdsey Quay. The final five miles were a nightmare as the sea wall, although a right of way, is almost impossible to walk. The shore is thick mud and so I moved in a little, but still had to struggle through the tall grass. The struggle was heightened by my extreme tiredness and by the fact that both achilles tendons were very sore, and had been for the past three weeks. But I was determined, with 6,350 miles walked and London just over a week away, that nothing was going to stop me reaching my goal. Talking to a passerby in Felixstowe Ferry I realized I hadn't put my watch back; it was the first day of Greenwich Mean Time.

Two miles of walking past the two Martello Towers took me to Felixstowe and the ferry point for the continent. After only five miles of coastline, I once again had to head inland in order to cross a river, so I walked along the sea walls of the river Orwell to reach Ipswich. From Felixstowe I could see Harwich just two miles away but I knew that it would be at least a day and a half before I got there. It was hardly encouraging when I arrived at Ipswich at eight o'clock, and with thirty-four miles walked from Woodbridge, to see that cross country Harwich was only eight miles away! Finding somewhere to stay in Ipswich was a problem, and after an hour's searching I walked into the centre and stayed at the Great White Horse Hotel. I was too tired to care.

30.10.78

After calling at the post office to collect my final correspondence, meet the press and do a recording for Radio Orwell, I began the long walk down the river Orwell and up and down the river Stour to reach Harwich; a walk of twenty-nine miles. Fortunately the weather was still mild and, although overcast, it was enjoyable walking by both path and lane. The highlight of the day was that on crossing the river Stour near Manningtree, I knew that I had entered my final county, Essex. I sat down near the river and ate a bar of chocolate to celebrate. At Mistley I stopped to look at the two towers which were originally part of a church designed by Robert Adam in 1776. When the church was pulled down the towers on the east and west side were left as the only examples of Robert Adam's ecclesiastical work in England.

A mile later I saw the first road sign to London: sixty-three miles away. Going round the coast, I walked 229 miles from that spot.

I reached Harwich in the dark and to my relief found somewhere to stay immediately. That night I delved deep into the rucksack and pulled out the two maps I had used to get out of London – I had carried them round the coast purposely for they were the only maps that I would need twice. It seemed very strange looking at them again after all this time.

31.10.78

I left Harwich early to begin the walk to Clacton-on-Sea. The weather was still very overcast. Shortly after leaving Harwich I joined the sea wall and began the tortuous route round Pewit Island, Hamford Water, Skipper Island, Horsey Island and Hedge-end Island to Walton on the Naze. I wasn't functioning very well. My thigh muscles were sore, my right ankle was stiff and both feet ached. Clacton-on-Sea was like a west coast Blackpool with its numerous bingo halls, amusement arcades and dozens of bed and breakfast establishments. I had no trouble finding somewhere to stay and after leaving the rucksack I went out for a fish and chip supper. Walking back to my lodgings I photographed, for the sake of contrast, the brightly lit amusement arcades.

1.11.78

After my weekly radio broadcast, I left Clacton-on-Sea in a rather emotional state. I was very tired and had mixed feelings about being so near the end of the walk; London was seven days away. The day's stop was Colchester, which I had to reach in order to cross the river Colne. Soon after leaving Clacton I had to take a detour, around Flag Creek, to reach Brightlingsea. From there, a long and difficult walk along the slippery and muddy banks of the river Colne took me to Colchester. I was surprised to find docks in the town and to see several small coasters being loaded with cargo. The river is barely wide enough for them and the open sea is ten miles away.

I was now drawing on my final reserves of will-power and strength. Inside I was in high spirits but, when I talked to anyone, tears formed because of the enormous strain I was under. I was physically drained and emotionally very turbulent. I knew that the end was in sight but I didn't want to get there; I had given everything to achieve my ambition and now an experience of a lifetime was about to end. I walked into Colchester like a robot and stayed at the youth hostel.

2.11.78

As I left Colchester I suddenly felt shooting pains in my right leg. I was alarmed, but walked on. Half a mile later I had pains in my left leg as well, and I began to wonder if I would actually make it. I walked on slowly, determined not to be stopped at the final hurdle.

Much of the day was spent walking inland to avoid the creeks round Mersea Island and all the creeks near Salcott and Tollesbury. I continued slowly to the banks of the river Blackwater and to Maldon where the largest collection of Thames sailing barges is moored. They are used in the annual races in July. I stopped for the day after walking just twenty-four miles.

3.11.78

As I approached Mundon Creek, I met Roger Smith, whom I had not seen since Edinburgh, a little over a month and 1,000 miles ago. I wasn't my usual cheerful self and he knew I was on my last legs. I tried to be cheerful but I was so torn between exhaustion and utter sadness that the walk was almost over, that it was difficult. We spent two hours walking the sea wall before he left. I learnt later that he told Christine I looked very tired and withdrawn and that my clothes were showing the signs of continuous wear. I was still wearing the same shirt and shorts that I had set out in so this wasn't surprising! Eight miles later I neared Bradwell-on-Sea where I was recognized by a couple who ran a small Christian centre. I had a snack with them, and, seeing my state, they suggested that I stay. That I couldn't do, because it was still too early in the day, so they very kindly agreed to pick me up from Sandbeach Farm, eight miles further round the coast.

I carried on along the sea wall to Bradwell Waterside and the nuclear power station at the mouth of the Blackwater river. From there I walked down a very remote section of the Essex marshes towards the river Crouch. At five o'clock, in growing darkness, I reached St Peter's Chapel. The chapel, often known as the Church of St Peter's on the Wall, was used as a barn until someone realized that it was the remains of a church built by St Cedd in about A D 650. It must be one of the oldest ecclesiastical sites in England. The nearby Othona Community use the church regularly. I carried on down the sea wall to the Sandbeach Outfall. As I reached the Sandbeach Farm track, the sky suddenly lit up as the setting sun tinged the clouds with red. My host was waiting for me at the farm and together we went back to his house. That night, the family lit their fireworks as 5 November fell on a Sunday.

4.11.78

The sun came out as I rejoined the wall from Sandbeach Farm and began the long walk along it to Burnham-on-Crouch. Essex has about 400 miles of sea wall but this includes islands such as Foulness. Eight miles along the wall I came to a group of workmen who were busy repairing the wall; it is a constant battle to maintain it in good order. The foreman spotted me and took a photograph. He had been expecting me and had his camera at the ready! After a welcome mug of tea I pressed on to Burnham. My legs seemed all right and I had no further twinges of pain.

To get round the river Crouch the only sensible way from Burnham was by following the lanes to Althorne and South Woodham Ferrers. From the map I saw it was possible actually to ford the river from there to Hullbridge and I hoped to reach South Woodham Ferrers that night. Two miles from there a caravanette caught up with me and the driver offered me a lift! It was the first time this had happened. I asked if he knew of anywhere to stay in South Woodham Ferrers and he promptly offered his house. He and his family rushed home and then walked back to escort me to their house. It was a wonderful evening and I sat down to a splendid meal. They had followed my progress right round the coast, so there was much to talk about.

5.11.78

They walked with me to the river Crouch, a mile and a half away, and waved goodbye as I paddled across the river. As it was low tide there was only a trickle of water. I rejoined the sea wall and began walking along the southern side of the river to Lion Wharf. There I began to use my London maps again. The sun came out and the temperature rose to 60°F; it was the warmest November day for twenty years. Not far from the wharf a photographer from *The Times* appeared and later photographed me sitting beneath a road sign saying 'Southend-on-Sea, two miles'. (In fact, to get there required a good ten miles of walking.)

Southend was technically my last town on the coastline, just as Herne Bay in Kent was my first. I reached Shoeburyness in the dark and across the river Thames I could see the lights of the Isle of Grain. In that moment the realization of what I had achieved flooded through me, and tears streamed down my face. For a long while I just sat staring at the scene, feeling intensely sad and humble. Half an hour later I walked into Southend and, needing to be with people to pull me out of my reverie, I booked into the first guest house I saw.

6.11.78

Before leaving Southend-on-Sea, I had to call at the post office for my mail and at a bank to replenish my dwindling money supply. I returned to the shore but, with the tide out and the yachts resting on the mud, it looked desolate. In front of me was the longest pier in Britain. I was just about to set off when a lorry pulled up. The driver leapt out and shook me by the hand. When I mentioned I was heading for Tilbury Docks, he offered to put me up for the night. I was most grateful and before I left he not only told me how to get there, but also handed me his door key, saying 'make yourself at home'. It was an extraordinarily generous and trusting gesture.

I left Southend-on-Sea in a happier mood and part of the

way up Benfleet I held a private ceremony on the mud flats. That morning I had put on my thirty-third and final pair of socks, and so I thought I would ceremoniously bury the penultimate pair as a symbolic gesture to the walk! This accomplished, I began to walk up the river Thames and reached my new-found friend's house at Stanford le Hope in late afternoon. That evening I rang all round the country to finalize details of my return to London. The police at Poplar were most helpful for I needed somewhere to stay the following night before the final few miles into the city. They arranged it all for me, and I was to stay at the Marshall Keate Inn, on the Isle of Dogs. The press and media now knew where I would be. All I had to do was to get there.

7.11.78

I didn't really have much time to reflect on the walk as I accomplished those final miles. I was extremely tired but still in good spirits. I walked thirty-four miles from Stanford le Hope, past Tilbury Docks and Grays and along the sea wall to Purfleet. Beyond were the Rainham marshes and firing was in progress. I had no alternative but to get onto the A13 road and walk along it. The road signs said 'London 13 miles'. In the dark I just plodded on, ticking the miles off as I went, getting more and more weary with every footstep. As I neared the inn the landlord was waiting to welcome me. Some reporters were waiting inside, and as I tucked into a huge steak I answered their questions. I also did a radio interview for BBC's World Service. I spent a couple of hours on the phone before trying to get some sleep, ready for the final few miles the next day.

8.11.78

I was up at seven o'clock and outside was bedlam: two radio vans and a film crew had already arrived. In the next three hours I did a major television story and twenty-five radio interviews. At around eleven o'clock, I set off to walk the final three miles to St Paul's Cathedral. On the way my friends Lewis and Barbara appeared and walked with me. All the while I could hear the whirr of the cameras. I arrived at St Paul's at midday, an hour earlier than had been announced to the press. This was a closely guarded secret for I had arranged to take Holy Communion quietly. The service moved me deeply, and I was close to tears as I thanked God for giving me the strength to overcome so many obstacles and to attain my goal. Before everyone left the chapel I was taken to the altar and prayers and a blessing were said for me. I was rather overawed by it, but I was grateful to be able to say thank you to God before I faced the media.

At one o'clock I walked through the undercroft and went outside, to come back up the cathedral steps as though I was just arriving. The police escorted me while the radio, television cameras and reporters recorded the event. As I approached the steps more than four hundred people were waiting and cameras clicked left, right and centre. Waiting at the top of the steps was Denis Howell, MP, the then Minister for Sport. I spent one and a half hours being filmed, interviewed and posing for photographs before getting into a taxi for a reception at the Cumberland Hotel.

The walk was over and a great chasm in my life opened up. It would take several weeks before I really started to adjust back to normal life. I am left with very deep memories of stunning coastline, friendly people, and the unique chance to see in one fell swoop the diverse character of the countryside and of the people of Britain. It is an experience I will never forget and something that I feel deeply humble at accomplishing.

Footnote
Five months from the end of the walk and thirty-six hours after completing this story, I climbed aboard a jet bound for America and the Appalachian Trail. At 2,049 miles it is the longest waymarked footpath in the world. Soon after my return I will be in the Alps to do a shorter walk before going to Scotland to marry Sheila in September.

Appendices

Appendix I

My Approach to Marathon Walking

In describing my approach to marathon walking in no way do I wish to appear dogmatic or belittle anyone else's achievements. It is simply that my methods have proved successful for me and have enabled me to complete all the long distance walks that I have set myself to date.

Planning and scheduling are an important part of my approach. I always plan my routes at least a year ahead. This is to give myself time to attune to the walk and also make sure it is prepared properly before I set out. I do extensive training walks and always break in the pair, or pairs, of boots that I will need with a minimum five hundred miles of walking per pair. The rhythm of the coastal walk, on which I used three pairs of boots, would have been seriously interrupted if I had had to break in each pair while actually on the walk.

I also make a daily schedule based on average mileage. This is important to me psychologically because it not only breaks down a long distance into feasible lengths, so making it less daunting and remote, but it also gives me a goal to attain each day. Without this the day would end with no sense of achievement. When I make out the schedule, and when I am actually on the walk, I do not take into account the contour lines, for the amount of climbing or downhill walking is of secondary importance to the goal I am striving for. To know that I still had three hills to climb at the end of a day could also make me feel tired and psychologically pull me down. I like to keep an element of surprise.

Before I set out I always ensure that the whole walk can be done on foot and that no other form of transport is necessary. Using any other form of motive power is unacceptable to me and would mean that the walk is not continuous. To make sure that I could complete the coastal walk on foot I devised a set of rules that would take me round the large number of 'obstacles' – such as estuaries – that I would encounter. On occasion I had to use a car to attend a charity function, but I always made sure I was returned to the spot I had been picked up from, to maintain continuity.

I prefer to camp out when possible, but never plan the sites ahead as it would be too restricting. On a walk of the variety and length of the coastal walk, I often found myself in a built-up area at the end of the day and so had to resort to guest houses or small hotels. I also used them if I needed to dry out my clothing and equipment at the end of a particularly wet day, and towards the end of the walk when I needed the light and space to make the final preparations for the arrival back to London.

On the walk itself I find it is important to develop an attitude of mind that will overcome the many problems and discomforts that will arise. For instance, I shut my mind off to the bad weather for if I worried or became depressed about each soaking, it would make those days seem very long and arduous and could even affect the next day's walking.

On all major walks (of over a thousand miles) I have always travelled by myself following the old adage 'he who travels alone, travels fastest'. This need neither imply a selfish attitude nor class me as a loner – I certainly have no wish to be the latter. But to find someone who walks at the same pace as myself, enjoys the same interests and who is totally compatible over a long period (in this case ten months) of mental and physical effort, is I think an impossible task. It puts a strain on the psychological factors of walking and also poses problems of loyalty if, for instance, my companion became ill.

I am constantly being asked if I get lonely or bored on these long walks, and the answer is simply 'No I don't'. For quite apart from trying to complete the scheduled mileage each day, I also take a great deal of interest in my surroundings: the geology, flora, fauna, historical buildings, churches, industrial archaeology, people and country life. By keeping my mind alert as well as constantly checking the route and looking at the map, photographing and observing through binoculars, I enjoy a full day.

Finally, I plan no rest days into my schedule. I find they do me no good at all, either mentally or physically. To rest properly would require at least a week by which time both fitness and mental concentration would be lost. To rest for just a day merely interrupts the rhythm of the walk. By walking seven days a week I can maintain my form and have found that I can generally cover about two thousand miles over a seventy-seven day period. With 50 or 60 lb of equipment I average about twenty-eight miles per day.

I can appreciate that to some this approach may seem too rigid. It has little to do with speed walking or with becoming a 'super-walker'. I only wish to emphasize that to me, my methods offer the ultimate challenge in long-distance walking.

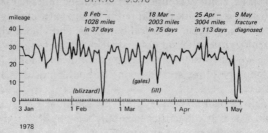

DAILY MILEAGE GRAPH
31.1.78 – 9.5.78

mileage

8 Feb –
1028 miles
in 37 days

18 Mar –
2003 miles
in 75 days

25 Apr –
3004 miles
in 113 days

9 May
fracture
diagnosed

(blizzard)

(gales)

(ill)

3 Jan   1 Feb   1 Mar   1 Apr   1 May

1978

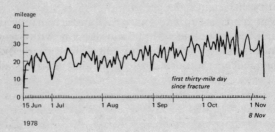

DAILY MILEAGE GRAPH
15.6.78 – 8.11.78

mileage

first thirty-mile day
since fracture

15 Jun   1 Jul   1 Aug   1 Sep   1 Oct   1 Nov

8 Nov

1978

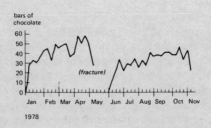

CHOCOLATE CONSUMPTION

bars of
chocolate

(fracture)

Jan Feb Mar Apr May Jun Jul Aug Sep Oct Nov

1978

266

Appendix II

Human Performance

Before I embarked on the coastal walk I had done several walks of 1,000 and 2,000 miles. Based on these experiences I knew that I needed to walk 500 miles before I even began to get into my stride, that at 1,000 miles I was attuned to what I was doing, but that I did not reach my peak until 1,500 miles. From that moment on I was capable of walking long distances daily.

The big question on the coastal walk was how was I going to react after 2,000 miles and would I reach a stage when I became fed up with walking? To answer the second part first I can definitely say that at no time on the 7,000-mile walk did I get fed up with walking. The first part is not so straightforward. Looking back and based on the graphs of my performance, I feel I reached my peak at 2,000 miles and held it until 2,500 miles. From then on it became a struggle to maintain 28 miles per day. By the time I had reached 3,000 miles I felt very tired and drained, and it was mainly my singlemindedness that drove me on to do 3,300 miles in 126 days. At that point I discovered I had pushed the body beyond the limit and I experienced the fatigue fracture; I suppose it acted as a safety valve.

Looking at the graph, it is interesting to see that the second half of the walk, the 3,700 miles back to London, followed a similar pattern. Because of my injured foot it took several weeks before I began to average 20 miles per day. Progress was steady until I was back up to walking 30 miles a day. By the time I reached John o'Groats I had walked 1,500 miles and was only just getting back into my stride. In fact, it was not until virtually three months after restarting that I actually walked

30 miles in one day. By the time I had walked 2,000 miles from the Firth of Clyde I was once more walking anything up to 40 miles in one day. In other words I was back at my peak level. But two weeks from London I was struggling again and both feet complained badly. Four days from London, at Colchester, I had stabbing pains in my calf and thigh muscles and wondered whether I would make it. Again I was on the edge of the limit of human performance. I struggled on and reached London.

Based on my experiences it would seem that I should try to lower my average of 28 miles per day with 50 lb of equipment. After the fracture I tried not to walk as far each day, but I soon felt restricted and reverted to my usual routine. I find the whole question of human performance a very interesting one, especially as I seem to do better on each walk. On my first three major walks I walked 20 miles a day. My 2,000-mile walk averaged 25 miles per day and on my Land's End to John o'Groats walk I averaged 28 miles per day. I also find it very interesting, mentally and physically, that after the fracture when the chips were down, I walked 3,700 miles at an average of 25 miles per day, whereas up to the fracture it was an average of 26 miles per day.

Prior to the coastal walk the maximum I had covered in one day with 50 lb of equipment was 38 miles. This time I covered the same distance often and on two occasions did 39 miles. Normally when I stretch myself this far I struggle to do 25 miles the following day. However, on the south coast near Exmouth I did 38 one day and 39 the next, and during the course of that week I did 225 miles – an average of just 32 miles per day. Three weeks from the end I was regularly doing 210 to 220 miles per week.

A number of marathon runners who have tried to run more than 200 miles a week have experienced fatigue fractures in the leg or foot. From this it would seem that perhaps the 200 miles a week figure could be critical. I don't think the weight of the rucksack adds greatly to the strain involved. Perhaps in future I will aim to walk 190 miles a week on average – just over 27 miles per day – but I won't know the answer until I've completed my next walk!

Appendix III

Equipment

The following is a list of all the equipment I used on the walk, together with comments on its performance. It was all new but my selection was usually based on past experience.

Tent: Blacks' Marriott Kamplite, made from rip-stop nylon inner and outer. Basically it was a standard tent but with an inner line for hanging clothes and double rings on the flysheet for extra strength. Out of 270 days on the walk I slept 170 of them in the tent in all weathers. It functioned very well indeed and did not leak once. The flysheet faded as the days passed and the only other visible signs of wear were the rubber rings on the flysheet which began to perish.

Rucksack: Berghaus Cyclops Serac No. 3. I have used this model of rucksack for the last three years, and personally I have never carried a load so comfortably upon my back. At first I used the very latest model available at the time (1978) but after 2,000 miles I found I was getting stomach ache. This was caused by the shoulder strap dimension which had been lengthened. At Tenby I changed rucksacks to the 1977 model and used it for the next 5,000 miles. I had used this sack for my 1977 training walks and altogether it did more than 8,000 miles before I 'retired' it. Apart from some of the straps fraying and the material fading it is still in remarkably good order.

Boots: Berghaus Scarpa Monte Rosa. I used three pairs, each of which had been broken in by 500 miles' walking. The first pair I wore to destruction (3,800 miles). The other two pairs were worn for 2,000 miles each. They were by far the most comfortable boot I have ever worn. I rarely got blisters and even breaking them in was a pleasure not a task. After about 2,500 miles the soles of the boot were very smooth and the heels worn through. The main damage to the boots was inside and around the heel. The inner leather wore through, so too did the padding to the outer leather.

Socks: Blacks' Norwegian Woollen Rag Socks. I used two pairs – an ankle pair underneath a pair of long hose with elasticated top. The elastic top prevented small stones from getting inside. Because I was walking anything up to twelve hours a day it was virtually impossible to wash them, and so I generally wore them for about three weeks, by which time they were very thin on the heels, and then threw them away. I wore out a total of thirty-three pairs.

Trousers: I had one pair of breeches and two pairs of shorts which were made specially for me by Clarke's, 'Craghoppers'. During January and February I wore the breeches which were perfect and withstood numerous soakings. From the beginning of March onwards I wore shorts and in fact wore the same pair for the next eight months. The only visible sign of wear was some fraying where friction had worn them through.

Shirts: I used two cotton shirts. I kept one for best and the other I wore for about nine months during which time it only had one wash! I tried to wear woollen shirts but they irritated my skin.

Pullover: Blacks' Norwegian. I wore the same pullover throughout the walk. After nine months of continuous wear several holes appeared, but this was caused by the constant rubbing of the cameras. It was warm in winter and like the shirts it was only washed once.

Anorak: Blacks' Ventile Highland Jacket. A really excellent item of clothing with plenty of pockets for maps, films, compass, whistle, cheque book and chocolate. Made with a cotton inner and a ventile outer, the garment with hood was both windproof and showerproof. In the final stages the full length zip began to wear, but after 7,000 miles who can complain?

Cagoule: Blacks' Grampian. I used two of these and although

I generated a lot of heat inside they kept the rain out. I also tested two Mistral Gore-Tex jackets by Berghaus. Both took a considerable hammering and I was unable to wash them. For me the material did not breathe but I think my test was unfair to the properties of Gore-Tex. It is a material I would like to test further before coming to any real conclusions.

Duvet: Blacks' Snowgoose. I carried and used this garment until the end of April. It was a splendid item of clothing and was essential in the cold weather that I experienced. I was very impressed by it and liked the outside pockets and the inner ones which were just the right size for an Ordnance Survey map. I also liked the waist band inside which made me feel very snug and warm.

Sleeping bags: As I would be walking through the seasons I used three different weights.

1. Blacks' Icelandic Mummy with 2 lb of duck down. A very warm bag which I used from January to early May. I felt the cold once, on the very coldest night.
2. Blacks' Tromso with $1\frac{1}{2}$ lb of duck down. I used this one in the autumn from September onwards and found it was just right for the colder temperature of that time of the year.
3. Blacks' Backpacker with $\frac{3}{4}$ lb of white goose down. I used this for four months right through the summer. Although very light I was impressed by its warmth and I couldn't have wished for a better bag.

Blacks' longlife Candles: During the winter months and autumn I used thirty longlife candles in the tent to cook and read by. On average they lasted eight hours and were better than using torches.

Stoves: During the winter months I used a Trangia stove burning methylated spirits. I liked the stove very much and it was very efficient. My only criticism was that it blackened the pans and was very messy to clean every morning. From early April onwards I used a Camping Gaz Globetrotter stove and eighty GT gas cylinders. At first the one-pint pans seemed too small but I soon adapted to them and in the end thought that the stove and size were ideal for one person. It operated faultlessly throughout the walk.

Odds and ends: I carried a first aid kit and elastoplast, crepe bandages, antiseptic cream, scissors, and aspirins. I also had a small torch, pedometer, whistle, jiffy can-opener, a Silva 4L compass, spoon and knife, toothpaste and brush, towel and sewing kit.

Food: Breakfast: this generally consisted of Alpen and a mug of tea. I estimate that I ate about 60 lb of cereal.

Lunch: I did not normally stop during the day, preferring to eat bars of chocolate or packets of Dextrosol. I ate the equivalent of 1,511 2 oz bars of chocolate.

Evening meal: I would usually drink a pint of milk before putting up the tent and often drink another before going to sleep. Altogether I drank 529 pints of milk. A typical evening meal would be a pint of soup, a tin of Irish stew or dehydrated meal, a tin of fruit or dehydrated dessert, a mug of tea and half a packet of biscuits.

I ate about 120 lb of sugar, drank 260 pints of soup, 150 tins of stew and fruit and 153 packets of biscuits. I also ate 120 dehydrated main meals and desserts made by Raven Foods. I selected about ten of each variety before I set off and packed them in parcels for sending on to the post offices along the way. Often I went six days on dehydrated food but when I could, I broke my routine and bought something locally. I found all the dehydrated meals very tasty and satisfying.

Daily Schedule (also Index)

To use this schedule as an index first look up the place name and then cross reference the date on the left-hand side of the page with those in the text.

Date	Route	Mileage	
3.1.78	St Paul's Cathedral – Mansion House – Tower Bridge – Southwark Park – Greenwich Park – Greenwich – Eltham Common – Welling – Bexley – Crayford – Dartford – Stone – Swanscombe – Northfleet – Gravesend	30	30
4.1.78	Gravesend – River Thames – Cliffe Marshes – Halston Marshes – St Mary's Marshes – Avery Farm – All Hallows – Lower Stoke – Stoke – North Street – Hoo – Findsbury – Strood	30	60
5.1.78	Wainscott – Strood – Rochester – Grange – Lower Rainham – Otterham Quay – Upchurch – Lower Halstow – Iwade – Grovehurst – Sittingbourne – Tonge – Blacketts – Conyer – Jarman's boatyard	26	86
6.1.78	Conyer – South Deep – Oare – Faversham – Nagden – Cleve Marshes – Seasalter – Whitstable – Swalecliffe – Herne Bay	25	111
7.1.78	Herne Bay – Reculver – Birchington – Westgate on Sea – Margate – North Foreland – Broadstairs – Ramsgate – Pegwell Bay	25	136
8.1.78	Pegwell Bay – Sandwich – Sandwich Bay – Deal – Walmer – Oldstairs Bay – St Margaret's Bay – Dover	25	161

Date	Route		Mileage
9.1.78	Dover – Shakespeare Cliff – Folkestone – Hythe – Dymchurch – St Mary's Bay	24	185
10.1.78	St Mary's Bay – Littlestone-on-Sea – Greatstone-on-Sea – Lydd-on-Sea – Lydd – The Forelands – Broomhill Sands – Camber – River Rother – Rye – Camber Castle – Winchelsea Beach	25	210
11.1.78	Winchelsea Beach – Cliff End – Fairlight Cove – Covehurst Bay – Hastings – West Marina – Bexhill – Norman's Bay – Pevensey Bay – Langney Point – Eastbourne – Wish Tower – Latham House Hotel	32	242
12.1.78	Eastbourne – Beachy Head – Seven Sisters – Exceat Bridge – Seaford – Newhaven – Peacehaven – Saltdean – Rottingdean – Brighton	31	273
13.1.78	Brighton – Hove – Shoreham – South Lancing – Worthing – Goring-by-Sea – Angmering-on-Sea – Littlehampton – Middleton-on-Sea	29	302
14.1.78	Middleton-on-Sea – Bognor Regis – Pagham – Pagham Harbour – Church Norton – Selsey Bill – Bracklesham Bay – East Wittering – West Wittering	26	328
15.1.78	West Wittering – West Itchenor – Chichester Yacht Basin – Dell Quay – Fishbourne – Bosham – Nutbourne – Prinsted – Hermitage – Warblington Castle – Langstone	22	350
16.1.78	Langstone – Farlington Marshes – Portsea Island – Portsmouth – Landport – Stamshaw – Cosham – Portchester – Fareham – Brockhurst – Gosport – Alverstoke	30	380
17.1.78	Alverstoke – Lee-on-the-Solent – Hill Head – Hook – Warsash – Sarisbury – Bursledon	18	398
18.1.78	Bursledon – Hamble – Netley – Itchen Bridge – Southampton – Totton – Eling – Marchwood	21	419
19.1.78	Marchwood – Hythe – Hardley – Fawley – Ower – Lepe – Exbury – Otterwood – Beaulieu	22	441
20.1.78	Hilltop – Beaulieu – Bucklers Hard – St Leonards Grange – Lisle Court – Lymington – Pennington Marshes – Keyhaven – Hurst Bridge – Milford on Sea	23	464

Date	Route	Mileage	
21.1.78	Milford on Sea – Barton on Sea – Highcliffe – Mudeford – Christchurch – Hengistbury Head – Southbourne – Boscombe – Bournemouth – Poole Head – Lilliput – Poole – Hamworthy Upton	30	494
22.1.78	Upton – Lytchett Minster – Wareham – Slepe Heath – Bushey – Brand's Bay – South Haven Point – Studland Bay – Studland – The Foreland – Ballard Cliff – Swanage – Durlston Head – Seacombe Cliff – St Alban's Head	38	532
23.1.78	St Alban's Head – Kimmeridge Bay – Steeple – East Lulworth – Lulworth Cove – Durdle Door – Osmington Mills – Weymouth	30	562
24.1.78	Bowleaze Cove – Weymouth – Ferry Bridge – Chesil – Portland Bill – Fortuneswell – Ferry Bridge	22	584
25.1.78	Ferry Bridge – Chesil Beach – Abbotsbury – Cogden Beach – Burton Beach – West Bay – Wear Cliffs – Golden Cap – Charmouth – Lyme Regis	38	622
26.1.78	Lyme Regis – Landslip – Charton Bay – Seaton – Beer – Beer Head – Branscombe Mouth – Coxe's Cliff – Dunscombe Cliff – Sidmouth – Ladram Bay – Budleigh Salterton – Straight Point – Exmouth	39	661
27.1.78	Exmouth – Topsham – Countess Wear Bridge – Exeter Canal – Powderham – Starcross – Dawlish Warren – Dawlish – Teignmouth	28	689
28.1.78	Teignmouth – Labrador Bay – Maidencombe – Watcombe – Torquay – Hope's Nose – Livermead Sands – Paignton – Broad Sands – Brixham	26	715
29.1.78	Brixham – Berry Head – Man Sands – Higher Brownstone Farm – Kingswear – Raddicombe – Churston – Waddeton – Port Bridge – Aish – Fleet Mill – Totnes	26	741
30.1.78	Totnes – Ashprington – Tuckenhay – Higher Tideford – Capton – Dartmouth – Stoke Fleming – Strete – Slapton Sands – Torcross – Beesands	27	768

Date	Route	Mileage	
31.1.78	Beesands – Hallsands – Start Point – Lannacombe Bay – Prawle Point – Gammon Head – Mill Bay – Goodshelter – South Pool – Frogmore – West Charleton – Kingsbridge – Collapit Bridge – Batson – Salcombe – Salcombe Youth Hostel	33	801
1.2.78	Salcombe Youth Hostel – Bolt Head – Soar Mill Cove – Bolt Tail – Outer Hope – Butter Cove – Bantham – Aunemouth – Stadbury – Bridge End – Tidal Road – Bigbury – Bigbury-on-Sea	23	824
2.2.78	Bigbury-on-Sea – Ayrmer Cove – Fernycombe Beach – Wonwell Beach – Torr Down – Clyng Mill – River Erme – Efford House – Mothecombe – Stoke House – The Warren – Noss Mayo – Bridgend – Wrescombe – Puslinch – A379 – Brixton	30	854
3.2.78	Brixton – Spriddlestone – Season Point – Wembury – Staddon Heights – Turnchapel – Hooe – Laira Bridge – Barbican – The Hoe – Plymouth – Stonehouse – Devonport – St Budeaux – Tamar Bridge – Saltash – Landrake – Tideford	26	880
4.2.78	Tideford – St Germans – Polbathic – Tredrossel – Sheviock – Millbrook – Cawsand Bay – Rame Head – Crafthole – Portwrinkle – Downderry – Seaton – East Looe – West Looe – Talland Bay – Polperro	26	906
5.2.78	Polperro – Lantivet Bay – Pencarrow Head – Lantic Bay – Polruan – Pont – Penpoll – Lerryn – Trewether – Lostwithiel – Castle – Castle Dore – Newtown – Fowey – Polridmouth – Gribben Head – Polkerris – Par Sands – Carlyon Bay – Charlestown	38	944
6.2.78	Charlestown – Porthpean – Trenarren – Pentewan Beach – Mevagissey – Chapel Point – Gorran Haven – Dodman Point – Porthluney Cove – Portholland – Portloe	25	969
7.2.78	Portloe – Nare Head – Pendower Beach – Portscatho – Zone Point – St Anthony – Gerrans – St Just Lane – St Mawes	27	996

276

Date	Route		Mileage

Date	Route		Mileage
8.2.78	St Mawes – St Just Lane – Trewithian – Ruan High Lanes – Ruan Lanihorne – Little Tregerrick – Tresillian – Truro – Carnon Downs – Devoran – Penryn – Falmouth	32	1,028
9.2.78	Falmouth – Pendennis Point – Swanpool Beach – Maen Porth – Rosemullion Head – Porthallack – Durgan – Porth Navas – Nancenoy – Gweek – Gear – Manaccan – Helford	25	1,053
10.2.78	Helford – Manaccan – Porthallow – Porthoustock – Lowland Point – Coverack – Black Head – Kennack Sands – Cadgwith – Landewednack – Lizard Point – Lizard	26	1,079
11.2.78	Lizard – Lizard Point – Kynance Cove – Vellan Head – Mullion Cove – Polurrian Cove – Poldhu Cove – Halzephron Cove – Loe Bar – Porthleven – Trewavas Head – Praa Sands – Bessy's Cove – Trenow Cove – Marazion	31	1,110
12.2.78	Marazion – Penzance – Newlyn – Mousehole – Lamorna Cove – St Loy – Penberth Cove – Porthcurno – Porth Loe – Mill Bay – Land's End – Sennen Cove – Sunny Corner	28	1,138
13.2.78	Sunny Corner – Aire Point – Polpry Cove – Cape Cornwall – Zawn a Bat – Pendeen Watch – Portheras Cove – Porthmoina Cove – Porthmeor Cove – Gurnard's Head – Pendour Cove – Zennor	22	1,160
14.2.78	Zennor – Wicca Pool – Clodgy Point – St Ives – Carbis Bay – Lelant – Hayle – Gwithian Beach – Godrevy Point – Navax Point – Hudder Down – Reskajeage Downs – Portreath	29	1,189
15.2.78	Portreath – Porthtowan – St Agnes Head – Perranporth – Perran Beach – Penhale Camp – Holywell Bay – Porth Joke – Crantock Beach – The Gannel – Newquay	28	1,217
16.2.78	Newquay – Watergate Bay – Mawgan Porth – Park Head – Constantine Bay – Trevose Head – Harlyn Bay – Gunver Head – Stepper Point – Gun Point – Padstow	27	1,244

Date	Route		Mileage
17.2.78	Padstow – Old Railway – Wadebridge – Gutt Bridge – Carlyon – Rock – St Enodoc's Church – Polzeath – Rumps Point – Port Quin – Port Isaac – Port Gaverne	29	1,273
18.2.78	Port Gaverne – The Mountain – Port William – Boscastle	17	1,290
19.2.78	*Snowbound! Worst blizzards since 1947.*	—	1,290
20.2.78	Tresparrett Posts – Boscastle – Rusey Cliff – High Cliff – Crackington Haven – Long Cliff – Millook – Widemouth Bay – Bude	24	1,314
21.2.78	Bude – Northcott Mouth – Duckpool – Stanbury Mouth – Lucky Hole – Marsland Mouth – Nabor Point – Mansley Cliff – Speke's Mill Mouth – Damehole Point – Upright Cliff	24	1,338
22.2.78	Upright Cliff – Hartland Point – Titchberry – Velly – Clovelly Cross – Buck's Cross – Horns Cross – Peppercombe – Babbacombe Cliff – Mermaid's Pool – Westward Ho! – Appledore – Northam	28	1,366
23.2.78	Northam – Bideford – Instow – Fremington – Bickington – Barnstaple – A361 – Braunton – Saunton – Croyde	27	1,393
24.2.78	Croyde – Baggy Point – Woolacombe Sand – Woolacombe – Mortehoe – Morte Point – Bull Point – Lee Bay – Ilfracombe – Watermouth – Combe Martin – Great Hangman – Trentishoe – Heddon's Mouth	32	1,425
25.2.78	Heddon's Mouth – Woody Bay – Lee Abbey – Valley of Rocks – Lynmouth – Foreland Point – County Gate – Culbone – Porlock Weir – Porlock	28	1,453
26.2.78	Porlock – Selworthy Beacon – North Hill – Minehead – Blue Anchor Bay – Watchet – West Quantoxhead – East Quantoxhead	28	1,481
27.2.78	East Quantoxhead – Hinkley Point – Wall Common – Steart – Otterhampton – Cannington – Wembdon – Bridgwater – A38 – Down End – Pawlett – Huntspill – Highbridge – Burnham on Sea	31	1,512

Date	Route		Mileage
28.2.78	Burnham on Sea – Brean – Bleadon Level sluice gates – Uphill – Weston-super-Mare – Sand Point – Woodspring – River Banwell sluice gates – River Yeo sluice gates – Clevedon – Portishead	31	1,543
1.3.78	Portishead – Easton in Gordano – Clifton Suspension Bridge – A4 – Avonmouth – A403 – Severn Beach – Aust	25	1,568
2.3.78	Aust – Littleton Warth – Oldbury-on-Severn – Hill – Upper Hill – Blackhall – Ham – Berkeley – Wanswell – Hinton – Purton – Gloucester and Sharpness Canal – Shepherd's Patch	21	1,589
3.3.78	Shepherd's Patch – Gloucester and Sharpness Canal – Gloucester – Minsterworth – Westbury-on-Severn	23	1,612
4.3.78	Westbury-on-Severn – Broadoak – Newnham – Lydney – Aylburton – Alvington – Woolaston – Tidenham – Chepstow – Pwllmeyric – Haysgate – Portskewett	30	1,642
5.3.78	Portskewett – West Pill – Cold Harbour Pill – Goldcliff – Newport – Transporter Bridge – Fair Orchard – St Brides Wentlooge – Peterstone Wentlooge – Rumney	30	1,672
6.3.78	Rumney – Cardiff – Llandough – Penarth – Lavernock Point – Sully Bay – Barry Island – Bull Cliff – Porthkerry	22	1,694
7.3.78	Porthkerry – Aberthaw Power Station – Summerhouse Point – St Donat's Bay – Nash Point – Cwm Mawr – Dunraven Bay – Ogmore-by-Sea – Ogmore	24	1,718
8.3.78	Ogmore – Merthyr Mawr – Candleston Castle – Porthcawl – Sker Point – Kenfig Sands – Margam Sands – Port Talbot – Neath Bridge – A483 – Swansea	30	1,748
9.3.78	Swansea – The Mumbles – Coastguard Station – Langland Bay – Caswell Bay – Pwlldu Bay – High Tor – Threecliff Bay – Oxwich Bay – Oxwich Point – Port-Eynon Bay – Port-Eynon Youth Hostel	25	1,773

Date	Route		Mileage
10.3.78	Port-Eynon Youth Hostel – Port-Eynon Point – Overton Cliff – Common Cliff – Thurba – Kitchen Corner – Rhossili – Rhossili Bay – Spaniard Rocks – Broughton Bay – Llanmadoc – Cheriton – Landimore – Llanrhidian – Crofty	25	1,798
11.3.78	Crofty – Pen-clawdd – Vernel – Yspitty – Llanelli – Pwll – Burry Port – Kidwelly – Llandyfaelog – Croesyceiliog – Carmarthen	33	1,831
12.3.78	Carmarthen – Cwrt Malle – Ffynnon – Pont-ddu – St Clears – New Mill – Cwmbrwyn – Pendine – Marros Sands – Telpyn Point – Amroth – Wiseman's Bridge – Saundersfoot	28	1,859
13.3.78	Saundersfoot – Monkstone Point – Tenby – Giltar Point – Lydstep – Manorbier	14	1,873
14.3.78	Manorbier – Freshwater East – Barafundle Bay – Broad Haven – St Govan's Head – Elegug Stacks – Castlemartin – Freshwater West – Angle	26	1,899
15.3.78	Angle – Angle Bay – Bullwell – Lambeeth – Hundleton – Pembroke – Neyland Bridge – Llanstadwell – Milford Haven – Hubberston	25	1,924
16.3.78	Hubberston – Herbrandston – Sandy Haven – Dale – St Ann's Head – Marloes Sands – Martin's Haven	24	1,948
17.3.78	Martin's Haven – St Brides Haven – Little Haven – Broad Haven – Nolton – Newgale – Solva	26	1,974
18.3.78	Solva – Caerfai Bay – Porth-clais – Ramsey Sound – St Justinian's Life Boat Station – Whitesand Bay – Penberry – Abereiddy – Porthgain – Trevine	29	2,003
19.3.78	Trevine – Abercastle – Aber-Mawr – Pwllderi – Strumble Head – Carregwastad Point – Goodwick – Fishguard	22	2,025
20.3.78	Fishguard – Penrhyn – Dinas Head – Fforest Bay – Newport – Pwll-coch – Ceibwr Bay – Cemaes Head – Poppit Sands – St Dogmaels – Cardigan	33	2,058

Date	Route		Mileage
21.3.78	Cardigan – Gwbert-on-Sea – Verwig – Felinwynt – Parcllyn – Aberporth – Tresaith – Penbryn Beach – Llangranog – Pendinas – Ciliau – Cwmtudu – New Quay	28	2,086
22.3.78	New Quay – Little Quay Bay – Llwyncelyn – Ffos-y-ffin– Aberaeron	10	2,096
23.3.78	Aberaeron – Aberarth – Llanon – Llanrhystud – Tynbwich – Morfa Bychan – Aberystwyth	20	2,116
24.3.78	Aberystwyth – Clarach Bay – Wallog – Borth – Ynyslas – Tre'r-ddôl – Furnace – Dovey Junction Station – Gogarth Halt – Penhelig – Aberdovey	25	2,141
25.3.78	Aberdovey – Bron-y-Môr – Aber Dysynni – Tonfanau – Llangelynin – Llwyngwril – Fairbourne – Morfa Mawddach Station – Toll Bridge – Barmouth – Llanaber – Tal-y-Bont – Dyffryn – Llanbedr	28	2,169
26.3.78	Llanbedr – Llanfair – Harlech – Llanfihangel-y-traethau – Llandecwyn Station – Toll Bridge – Penrhyndendraeth – Minffordd – Toll Bridge – Portmadoc – Morfa Bychan – Criccieth – Llanystumdwy – Afon Wen – Butlin's Camp	26	2,195
27.3.78	Butlin's Camp – Pwllheli – Traeth Crugan – Llanbedrog – Abersoch – Marchros – Llanengan – Hell's Mouth – Treheli – Blawdty – Aberdaron	28	2,223
28.3.78	Aberdaron – Port Meudwy – Gwyddel – Llanllawen – Anelog – Carreg – Porthor (Whistling Sands) – Port Iago – Porth Tŷ-Mawr – Porth Colmon – Porth Towyn – Porth Dinllaen – Porth Nefyn – Nefyn	24	2,247
29.3.78	Nefyn – Pistyll – Craig Ddû – Trevor – Gurn Gôch – Clynnogfawr – Aberdesach – Pontlyfni – Penygroes – Talysarn – Nanlle – Drws-y-Coed – Llyn Cwellyn – Snowdon Ranger Youth Hostel	27	2,274
30.3.78	Snowdon Ranger Youth Hostel – Snowdon Ranger Path – Snowdon – Snowdon Ranger Youth Hostel – Drwy-y-Coed – Nantle – Talysarn – Penygroes – Dinas Dinlle	25	2,299
31.3.78	Dinas Dinlle – Morfa Dinlle – Saron – Ysgubor Isaf – Caernarvon – Port Dinorwic – Menai Bridge – Bangor	21	2,320

Date	Route		Mileage
1.4.78	Bangor – Penrhyn Castle – Aber – Llanfairfechan – Penmaenmawr – Penmaen-bach Point – Conwy Morfa – Bodlondeb – Conwy – Deganwy – Llandudno	26	2,346
2.4.78	Llandudno (West) – Marine Drive (Great Ormes Head) – Llandudno (East) – Penrhyn – Rhos-on-Sea – Colwyn Bay – Llanddulas – Abergele Roads – Kinmel Bay – Rhyl	26	2,372
3.4.78	Rhyl – Prestatyn – Point of Ayr – Coal Mine – Ffynnongroew – Mostyn – Greenfield – Bagillt – Flint – Oakenholt	25	2,397
4.4.78	Oakenholt – Connah's Quay – Shotton – Queensferry Bridge – BSS Shotton – Burton Point – Denhall House Farm – Little Neston – Neston – Wirral Way – Parkgate – Heswall – Thurstaston – Caldy – West Kirby	23	2,420
5.4.78	West Kirby – Hoylake – Mockbeggar Wharf – New Brighton – Egremont – Birkenhead – Tranmere – Rock Ferry – New Ferry – Port Sunlight – Bromborough – Eastham – Overpool – Ellesmere Port – Stanlow – Elton	30	2,450
6.4.78	Elton – Ince Marshes – Marsh Green – Frodsham – Runcorn – Runcorn Bridge – Ditton Junction Station – Hale – Speke – Garston – Aigburth – Dingle – Liverpool (Central)	28	2,478
7.4.78	Liverpool – Bootle – Crosby – Hightown – Altcar Ranges – Formby Point – Ainsdale Sands – Birkdale Sands – Southport	28	2,506
8.4.78	Southport – Banks – Hesketh Bank – Beconsall – Tarleton – Much Hoole – Longton – Hutton – Preston – A583 – A584 – Freckleton	29	2,535
9.4.78	Freckleton – Warton – Lytham St Anne's – South Shore – Blackpool – North Shore – Cleveleys – Fleetwood – A585 (Nautical College)	29	2,564
10.4.78	Fleetwood (Nautical College) – A585 – Thornton – Little Thornton – Shard Bridge – Hambleton – Staynall – Heads – Knott End-on-Sea – Fluke Hall – Pilling – A588 – Braides – Pattys Farm – Bank Houses – Crook Farm – Glasson	27	2,591

Date	Route		Mileage
11.4.78	Glasson – Ashton – Lancaster – Ovangle Farm – Oxcliffe – Heaton – Overton – Sunderland – Potts Corner – Ocean Edge caravan park – Heysham – Morecambe	25	2,616
12.4.78	Morecambe – Bolton-le-Sands – Lancaster Canal – Carnforth – Warton – Silverdale – Arnside – Milnthorpe – Heversham – Levens Bridge – Sampool caravan site	26	2,642
13.4.78	Sampool caravan site – Longhowe End – Meathop – Blawith – Grange-over-Sands – Kents Bank – Flookburgh – Cark – Holker Hall – Stribers – Fish House – Greenodd – Arrad Foot – Newland – Ulverston	28	2,670
14.4.78	Ulverston – Bardsea – Baycliff – Aldingham – Newbiggin – Rampside – Roa Island – Westfield – Barrow-in-Furness – Sowerby – Roanhead Farm – Askam in Furness – Dunnerholme – Duddon Sands – Foxfield – Broughton in Furness	32	2,702
15.4.78	Broughton – Lady Hall – Millom Marsh – Millom – Haverigg – Haverigg Point – Sands – Gutterby Spa – Selker Coastguard Lookout – Marshside – Eskmeals – Ravenglass	29	2,731
16.4.78	Ravenglass – Chapel Hill – Ross's Camp – Eskdale Green – Dalegarth – Woolpack Inn – Brotherilkeld – Throstle Garth – Cam Spout – Mickledore – Scafell Pike – Mickledore – Cam Spout – Throstle Garth – Brotherilkeld – Dalegarth – Eskdale Green – Ross's Camp – Chapel Hill – Ravenglass	34	2,765
17.4.78	Ravenglass – Drigg Holme Bridge – Seascale – Sellafield Station – Braystones – Nethertown Beach – Seamill – St Bees Head – Saltom Bay – Whitehaven	24	2,789
18.4.78	Whitehaven – Parton – Lowca – Harrington – Workington – Siddick – Flimby – Maryport – Brown Rigg – Allonby	23	2,812

Date	Route		Mileage
19.4.78	Allonby – Mawbray – Beckfoot – Silloth – Skinburness – Calvo – Abbeytown – Moss Side – Newton Arlosh – Angerton – Whitrigg – Anthorn – Cardurnock – Bowness-on-Solway – Port Carlisle – The Cottage camp site	37	2,849
20.4.78	The Cottage camp site – Glasson – Drumburgh – Burgh by Sands – Monkhill – Carlisle – Stanwix – Rockcliffe – Floristonrigg – Metal Bridge – A74 – Gretna	25	2,874
21.4.78	Gretna – Old Graitney – Redkirk – Browhouses – Torduff Point – Dornockbrow – Battlehill – Seafield – Waterfoot – Annan – Barnkirk Point – Newbie Mains – Powfoot – Moss-side – Priestside – Ruthwell – Stanhope	27	2,901
22.4.78	Stanhope – B725 – Bankend – Caerlaverock Castle – Scarn Point – Glencaple – B725 – Dumfries – A710 – Islesteps – Whinny Hill – New Abbey	25	2,926
23.4.78	New Abbey – Kirkbean – Southerness – Caulkerbush – Sandyhills – Port O'Warren Bay – Barcloy Hill – Rockcliffe – Kippford – Barnbarrock – Dalbeattie	26	2,952
24.4.78	Dalbeattie – Palnackie – Screel – Auchencairn – Balcary Point – Rascarrel Bay – Barlocco Bay – Orroland Lodge – Fagra – Dundrennan – Mutehill – Kirkcudbright	28	2,980
25.4.78	Kirkcudbright – Gull Craig – Senwick House – Ross Bay – Meikle Ross – Fauldbog Bay – Brighouse Bay – Borness – Muncraig – Kirkandrews – Knockbrex – Carrick – Sandgreen – Cally Mains – Cally Hotel – Gatehouse of Fleet	24	3,004
26.4.78	Gatehouse of Fleet — Skyreburn Bay – Dalavan Bay – Mossyard Bay – Ravenshall – Kirkdale Port – Carsluith – Creetown – Blairs – Croft – Blackcraig – Newton Stewart	24	3,028
27.4.78	Newton Stewart – A174 – Wigtown – Bladnoch – Kirkinner – Inerwell Port – Port McGean – Garlieston – Rigg Bay – Port Allen – Portyerrock Bay – Isle of Whithorn – Burrow Head camp site	31	3,059

Date	Route	Mileage	
28.4.78	Burrow Head – St Ninian's Cave – Lochans of Cairndoon – Back Bay – Monreith Bay – A747 – Port William – West Barr – Chippermore Point – Cock Inn – Mull of Sinniness – Stair Haven – Glenluce	28	3,087
29.4.78	Glenluce – A75 – A715 – Sandhead – Dyemill – Chapel Rossan Bay – Portacree – New England Bay – Kilstay Bay – Drummore – Cailliness Point – Maryport Bay – Portankill – East Tarbert – Mull of Galloway	28	3,115
30.4.78	Mull of Galloway – West Tarbert – Port Mona – Portencorkrie – Clanyard Bay – Port Logan – Drumbreddan Bay – Ardwell Bay – Float Bay – Knockinaam Lodge – Portpatrick (Galloway Point camp site)	27	3,142
1.5.78	Portpatrick – Black Head – Knock Bay – Broadsea Bay – Strool Bay – Dally Bay – Corsewall Point – Milleur Point – Lady Bay – Clachan Heughs – The Scar – The Wig	29	3,171
2.5.78	The Wig – Stranraer – Cairnryan – Finnarts Bay – Portandea – Currarie Port – Downan Point – Ballantrae	24	3,195
3.5.78	Ballantrae – Bennane Head – Lendalfoot – Girvan – Dipple – Turnberry – Maidens	24	3,219
4.5.78	Maidens – Culzean Castle – Culzean Bay – Dunure – Bracken Bay – Heads of Ayr – Cunning Park – Ayr Youth Hostel	20	3,239
5.5.78	Ayr Youth Hostel – Woodfield Beach – Prestwick Beach – St Andrews House – South Bay – Troon – North Bay – Barassie – Irvine Bay Beach – Fullarton – Nethermains – Stevenston – Saltcoats – South Bay	27	3,266
6.5.78	South Bay (Saltcoats) – Ardrossan – North Bay	3	3,269
7.5.78	*Immobilized at Ardrossan North Bay.*	1	3,270
8.5.78	Ardrossan North Bay – Seamill – Ardneil Bay – Portencross – Stoney Port – Poteath – Southannan – Fairlie – Monument – Castle Bay – Largs – Largs Bay – A78 – Meigle Bay – Skelmorlie Mains camp site	21	3,291

Date	Route		Mileage
9.5.78	Skelmorlie Mains – Skelmorlie – Wemyss Bay	5	3,296
10.5– 14.6.78	*Fatigue fracture diagnosed; retired to Drymen with right foot in plaster for four weeks and one week 'breaking in' foot after plaster removed.*	24	3,320
15.6.78	Skelmorlie post office – Wemyss Bay – Inverkip – Cloch Point Lighthouse – Gourock – Greenock	15	3,335
16.6.78	Greenock – Port Glasgow – Langbank – Erskine Golf Course – Erskine Bridge – Old Kilpatrick	17	3,352
17.6.78	Old Kilpatrick – Bowling – Dumbarton – Cardross – Ardmore – Craigendoran	17	3,369
18.6.78	Craigendoran – Helensburgh – Rhu – Shandon – Faslane Bay – Garelochhead – Mambeg – Greenlea – Clynder	15	3,384
19.6.78	Clynder – Rosneath – Rosneath Bay – Kilcreggan Cove – Peaton House – Trig (217 metres) – Lochan Ghlas Laoigh – Portincaple – Arddarroch – Glenmallan	22	3,406
20.6.78	Glenmallan – Craggan – Ardmay – Arrochar – Ardgartan	11	3,417
21.6.78	Ardgartan – Ardgartan Forest – Corran Lochan – Ardgoil Forest – Lochgoilhead – Douglas Pier – Cormonanchan – Carrick	21	3,438
22.6.78	Carrick – Knap – Finart Bay – Ardentinny – Gairletter Point – Blairmore – Strone – Kilmun – Dalinlongart – Sandbank – Hunter's Quay – Dunoon – McColls Hotel (West Bay)	23	3,461
23.6.78	Dunoon – Bullwood – Dunan – Innellan – Toward Point – Ardyne Point – Port Lamont – Loch Striven – Finnart Point – Invervegain – The Craig Bothy	20	3,481
24.6.78	The Craig Bothy – Loch Striven – Lochhead – Loch Striven – Ardbeg – Troustan – Baingortan – Coustonn – Strone Point – Bargehouse Point – Upper Altgaltraig – Colintraive	20	3,501
25.6.78	Colintraive – Auchenbreck – Auchnagarron – Ormidale – Lochead – Caladh Bay and Farm – Forest Trail – Rubha Bàn – Port Driseach – Tighnabruaich Youth Hostel	17	3,518

Date	Route		Mileage
26.6.78	Tighnabruaich – Kames – Blair's Ferry – Carry Point – Ardlamont Point – Kilbride Bay – Asgog Bay – Port Ghabhar – Glenan Bay – Ardmarnock Bay – Auchalick Bay – Kilfinan Bay – Otter Ferry	24	3,542
27.6.78	Otter Ferry – Largiemore – Lephinchapel – Lephinmore – Lachlan Bay – Leack – Strachur Bay – Creggans – St Catherines – Tighcladich	22	3,564
28.6.78	Tighcladich – Ardkinglas House – Cairndow – Ardgenavan – Dundarave Castle – Loch Shira – Inveraray – Dalchenna – Battlefield camp site	20	3,584
29.6.78	Battlefield camp site – Pennymore – Furness – Crarae Bay – Minard Castle – Loch Gair	17	3,601
30.6.78	Loch Gair – Port Ann – Ballimore – Lochgilphead – Ardrishaig – Brenfield Bay – Bàgh Tigh-an-Droighinn – Clach an Easbuig	18	3,619
1.7.78	Clach·an Easbuig – Stonefield Castle Hotel – Tarbert	7	3,626
2.7.78	Tarbert – Cruach Bhreac – Guallann Mhór – Cnoc na Mèine – Skipness Castle – Skipness – Sgeir na Luing	11	3,637
3.7.78	Sgeir na Luing – Claonig Bay – Port Fada – Crossaig – Cour Bay – Grogport – Grianain Island – Carradale	16	3,653
4.7.78	Carradale – Dippen – Waterfoot – Torrisdale Bay – Saddell Abbey – Saddell Castle – Ugadale Point – Black Bay – Ardnacross Bay – Lower Smerby – Campbeltown	18	3,671
5.7.78	Campbeltown – Glenramskill – Davaar House – Achinhoan – Ru Stafnish – Johnston's Point – Glenchervie – Polliwilline Bay – Macharioch Bay – Cove Point – Brunerican Bay – Dunaverty Bay (Southend)	19	3,690
6.7.78	Southend – Carskey Bay – Feorlan – The Gap – Mull Lighthouse – Corr Bhàn – Trig 289 – Cnoc Moy – Ballygroggan – High Lossit – Machrihanish	20	3,710

Date	Route		Mileage
7.7.78	Machrihanish – Machrihanish Bay – Westport – Port Corbert Bellochantuy – Dalkeith – Glenacardoch Point – Muasdale – Killean – Tayinloan – Ferry – Point Sands camp site	21	3.731
8.7.78	Point Sands – Rhunahaorine Point – Ballochroy – Dunskeig Bay – Clachan – Whitehouse – Rhu Point – Escart caravan site	18	3,749
9.7.78	Escart – West Tarbert – Avinagillan – Torintùrk – Dunmore – Ardpatrick – Ardminish – Loch Stornoway – The Coves – Kilberry Bay – Port Bàn caravan site	19	3,768
10.7.78	Port Bàn – Stotfield Bay – Ormsary – Loch Caolisport – Ellary – Balimore – Kilmory – Castle Sween	20	3,788
11.7.78	Castle Sween – Dunrostan – Daltot – Ashfield – Achanamara – Loch Barnluaggan – Tayvallich – Keillbeg – Port an Sgadain – Carsaig Bay	26	3,814
12.7.78	Carsaig Bay – Ardnackaig – Dounie – Ardnoe Point – Crinan – Islandadd Bridge – Duntrune Castle – Ardifuir – Benan Ardifuir – Port Mòine – Ormaig Bay – Kintraw – Ardfern	25	3,839
13.7.78	Ardfern – Duine – Kirkton – Craignish Point – Craignish Castle – Bàgh Bàn – Port Caol – Lunga – Asknish Bay – Kames Bay – Melfort – Kilchoan	22	3,861
14.7.78	Kilchoan – Degnish – Caddleton – Ardmaddy Castle – Clachan Bridge – Loch Seil – Kilninver – Loch Feochan – Cleigh – Kilbride – Lerags – Lochan na Croise – Gallanach Bay – Sound of Kerrera	22	3,883
15.7.78	Sound of Kerrera – Oban – Ganavan – Dunstaff-nage Castle – Dunbeg – Connel Bridge – Ledair – Benderloch – Tralee Bay camp site	15	3,898
16.7.78	Tralee Bay – Barcaldine Castle – Loch Creran – Creagan – Inverfolla – Rubha Garbh – North Shian – Port Appin	15	3,913
17.7.78	Port Appin – Portnacroish – A828 – Cuil Bay – Ardsheal – Kentallen – Rubh'a'Bhaid Bheithe – Collum Beg	15	3,928

Date	Route		Mileage
18.7.78	Collum Beg – South Ballachulish – Ballachulish Bridge – North Ballachulish – Onich – A82 – Corrychurrachan – Druimarbin – Fort William – Glen Nevis camp site	17	3,945
19.7.78	Glen Nevis – Ben Nevis – Glen Nevis – Inverlochy – Caledonian Canal – Banavie camp site	16	3,961
20.7.78	Banavie – Corpach – A830 – Fassfern – Loch Eil – Kinlocheil – Drumsallie – South Garvan – Duisky – Blaich – Achaphubuil – Trislaig – Stronchreggan	23	3,984
21.7.78	Stronchreggan – Inverscaddle Bay – Ardgour – Clovullin – Sallachan – Inversanda Bay – Camas Chil-Mhalieu – Ceanna Mór	23	4,007
22.7.78	Ceanna Mór – Kingairloch – Loch Uisage – B8043 – A884 – Clounlaid – Gleann Geal – Larachbeg – Lochaline – B849 – Achabeg	20	4,027
23.7.78	Achabeg – Fiunary – Glenmorven – Drimnin – Auliston – Portabhata – Doirlinn – Loch Teacuis – Rahoy – Kinloch	24	4,051
24.7.78	Kinloch – Beinn Ithearlan – Glencripesdale – Camas Salach – Laudale – Liddesdale – A884 – Strontian	22	4,073
25.7.78	Strontian – Camuschoirk – A861 – Resipole – Salen – B8007 – Camasinas – Laga Bay – Glenborrodale – Glenmore	20	4,093
26.7.78	Glenmore – Camas nan Geall – Maclean's Nose – Mingary – Kilchoan – Ormsaigbeg – Ardnamurchan Lighthouse	18	4,111
27.7.78	Ardnamurchan – Portuairk – Sanna Bay – Plocaig – Glendrian Caves – Fascadale Bay – Achateny – Kilmory – Swordle – Ockle – Acarsaid – Gortenfern – Arivegaig – Acharacle – Ardshealach Farm	25	4,136
28.7.78	Ardshealach – Acharacle – Cliff – Castle Doirlinn – Loch Moidart – Ardmolich – Kinlochmoidart – Kylesbeg – Glenuig – Samalaman – Glenuig – Forsay caravan site	16	4,152

Date	Route		Mileage
29.7.78	Forsay – Alisary – Loch Ailort – A830 – Polnish – Ardnish – Polnish – Prince Charlie's Cave – Arisaig House – Glen Cottage – Camas an t-Salainn	22	4,174
30.7.78	Camas an t-Salainn – Millburn Cottage – Rhue House – Trig 103 – Camas Leathann – Camas an t-Salainn – Arisaig – Keppoch – Portnaluchaig – Garramor Youth Hostel	12	4,186
31.7.78	Garramor Youth Hostel – Morar – Mallaig – Mallaigmore – Mallaig – Morar – Bracora – Loch Morar – Swordland – Tarbet – Kylesmorar	19	4,205
1.8.78	Kylesmorar – Ardnamurach – Finiskaig – Sourlies – Carnoch – Màm Meadail – Glen Meadail – Inverie	17	4,222
2.8.78	Inverie – Scottas – Sandaig Bay – Airor – Inverguseran – Croulin – Rubha Ruadh – Li	21	4,243
3.8.78	Li – Barrisdale Bay – Barrisdale – Caolas Mór – Runival – Skiary – Loch Beag – Kinloch Hourn – Lochan Torr a Choit – Gleann Dubh Lochain – Glen Arnisdale – Corran – Arnisdale	21	4,264
4.8.78	Arnisdale – Creag Ruadh – Màm an Staing – Upper Sandaig – Sandaig – Upper Sandaig – Màn Uranan – Eilanreach – Glenelg	14	4,278
5.8.78	Glenelg – Kyle Rhea Ferry – Ardintoul – Broch – Totaig – Letterfearn – Ratagan – Shiel Bridge	17	4,295
6.8.78	Shiel Bridge – A87 – Inverinate – Castle Eilean Donan – Dornie – Nostie – Kirton – Balmacara – Kyle of Lochalsh – Kyleakin (Isle of Skye)	19	4,314
7.8.78	Kyleakin – Kyle of Lochalsh – Drumbuie – Duirnish – Plockton – Duncraig Castle – Achmore – Stromeferry	14	4,328
8.8.78	Stromeferry – Ardnarff – A890 – Attadale – Strathcarron – A896 – Lochcarron – Strome Castle – Leacanashie – Reraig Achintraid – Ardarroch – Kishorn Post Office	21	4,349
9.8.78	Kishorn – Tornapress – Loch Kishorn Site – Airigh-drishaig – Loch Airigh Alasdair – Toscaig – Culduie – Camusterrach – Milton – Applecross	16	4,365

Date	Route		Mileage
10.8.78	Applecross – Cruarg – Sand – Salacher – Lonbain – Kalnakill – Cuaig – Fearnmore – Fearnbeg – Kenmore – Ardheslaig – Inverbain – A896 – Shieldaig	25	4,390
11.8.78	Shieldaig – Upper Loch Torridon – Annat – Torridon – Inveralligin – Port Laire – Loch Diabaig – Lower Diabaig – Craig Youth Hostel	20	4,410
12.8.78	Craig – Redpoint – South Erradale – Opinan – Port Henderson – Badachro – Shieldaig – Kerrysdale – Charlestown – Gairloch	18	4,428
13.8.78	Gairloch – Strath – Carn Dearg – Big Sand – Rubha Bàn – North Erradale – Peterburn – Melvaig – Rubha Reidh	13	4,441
14.8.78	Rubha Reidh – Camas Mór – Loch an Draing – Loch Sguod – Midtown – Naast – Poolewe – Inverewe – Tournaig – Drumchork – Aultbea Youth Hostel	20	4,461
15.8.78	Aultbea – Mellon Charles – Slaggan Bay – Greenstone Point – Opinan – Mellon Udrigle – Laide – Second Coast – Gruinard House	22	4,483
16.8.78	Gruinard House – Carn Dearg an Droma – Badluarach – Durnamuck – Badcaul – Camus-magaul – Dundonnell – Badrallach	19	4,502
17.8.78	Badrallach – Scoraig – Cailleach Head – Annat Bay – Badrallach – Loggie – Letters – Head of Loch Broom	22	4,524
18.8.78	Loch Broom – Ullapool – Keanchulish – Geodha Mór – Achduart – Acheninver Youth Hostel	22	4,546
19.8.78	Acheninver – Achiltibuie – Polbain – Altandhu – Reiff – Rubha Coigeach – Achnahaird Bay – Garvie Bay – Inverpolly Salmon Farm	25	4,571
20.8.78	Inverpolly Salmon Farm – Polly More – Loch Kirkaig – Strathan – Lochinver – Baddidarach – Ardroe – Achmelvich – Clachtoll	19	4,590
21.8.78	Clachtoll – Stoer – Balchladich – Raffin – Lighthouse – Point of Stoer – Culkein – Clashnessie Bay – Oldany – Drumbeg – Nedd	20	4,610

Date	Route		Mileage
22.8.78	Nedd – Gleann Ardbhair – Loch Unapool – Loch na Gainmhich – Eas a Chuál Aluinn Waterfall – Loch Beag – Glencoul	18	4,628
23.8.78	Glencoul – Loch Glendhu – Glendhu – Kylestrome – Kylesku Ferry – Kylestrome – Duartmore Bridge – Duarbeg – Lower Badcall – Scourie	20	4,648
24.8.78	Scourie – Lochan Bealach an Eilein – Tarbet – Fanagmore – Foindle – Lochan an Fhéidh – A894 – Laxford Bridge – Skerricha Loch Inchard – Rhiconich – Achriesgill – Badcall Kinlochbervie – Oldshoremore – Sheigra Beach	25	4,673
25.8.78	Sheigra Bay – Am Buachaille – Sandwood Bay – Bay of Keisgaig – Am Bodach – Cape Wrath – Kearvaig Bay – Clò Mór – Daill	25	4,698
26.8.78	Daill – Ferry Point – Kyle of Durness – Sarsgrum – Keoldale – Balnakeil – Balnakeil Bay – Faraid Head – Aodann Mhór Durness – Smoo (Durness Youth Hostel)	18	4,716
27.8.78	Durness – Samgobeg – Rispond – Souterrain – Laid – Loch Eriboll – A838 – Eriboll – Kempie – Hope – Loch Maovally – Moine House – A838 – Kyle of Tongue – Tongue Youth Hostel	28	4,744
28.8.78	Tongue Youth Hostel – Tongue Village – Tongue Youth Hostel – A838 – Moine House – Cnoc nan Gobhar – Freisgill – Whiten Head – Strathan – Talmine – Midtown – Melness – Kyle of Tongue – Tongue Youth Hostel	24	4,768
29.8.78	Tongue Youth Hostel – Rhitongue – Skullomie – Sletell – Strathan Skerray – Skerray – Airdtorrisdale – Torrisdale Bay – Bettyhill – Farr – Swordly – Kirtomy – Armadale – Armadale House	21	4,789
30.8.78	Armadale House – Lednagullin – Aultiphurst – Aultivullin – Strathy Point – Strathy – Portskerra – Melvich – Bighouse – Sandsite Head – Reay – Balmore – Bridge of Forss – Brims – Scrabster Loch – Scrabster	28	4,817
31.8.78	Scrabster – Thurso – Clardon Hill – Murkle Bay – Castlehill – Dunnet Beach – Dunnet	12	4,829

292

Date	Route		Mileage

Date	Route		Mileage
1.9.78	Dunnet – Loch of Bushta – Briga Head – Dunnet Head – Scarfskerry – Castle of Mey – Gills – Kirkstyle – Huna – John o'Groats Hotel	21	4,850
2.9.78	John o'Groats – Duncansby Head – Wife Geo – Skirza – Freswick Castle – Auckengill – Keiss – Tang Head – Keiss Sands – Ackergill Links – Noss – Noss Head – Staxigoe – Wick camp site	23	4,873
3.9.78	Wick – South Head – Castle of Old Wick – Helman Head – Sarclet – Mains of Ulbster – Ulbster – Whaligoe – Bruan – Mid Clyth – Lybster – Forse – Latheron – Latheronwheel Hotel	22	4,895
4.9.78	Latheronwheel – Dunbeath – Borgue – Berriedale – Badbea – Ord of Caithness – Navidale – Helmsdale Youth Hostel	20	4,915
5.9.78	Helmsdale – Portgower – Lothmore – Lothbeg – Dalchalm Beach – Brora – Strathsteven Beach – Dunrobin Castle – Golspie – The Mound – Loch Fleet – Skelbo Castle – Coul Farm – Embo camp site	28	4,943
6.9.78	Embo – Dornoch – Lonemore – Loch Evelix – Loch Ospisdale – Skibo Castle – Whiteface – A9 – Spinningdale – A9 – Bonar-Bridge – Ardgay – Bonar-Bridge Station	20	4,963
7.9.78	Ardgay – Kincardine – A9 – Ardvannie – Edderton – Tain – Balnagall – Inver – Roy's Bay – Portmahomack	25	4,988
8.9.78	Portmahomack – Hilton – Tarbat Ness – Rockfield – Hilton of Cadboll – Shandwick – Hill of Nigg – Ankerville Corner – Arabella – Ballchraggan – Kilmuir – Barbaraville – Balintraid – Saltburn – Invergordon	27	5,015
9.9.78	Invergordon – Belleport – Alness – Novar – Evanton – Ardullie Lodge – A9 – Dingwall – Maryburgh – Conon Bridge	17	5,032
10.9.78	Conon Bridge – Alcaig – Shoretown – Cullicudden – Balblair – Udale Bay – Jemimaville – Shoremill – Cromarty	22	5,054

Date	Route		Mileage
11.9.78	Cromarty – Sutors Stacks – Gallow Hill – Navity – Ethie – Rosemarkie – Fortrose – Avoch – Crosshill – Drum – Munlochy – Kessock Forest – Kilmuir – Craigton – North Kessock – Charlestown	27	5,081
12.9.78	Charlestown – Corgrain Point – Redcastle – Whitewells – Bellevue – Windhill – A9 – Beauly – Lovat Bridge – Kirkhill – A9 – Mains of Bunchrew – Clachnaharry – Inverness	24	5,105
13.9.78	Inverness – A96 – B9039 – Ardersier – Fort George – Baddock – B9092 – A96 – Nairn – Kingsteps – Maviston – Cothill – Castle – Brodie (Mill Inn camp site)	30	5,135
14.9.78	Brodie – Findhorn Bridge – Forres – Mill of Grange – Kinloss – B9011 – Findhorn – Burghead Bay – Burghead – Newtown – Hopeman	20	5,155
15.9.78	Hopeman – Gow's Castle – Covesea Skerries Lighthouse – Branderburgh – Lossiemouth – Spey Bay – Kingston – Old Railway Bridge – Spey Bay – Portgordon – Buckie – Portessie – Strathlene camp site	26	5,181
16.9.78	Strathlene – Findochty – Portknockie – Cullen Bay – Findlater Castle – Sandend – Portsoy – Boyne Bay – Whitehills – Banff	21	5,202
17.9.78	Banff – Macduff – Melrose – More Head – Gardenstown – Crovie – Troup Head – Pennan – Mill Farm – Braco Park – Rosehearty	23	5,225
18.9.78	Rosehearty – Sandhaven – Fraserburgh – Inverallochy – St Combs – Back Bar – Rattray Head – Scotstown Head – Kirkton Head – Peterhead	25	5,250
19.9.78	Peterhead – Burnhaven – Boddam – Long Haven – North Haven – Cruden Bay – Whinnyfold – Mains of Slains – Collieston – Sands of Forvie – Newburgh	22	5,272
20.9.78	Newburgh – Foveran Links – Menie Links – Drumside Links – Eigie Links – Blackdog Range – Balgownie Links – Bridge of Don – Old Town – Aberdeen – Blacks' Shop – Aberdeen Youth Hostel	18	5,290

Date	Route		Mileage
21.9.78	Aberdeen Harbour – Girdle Ness – Greg Ness – Cove Bay – Findon – Portlethen – Downies – Newtonhill – Muchalls – A92 – Cowie – Stonehaven	22	5,312
22.9.78	Stonehaven – Dunnottar Castle – Crawton – Catterline – Whistleberry – Grange – Inverbervie – Gourdon – Johnshaven – Milton Ness – St Cyrus Nature Reserve – Fisherhills – Montrose (Links)	27	5,339
23.9.78	Montrose – Ferryden – Mains of Dunninald – Braehead – Lunan – Lunan Sands – Ethie Haven – Red Head – Auchmithie – Carlingheugh Bay – Arbroath – Sands – East Haven – West Haven – Carnoustie – Barry	27	5,366
24.9.78	Barry – Monifieth – Broughty Ferry – Stanner-gate – Dundee – Tay Road Bridge – Tayport – Tentsmuir Sands – River Eden – Shelly Point – Inner Bridge – Guardbridge – West Sands – St Andrews	34	5,400
25.9.78	St Andrews – Buddo Rock – Babbet Ness – Kingsbarns – Fife Ness – Crail – Anstruther Easter and Wester – Pittenweem – St Monance – Elie	28	5,428
26.9.78	Elie – Earlsferry – Shell Bay – Largo Bay – Lower Largo – Leven – Methil – Buckhaven – East Wemyss – West Wemyss – Dysart – Kirkcaldy	23	5,451
27.9.78	Kirkcaldy – Linktown – Kinghorn – Pettycur – Burntisland – Silversands Bay – Aberdour – Dalgety Bay – Donibristle Bay – St Davids Harbour – Inverkeithing – Inner Bay – Forth Road Bridge – Queensferry – Peatdraught Bay – Dalmeny House – Eagle Rock – Cramond Bridge	28	5,479
28.9.78	Cramond Bridge – Cramond – Muirhouse – Granton Harbour – Royal Botanic Garden – Queen Street (BBC Scotland) – Leith Walk – Portobello – Joppa – Musselburgh – Prestonpans – Port Seton – Gosford Bay – Aberlady	29	5,508

Date	Route		Mileage
29.9.78	Aberlady – Gullane Sands – Gullane Bay – Black Rocks – Weaklaw Rocks – Broad Sands – North Berwick – Tantallon Castle – Seacliff Beach – Scoughall Rocks – Peffer Sands – Tyne Sands – Belhaven Bay – Dunbar	28	5,536
30.9.78	Dunbar – White Sands – Barns Ness – Skateraw Harbour – Thorntonloch – A1 – Cove – Pease Bay – Redheugh – Fast Castle – St Abb's Head – St Abbs – Coldingham Bay	24	5,560
1.10.78	Coldingham Bay – Hairy Ness – Eyemouth – Nestends – Fancove Head – Burnmouth – A1 – The Border – Marshall Meadows – Berwick-upon-Tweed	17	5,577
2.10.78	Berwick – Spittal – Seahouse – Cheswick Sands – Goswick Sands – Beal Point – Granary Point – Tealhole Point – Ross Point – Ross Back Sands – Budle Bay – Waren Mill – Budle Point – Bamburgh – Greenhill	29	5,606
3.10.78	Greenhill – Seahouses – Beadnell – Beadnell Bay – Newton Links – Low Newton-by-the-Sea – Craster – Howick Haven – Boulmer – Seaton Point – Alnmouth – Hipsburn – Birling Carrs – Warkworth	27	5,633
4.10.78	Warkworth – Amble – Hauxley Haven – Druridge Bay – Cresswell – Lynemouth – Beacon Point – Newbiggin-by-the-Sea – River Wansbeck – A189 – Cowpen – Blyth – South Beach – Seaton Sluice – Whitley Bay	34	5,667
5.10.78	Whitley Bay – Tynemouth – North Shields – Willington Quay Wallsend – Byker – Newcastle – Felling – Hebburn – Jarrow – Tyne Dock – South Shields – South Pier	27	5,694
6.10.78	South Shields – Frenchman's Bay – Marsden Bay – Lizard Point – Souter Point – South Bents – Whitburn Bay – Roker – Sunderland – Salterfen Rocks – Ryhope – Seaham – Hawthorn Hive – Easington Colliery – Horden	25	5,719

Date	Route		Mileage
7.10.78	Horden – Blackhall Colliery – Crimdon Park – North Sands – Parton Rocks – Hartlepool – Seaton Carew – A178 – Port Clarence – Transporter Bridge – Middlesbrough – Cargo Fleet – South Bank – Warrenby – Coatham – Redcar	30	5,749
8.10.78	Redcar – Marske Sands – Saltburn Sands – Cleveland Way – Skinningrove – Boulby Cliffs – Boulby – Staithes – Port Mulgrave – Runswick – Kettleness – Sandsend – Whitby Sands – Whitby Youth Hostel	30	5,779
9.10.78	Whitby – Lighthouse – Robin Hood's Bay – Boggle Hole – Ravenscar – Beast Cliff – Hayburn Wyke – Cloughton Wyke – Cromer Point – North Bay – Scarborough	25	5,804
10.10.78	Scarborough – South Sands – Cayton Bay – Gristhorpe Cliff – Filey – Muston Sands – Hunmanby Sands – Reighton Sands – Speeton Sands – Speeton Cliffs – Buckton Cliffs – Bempton Cliffs – North Cliff – Flamborough Head – South Landing – Sewerby Rocks – North Sands – Bridlington	35	5,839
11.10.78	Bridlington – South Sands – Fraisthorpe Sands – Barmston Sands – Ulrome Sands – Skipsea Sands – Atwick Sands – Hornsea – Rolston – Mappleton – Cowden Parra – Aldbrough	24	5,863
12.10.78	Aldbrough – East Newton – Ringbrough – Grimston – Monkwith – Waxholme – Withernsea – Holmpton – Dimlington – Easington – Kilnsea – Spurn Head – Kilnsea – Easington	34	5,897
13.10.78	Easington – Weeton – Welwick – Patrington – Ottringham – Keyingham – Thorngumbald – Hedon – Marfleet – Hull	27	5,924
14.10.78	Hull – Hessle – Redcliff Sand – East Clough – Brough Roads – Brough – Cave Sands Farm – Weighton Lock – Blacktoft – Yokefleet – Laxton – Goole Bridge – Goole	31	5,955
15.10.78	Goole – Swinefleet – Mount Pleasant – Reedness Grange – Crowle Cottage – Crowle – A18 – Althorpe – Gunness – Scunthorpe	22	5,977

Date	Route		Mileage
16.10.78	Scunthorpe – Steel Works – Low Santon – B1207 – Appleby – Saxby All Saints Bridge – Saxby Wolds – B1218 – Beacon Hill – Barton-upon-Humber – Sea Wall – New Holland – Goxhill Haven – East Halton Skitter – North Killingholme Haven – South Killingholme Haven – Immingham Dock	36	6,013
17.10.78	Immingham Dock – Sea Wall – Grimsby Docks – Cleethorpes – Humberston Fitties – Tetney Haven – Northcoates Point – Horse Shoe Point – Pye's Hall – Donna Nook – Samphire Bed – Saltfleet	30	6,043
18.10.78	Saltfleet – Coastline – Mablethorpe – Trusthorpe – Sutton on Sea – Sandilands – Anderby Creek – Chapel Point – Ingoldmells Point – Seathorne – Skegness	25	6,068
19.10.78	Skegness – Gibraltar Point – Clough Farm – Wainfleet Sand – Sea Wall – The Horseshoe – Wrangle Flats – The Delph – Clay Hole – The Haven – Skirbeck – Boston	31	6,099
20.10.78	Boston – The Haven – Sea Wall – Frampton Marsh – Fosdyke Wash – Sea Wall – Fleet Haven – Sea Wall – Old Lighthouses – Nene Outfall Cut – Sutton Bridge Hotel	33	6,132
21.10.78	Sutton Bridge – River Nene – Old Lighthouses – Breast Sand – Admiralty Point – Lynn Channel – River Great Ouse – West Lynn – King's Lynn	21	6,153
22.10.78	King's Lynn – South Wootton – North Wootton – Sea Wall – Snettisham Scalp – Stubborn Sand – Hunstanton – Gore Point – Broad Water – Thornham – Titchwell – Brancaster – Burnham Deepdale – Burnham Market – Burnham Overy – Overy Staithe – Holkham	39	6,192
23.10.78	Holkham – West Sands – Wells-next-the-Sea – Warham Greens – Stiffkey Greens – Agar Creek – Blakeney – Cley next the Sea – Cley Eye – Salthouse Broads – Weybourne Hope – Sheringham Youth Hostel	26	6,218
24.10.78	Sheringham – East Runton Gap – Cromer – Overstrand – Marl Point – Mundesley – Bacton – Walcott	20	6,238

Date	Route		Mileage
25.10.78	Walcott – Happisburgh – Eccles Beach – Sea Palling – Marram Hills – Winterton Ness – Winterton-on-Sea – Newport – California – Caister-on-Sea – Britannia Pier Great Yarmouth	25	6,263
26.10.78	Great Yarmouth – Southtown – Gorleston on Sea – Corton Cliffs – Corton – Lowestoft – Pakefield Cliffs – Kessingland	20	6,283
27.10.78	Kessingland – Benacre Ness – Covehithe – Easton Cliffs – Southwold – Tinker's Marshes – Walberswick – Reedland Marshes – Dunwich – Minsmere Haven – Sizewell Power Station – Thorpeness – The Haven – Aldeburgh	26	6,309
28.10.78	Aldeburgh – South Warren – Black Heath Wood – Shape Street – Ikencliff – Tunstall Forest – Chillesford – Butley Abbey – Ely Hill – Oak Hill – Oxley Marshes – Shingle Street – Martello Tower – Bawdsey Manor – Bawdsey – Alderton – Shottisham – Sutton – B1083 – Wilford Bridge (Melton)	32	6,341
29.10.78	Wilford Bridge – Martlesham Creek – Waldringfield – Hemley Kirton Creek – Deben River Wall – Felixstowe Ferry – Sea Wall – Felixstowe – Waltonferry – Levington – Nacton – Ipswich (centre)	34	6,375
30.10.78	Ipswich – A137 – B1456 – Woolverstone – Holbrook – Stutton – Seafield Bay – Cattawade – Manningtree – Mistley – Bradfield – Wrabness – Ramsey – Harwich	29	6,404
31.10.78	Harwich – Sea Wall – Little Oakley Hall – Great Oakley – Beaumont-Cum-Moze – Kirby le Soken – Walton on the Naze – Frinton-on-Sea – Holland-on-Sea – Clacton-on-Sea	25	6,429
1.11.78	Clacton-on-Sea – Jaywick Sands – St Osyth Beach – Lee-over-sands – Point Clear – St Osyth – Hollybush Hill – Brightlingsea – Alresford Creek – Wivenhoe – River Colne – Colchester Youth Hostel	25	6,454
2.11.78	Colchester – B1025 – Blackheath – Abberton – Peldon – Great Wigborough – Salcott – Tolleshunt D'Arcy – Goldhanger – Maldon	24	6,478

Date	Route		Mileage
3.11.78	Maldon – Sea Wall – Limbourne Creek – Southey Creek – Maylandsea – Steeple – St Lawrence Bay – Bradwell Waterside – Sea Wall – St Peter's Chapel – Sandbeach Outfall – Sandbeach Farm	25	6,503
4.11.78	Sandbeach Farm – Howe Outfall – Grange Outfall – Sea Wall – Coate Outfall – Holliwell Point – Sea Wall – Burnham-on-Crouch – Althorne – Uleham's Farm – Great Hayes – South Woodham Ferrers	26	6,529
5.11.78	South Woodham Ferrers – River Crouch ford – Hullbridge – The Dome – Fambridge – Sea Wall – Black Point – Lion Wharf – Ballards Gore – Great Stambridge – Rochford Mill – Sutton Hall – Barling – Great Wakering – Shoeburyness – Thorpe Bay – Southend-on-Sea	31	6,560
6.11.78	Southend-on-Sea – Leigh-on-Sea – Hadleigh Marsh – Benfleet Creek – St Margaret's Church – Pitsea – Vange – Fobbing – Stanford le Hope	20	6,580
7.11.78	Stanford le Hope – Mucking – East Tilbury – Sea Wall – Tilbury – Little Thurrock – Grays – Sea Wall – Purfleet – Wennington – Rainham – A13 – Dagenham – A13 – Barking Creek – South Bromley – Poplar	34	6,614
8.11.78	Poplar – City of London – St Paul's Cathedral	10	6,624

Malfunction of pedometer on north-west coast of Scotland: estimated additional mileage   200

Total Mileage   6,824

Appendix V

Weather

As a general survey of the weather encountered on the walk between 3 January and 8 November 1978, the first three months were very poor with rain and galeforce winds much of the time. Cornwall suffered the worst blizzards for thirty years. The summer on the west coast of Scotland was the worst for ten years, but autumn everywhere proved to be the best for sixty years.

The following is an attempt to summarize the weather throughout the walk:

| Date | Number of days | | | | | |
	sunny and dry	gale-force winds	cloudy	rain	snow	soaked
3 Jan. – 9 Feb.	20	11	4	14	2	5
10 Feb. – 17 Mar.	9	13	9	16	5	4
18 Mar. – 21 Apr.	16	12	5	10	2	3
22 Apr. – 16 June	48	4	2	4		
17 June – 20 July	14	2	10	8		3
21 July – 16 Aug.	12	1	9	6		2
17 Aug. – 8 Nov.	30	15	25	17		9
Total	149	58	64	75	9	26

Notes

Sunny and dry: Dry days with long periods of sunshine. When strong or galeforce winds blew, this is given as a separate entry in the appropriate column.

Galeforce winds: Winds of force four and upwards.

Cloudy: Overcast days, usually with gentle breeze.

Rain: Days when more than four hours of rain fell.

Snow: Days when snow fell.

Soaked: Number of days when I was literally soaked to the skin.

Appendix VI

Flora and Fauna

Below is a list of birds seen on the walk, in alphabetical order, and not in order of sighting to avoid duplication. Unfortunately I missed some of the sea birds in the early summer because of the fracture, and sadly I did not see a puffin.

Birds

Arctic tern
Avocet
Barnacle geese
Barn owl
Black-backed gull
Blackbird
Black-fronted geese
Black guillemot
Black-headed gull
Black swan
Black-throated diver
Blue tit
Brent geese
Buzzard
Canada geese
Carrion crow
Chaffinch
Chough
Collared dove
Coot
Common gull
Common sandpiper
Common tern
Cormorant

Crested tit
Cuckoo
Curlew
Dipper
Dotteril
Dunlin
Eider duck
Fulmar
Gannet
Goldcrest
Golden eagle
Goldfinch
Great black-backed gull
Great northern diver
Great skua
Great spotted
   woodpecker
Great tit
Greenfinch
Green woodpecker
Grey heron
Grey wagtail
Grouse
Guillemot

Hedge sparrow
Herring gull
Hooded crow
House martin
House sparrow
Jackdaw
Jay
Kestrel
Kingfisher
Kittiwake
Knot
Lapwing
Little stint
Long-tailed tit
Magpie
Mallard
Meadow pipit
Merlin
Mistle thrush
Moorhen
Mute swan
Oyster-catcher
Partridge
Peregrine falcon

Pheasant
Pied wagtail
Pinkfoot geese
Raven
Razorbill
Red-breasted merganser
Redshank
Red-throated diver
Redwing
Ringed plover
Ring ouzel
Robin
Rock dove
Rock pipit

Rook
Sanderling
Shag
Shelduck
Short-eared owl
Skylark
Snipe
Song thrush
Sparrow
Sparrowhawk
Starling
Stonechat
Swallow
Swift

Teal
Tree creeper
Tree sparrow
Turnstone
Wheatear
Whimbrel
Whinchat
Woodcock
Wood pigeon
Wren
Yellow wagtail

Animals, Mammals and Reptiles

Adder
Atlantic seal
Basking shark
Dolphin
Grey seal
Grey squirrel

Hare
Hedgehog
Jacob sheep
Otter
Pine marten
Rabbit

Red deer
Red fox
Red squirrel
Roe deer
Slow-worm
Stoat

Butterflies

Brimstone
Common blue
Large white

Peacock
Red admiral
Small blue

Small white
Tortoiseshell (small)

Flowers

Aconite
Bell heather
Bird's foot trefoil
Bistort
Blackthorn
Bluebell
Bog asphodel
Broom
Bugle
Butterbur
Clover
Coltsfoot

Comfrey
Common mallow
Common vetch
Corn marigold
Cotton grass
Cross-leaved heath
Crocus
Cuckoo pint
Daffodil
Daisy
Dandelion
Dock

Dog rose
Early purple orchid
Field scabious
Forget-me-not
Foxglove
Fuschia
Germander speedwell
Gipsy wort
Goatsbeard
Gorse
Harebells
Harts tongue fern

Herb robert
Honesty
Honeysuckle
Jacob's ladder
Kidney vetch
Lady's smock
Lesser celandine
Ling
Long-leaved scurvy grass
Marsh marigold
Meadow cranesbill
Meadow saxifrage
Mistletoe
Monkey flower
Old man's beard
Ox-eye daisy
Pansy
Periwinkle (lesser &
    greater)
Poppy

Primrose
Purple loosestrife
Pussy willow
Ragged robin
Red campion
Rock anemone
Rosebay willowherb
Roseroot
Sea bindweed
Sea campion
Sea holly
Sea kale
Sea saxifrage
Sea pink (thrift)
Sheep's bit
Snowdrop
Spotted heath orchid
Stinging nettle
Stitchwort
St John's wort

Teazle
Toadflax
Tormentil
Tree mallow
Tufted vetch
Violet
White campion
White deadnettle
White stonecrop
White waterlily
Wild strawberry
Wood anemone
Wood avens
Wood garlic (ransomes)
Wood sorrel
Yellow archangel
Yellow flag iris
Yellow horned poppy
Yellow loosestrife
Yellow stonecrop

Appendix VII

Photography

On the walk I carried and used the following 35 mm equipment:

A Practica LTL3 single lens reflex camera
A Chinon Memotron single lens reflex camera
A 2-times auto teleplus converter
A 35 mm Prinzgalaxy telephoto lens
A 135 mm Pentacon 2.8 telephoto lens
A pair of 10 × 50 binoculars

I took 3,500 35 mm colour slides using 50 ASA Orwochrom film. I was very pleased with the results, especially as they were taken in varying light conditions, and some were taken inside churches without flash. On the odd occasion where I ran out of film I used Fuji colour and Kodak 25. Again both gave very good results. The black and white film was exclusively Ilford HP5 (400 ASA). I took about 2,500 shots and again the results are very good. All the cameras and lenses worked faultlessly. The Chinon had to have another battery in it, but that was all.

The only items of equipment that I wished I had taken were some close-up rings so that I could get closer shots of the flowers and insects. I found the 135 mm lens very useful and when needed I could put the 2x converter with it. The 300 mm lens I used only rarely and then for bird photography. The binoculars were invaluable for bird watching, and also for looking ahead and seeing what the terrain was like, especially in Scotland.

Appendix VIII

Logistics

Parcels
I sent out nineteen parcels to different post offices on the coastline as shown below. Each contained:

6–8 1:50,000 Series OS Maps
4 packets of Dextrosol
4 longlife candles (only in first six parcels)
1 rice and curry main meal
1 vegetable stew main meal
1 pasta and vegetable bolognese main meal
1 shrimp curry main meal
1 spicey beef and potato main meal
1 chicken and mushroom and rice main meal
2 rice pudding desserts
2 apple and strawberry desserts
2 banana and custard desserts
7 Gaz cylinders, GT (from April onwards)

Maps (Ordnance Survey 1:50,000)
   3 January London
Map nos 177, 178, 179, 189, 199, 198
   12 January Brighton, Sussex
Map nos 197, 196, 195, 194, 193, 192
   27 January Budleigh Salterton, Devon
Map nos 202, 201, 200, 204
   9 February Mevagissey, Cornwall
Map nos 203, 200, 190
   23 February Bude, Cornwall

Map nos 180, 181, 182, 171, 172, 162

9 March Cardiff, Glamorgan

Map nos 170, 159, 158, 157, 145

24 March Cardigan, Dyfed

Map nos 146, 135, 124, 123, 115, 116

6 April Prestatyn, Gwynedd

Map nos 117, 108, 102, 97, 96, 89

(Collect first pair of boots)

20 April Whitehaven, Cumbria

Map nos 85, 84, 83, 82

1 May Portpatrick, Galloway

Map nos 76, 70, 63, 64, 65, 56, 62, 55, 56

19 May Inveraray, Strathclyde

Map nos 68, 49

1 June Oban, Strathclyde

Map nos 50, 41, 40, 47

14 June Mallaig, Highland

Map nos 33, 24, 25, 19, 20

29 June Ullapool, Highland

Map nos 15, 9, 10, 12

(Collect second pair of boots)

13 July Wick, Highland

Map nos 11, 17, 21, 26, 27, 28, 29, 30

27 July Fraserburgh, Grampian

Map nos 38, 45, 54, 59, 66, 67, 75, 81, 88

11 August Newcastle upon Tyne, Tyne and Wear

Map nos 93, 94, 101, 107, 113, 106, 112

24 August Cleethorpes, Humberside

Map nos 122, 131, 132, 133, 134, 156, 169

6 September Ipswich, Suffolk

Map nos 168, 167, 178, 177

Appendix IX

Charity Involvement

I realized at an early stage that my British coastal walk would be an ideal vehicle for raising money for a charity. I approached several charities and was surprised when in each case my suggestions were met with lukewarm response and when in some cases my letters were not even acknowledged.

It was not until I was giving a lecture to my own rotary club in December 1976, to raise money for the Royal Commonwealth Society for the Blind, that my idea was taken seriously at all. A representative from the charity attended the lecture and I mentioned the idea to her afterwards. She immediately agreed it was worth following through and it was subsequently confirmed.

They were very enthusiastic about the schedule and did their utmost to cooperate. I did not want to get involved with the organization and planning as I already had enough of my own, but in the event I had to. My first major breakthrough was when I obtained the support of the rotary movement throughout Britain. Once that had been achieved, I wrote to all the rotary clubs on or within twelve miles of the coast. There were 700 in all and to each I explained my aims and proposed that money could be raised in the following ways:

1. A rotary president and a maximum of four others from the club could walk a maximum of five miles with me provided they were sponsored.
2. A lottery could be held on the time that I reached a specific point of the walk or on how long it took me to walk a particular section.

3. A fund-raising evening could be held.

The connection with the fund raising and the involvement of the rotary clubs proved to be a mixed blessing throughout the walk. Within a month I was absolutely shell-shocked by the attention both from the clubs and the people sponsored to walk with me. The events that I had been told about, I could cope with because I had been able to prepare myself – after all, it necessitated quite a lot of adapting on my part to emerge from twenty or so miles of walking along remote coastline into hordes of people, or to have people accompanying me on the walk when I was used to being by myself. But on countless occasions events had been arranged about which I knew nothing and then the shock was too great and I often felt strained. After four weeks of relentless attention I was forced to complain to the RCSB, but I didn't gain effective control until I reached Scotland. Then I agreed to do only three events on my return journey. It was a difficult decision to make, especially as I knew the fund raising would be seriously affected, but I was terrified that I might receive the same attention for the rest of the walk, and I knew I wouldn't be able to cope.

I say it was a mixed blessing, for apart from this I received many instances of help from rotary club members throughout the country – especially in the form of meals and accommodation.

But taken over all, I would have to think seriously before letting a charity get involved in any future major walks. It had created a conflict of interests: for me a major walk is a personal challenge as a marathon walker, and the fund raising is very much a secondary thing, whereas to a charity of course the fund raising is a primary consideration.

The coastal walk raised a little over £40,000 of which I collected £3,000 in cash and cheques from individuals I met on the way. This will restore sight to approximately 14,000 people in India.

MORE ABOUT PENGUINS
AND PELICANS

For further information about books available from Penguins please write to Dept EP, Penguin Books Ltd, Harmondsworth, Middlesex UB7 0DA.

In the U.S.A.: For a complete list of books available from Penguins in the United States write to Dept CS, Penguin Books, 625 Madison Avenue, New York, New York 10022.

In Canada: For a complete list of books available from Penguins in Canada write to Penguin Books Canada Ltd, 2801 John Street, Markham, Ontario L3R 1B4.

In Australia: For a complete list of books available from Penguins in Australia write to the Marketing Department, Penguin Books Australia Ltd, P.O. Box 257, Ringwood, Victoria 3134.

In New Zealand: For a complete list of books available from Penguins in New Zealand write to the Marketing Department, Penguin Books (N.Z.) Ltd, P.O. Box 4019, Auckland 10.

Look out for these from Penguins!

CARNIVAL IN ROMANS
A People's Uprising at Romans 1579–1580
Emmanuel Le Roy Ladurie

'In February 1580, Carnival in Romans was a time of masks and massacres for the divided citizenry.' Concentrating on two colourful and bloody weeks, the author of *Montaillou* vividly resurrects the social and political events that led to the tragedy of 1580.

'Professor Le Roy Ladurie is one of the greatest historians of our time . . . this is a book not to be missed' – Christopher Hill

THE VIEW IN WINTER
Reflections on Old Age
Ronald Blythe

'Old age is not an emancipation from desire for most of us; that is a large part of its tragedy. The old want their professional status back or their looks . . . most of all they want to be wanted.' Ronald Blythe listened to all kinds of people who are in and around their eighties as they talked about their old age, to make this marvellous, haunting record of an experience that touches us all.

'Beautifully written . . . Moving but unsentimental and even oddly reassuring, it deserves, like *Akenfield*, to become a classic' – A. Alvarez in the *Observer*

THE OLD PATAGONIAN EXPRESS
By Train through the Americas
Paul Theroux

From blizzard-stricken Boston to arid Patagonia; travelling by luxury express and squalid local trucks; sweating and shivering by turns as the temperature and altitude shot up and down; Paul Theroux's vivid pen clearly evokes the contrasts of a journey 'to the end of the line'.

'One of the most entrancing travel books written in our time' – C. P. Snow in the *Financial Times*

Look out for these from Penguins!

CHARMED LIVES
Michael Korda

The story of Alexander Korda and the fabulous Korda film dynasty starring Garbo, Dietrich, Churchill and a cast of thousands.

'Charmed lives, doubly charmed book . . . Comments, jokes, experiences; and at the heart of it all there is Alexander Korda, powerful, brilliant, extravagant, witty, charming. And fortunate: fortunate in his biographer. Few men have the luck to be written about with so personal an appreciation, so amused, yet so deep an affection' – Dilys Powell in *The Times*

THE WHITE ALBUM
Joan Didion

In this scintillating epitaph to the sixties Joan Didion exposes the realities and mythologies of her native California – observing a panorama of subjects and events, ranging from Manson to bikers to Black Panthers to the Women's Movement to John Paul Getty's museum, the Hoover Dam and Hollywood.

'A richly worked tapestry of experiences' – Rachel Billington

THE SEVENTIES
Christopher Booker

From the rise of Mrs Thatcher to the murder of Lord Mountbatten, from the energy crisis to the trial of Jeremy Thorpe, from the Cult of Nostalgia to the Collapse of the Modern Movement in the Arts : . . In this series of penetrating essays Christopher Booker explores the underlying themes which shaped our thoughts and our lives in the seventies.

'Booker is quite compulsive' – *Punch*
'Constantly stimulating . . . savagely funny' – *Evening Standard*

Look out for these from Penguins!

THE HISTORY OF MYDDLE
Richard Gough

The Parish of Myddle in 1701 was as full of life, gossip, intrigues, births, marriages and deaths as any other small community in Stuart England. What made Myddle different was that one of its parishioners, Richard Gough, decided to write down the family history of the occupants of each pew in the church. And, as he was gifted with a remarkable ear for anecdote, a sharp eye for foible and a pithy pen for a telling phrase, his history gives us a quite incredible glimpse into the seventeenth-century family and parish, and into the characters of the people who seem to live and breathe on his pages today as they did then.

LARK RISE TO CANDLEFORD
Flora Thompson

The endearing and precise record of country life at the end of the last century – a record in which Flora Thompson brilliantly engraves the fast-dissolving England of peasant, yeoman and craftsman and tints her picture with the cheerful courage and the rare pleasures that marked a self-sufficient world of work and poverty.

GREENVOE
George Mackay Brown

Greenvoe, the community on the Orkney Island of Hellya, has existed unchanged for generations. In this, his first novel, George Mackay Brown has recreated a week in its life, mixing history with personality – from minister to Marxist – in a brilliantly sparkling mixture of prose and poetry.
'Poetic, distinguished and totally delightful . . . full of humour and sensitivity and of the unsentimental poetry of raw experience' – *Sunday Times*

Look out for these from Penguins!

A TIME OF GIFTS
Patrick Leigh Fermor

'Like a tramp, a pilgrim, or a wandering scholar', Patrick Fermor set out from Irongate Wharf one wet December day to walk to Constantinople. This book covers his journey as far as Hungary; unfolding the languages, arts, landscapes, religions, histories and, above all, the people of a dozen civilizations – life as it was lived before the onslaught of the Second World War.
'Nothing short of a masterpiece' – Jan Morris in the *Spectator*

A PLACE APART
Dervla Murphy

Dervla Murphy, a southern Irishwoman and well-known travel-writer, crossed the border and explored Northern Ireland on a bicycle. Her travelogue, said *The Times Literary Supplement*, is 'an extraordinarily successful attempt to present Northern Ireland from the inside out, with honesty, sympathy and understanding'.

JUPITER'S TRAVELS
Ted Simon

One black and rainy night in London, Ted Simon got on his motorbike and set off to ride round the world. Four years, 60,000 miles and 50 countries later, *Jupiter's Travels* celebrates his discoveries . . .
'A rattling good read' – *Guardian*

Look out for these from Penguins!

MY MUSIC
Steve Race

Here are the ripest plums – the outrageous puns, the nonsense, the sparkling repartee – from thirteen glorious years of the internationally famous BBC Radio and Television quiz game, starring Frank Muir, Denis Norden, John Amis and Ian Wallace and chaired by Steve Race.

THE BEST OF JAZZ
Humphrey Lyttelton

'A kaleidoscope of anecdote, analysis, history, interpretation and background colour which should please beginner and expert alike . . . a smashing book' – Miles Kington in *Punch*
Crammed with anecdote, wit and erudition, here is a complete run-down on the history, the personalities – Louis Armstrong, Sidney Bechet, Jelly Roll Morton, Bessie Smith, Bix Beiderbecke – and the masterpieces which have bedecked a music whose golden notes and subtle rhythms have found a permanent home in modern culture.

THE Q ANNUAL
Spike Milligan

If you've seen Spike Milligan's hilarious Q Series on television, you'll enjoy this book . . .
In glorious black and white Spike sings his evening dress to sleep; measures Napoleon for half a coffin; impersonates John Hanson in 'On the Buses'; speaks out on behalf of oppressed minorities from the Royal Family to the Lone Ranger. There is a rare photograph of Ivan's wife Mrs Ethel Terrible, and dramatic new evidence on the liquefaction of Harry Secombe, Princess Anne's birthday, the electric banana . . .

Autobiographies with a flavour of Ireland

WOODBROOK
David Thomson

Woodbrook is a house that gives its name to a small, rural area in Ireland, not far from the old port of Sligo. In 1932 David Thomson, aged eighteen, went there as a tutor and stayed for ten years. His autobiography grew out of two great loves, for the house and for Phoebe, his pupil.

'A marvellous conjuring up of a past age, of a beautiful decaying house . . . an innocent and idyllic love' – *The Times*

HOME BEFORE NIGHT
Hugh Leonard

A delightful evocation of his Dublin childhood in the thirties and forties, Hugh Leonard's autobiography is like an Irish *Cider With Rosie* – crammed with people and conversations, rich in poetry, full of love, laughter and rare pleasures.

'Superb . . . moving and very funny' – William Trevor

WHEELS WITHIN WHEELS
Dervla Murphy

Intrepid cyclist and traveller, and a writer whose work is marked by stringent commonsense, riotous honesty and subtle bewitching prose, Dervla Murphy writes here about her richly unconventional first thirty years.